My Best Work is Done at the Office

Skyline Publishing is a fully owned subsidiary of Roland and Jane Cheeks' lives, staffed entirely with 2.6974 human beings striving endlessly to find a profession in which we can succeed. *Skyline Publishing* was birthed in a remote wilderness tent camp where the principals practiced servitude to 28 assorted horses and one spaniel dog. Our objective was to achieve fame and sufficient fortune to enable us to afford six plough horses and a Labrador retriever.

We're down, now, to four aging ponies and one photograph of the greatest dog who ever lived—the task of turning dream to reality is illusive and requires modification.

Our revised business plan is, thus, to continue producing the best-looking, best written, most informative books ever compiled. It also includes limiting extraneous expenses, such as food, clothing, and shelter.

We're succeeding.

My Best Work is Done at the Office

Roland Cheek

a Skyline Publishing Book

Copyright 2000 by Roland Cheek

Editing by Bob Elman
Cover design by Laura Donovan
Text design and formatting by Michael Dougherty
Copy editing by Jennifer Williams

Publisher's Cataloging in Publication
(Prepared by Quality Books, Inc.)

Cheek, Roland.
   My Best Work is Done at the Office / Roland
Cheek. — 1st ed.
   p. cm.
   LCCN: 989-76467
   ISBN: 0-91898106-9

   1. Outdoor life—Rocky Mountains—Anecdotes.
   2. Rocky Mountains—Anecdotes.   3. Cheek, Roland
   I. Title.

   GV191.42.A17C44 2000   796.5'0978
                                QBI00-160

Published by   Skyline Publishing
                  P.O. Box 1118
                  Columbia Falls, Montana 59912

2nd Printing November 2000

Printed in Canada

ATTENTION SCHOOLS, ORGANIZATIONS, AND NON-PROFIT GROUPS: Quantity discounts are available on bulk purchases of this book for educational purposes or fund raising. For information, please contact Skyline Publishing, P.O. Box 1118, Columbia Falls, MT 59912. Phone: (406) 892-5560.

Dedication

No writer, *especially* one engaged in self-publishing his or her own stuff, should see that stuff into print without first passing the prose under the baleful glare of a merciless editor.

I have such an editor. When I allow myself to fantasize, I see him rubbing his hands and chortling as the post delivers my latest manuscript. I see him hanging a "Do Not Disturb" sign on his office door then reaching for his sharpest knife and his bluest pencil. And lastly, in my fantasy, I see him spewing bile all over my cherished pages because after all the effort he's spent with me, I still haven't attained the level of craft skills that he *knows* is there.

I love him for it. He clears up occasional punctuation and straightens out stray syntax. He does so, not to impose his voice on my work, but to better portray mine by bringing out rhythm and flow and intent. He decries false modesty. And he's positively dedicated to search-and-destroy missions to take out the use of superflous words, or four-bit ones when two-bit ones will do. He makes my work sing.

Bob Elman is editor, friend, and mentor. He's a guy who sits high on the mountainside of literary intuitiveness and craft understanding to which I aspire. This book, then, is dedicated to him.

Author's Note

What you are about to read was written piecemeal during the last two decades of the 20th Century. Those pieces were drafted as newspaper columns or radio scripts. Events, people, and places depicted herein were products of both observation and imagination. Taken collectively, they provide a peek at how the mind works for a guy who spends an inordinate amount of time alone in the wilderness.

Unlike my previous books, this one has no storyline and no resolution. Rather, its chapters are all vignettes. Thus the reader can pause often and contemplate long without interrupting flow. In short, it's a bathroom book, or one in which to dip during brief windows of opportunity: at breakfast or lunch, say, or during morning or evening subway commutes. It's a work that cries out to be read as it was drafted—piecemeal.

As you will see, I'm still struggling to understand. When I get a solid grasp on life and meaning and man's mortality I'll share it with you. Until then—until the ultimate feast—we may have to content ourselves with mere snacks.

Have another cheese and cracker?

Foreword

There are folks who actually believe I'm a *natural* storyteller. Perhaps it would be more accurate to say I had lots of on-the-job training: entertaining guests around flickering campfires was expected of a wilderness guide. And if twenty years of spine-tingling adventures facing an array of wild animals amid incredibly rugged mountains left listeners hanging on every word, why not accept plaudits when offered?

That those adventures turned out to be marketable as newspaper columns and radio shows is what mystified me.

Even after that beginning, I gave no thought to producing an entire book of those tales. Instead of concentrating on a collection of my stories, I first wrote and photographed a book about the mountain wild country that became my living room; followed that with a book on grizzly bears; then turned to one about elk; and after that wrote a memoir about my matrimonial sidekick, Jane, and our life of adventure.

Wonder of wonders, all four of those books have gained wide audiences, for which I'm very grateful. But a great many readers let me know they wanted something else—something along the lines of my columns and radio shows. Alice Royce of Belfry, Montana, wrote: "I received the Bob Marshall Wilderness book and it is great, but I really thought it would have the tales in it that you give on the radio. Are they available?"

Jan Davis of Gunnison, Colorado, was dissatisfied with one of my books because it didn't provide such stories. Eldon Hamlin of Newburg, Oregon, said he enjoyed *Learning to Talk Bear* very much, but was "really looking forward to the one with short stories." Joel Eikomstead of East Helena, Montana, agreed with Hamlin by writing, "Am looking forward to the future publishing of [a] 'Storybook'."

Though I'd written a weekly outdoors column for several newspapers since 1982 and for over seven years, hosted a daily outdoors show for radio stations scattered across America, I still had no plans to put together a printed collection of stories. But after the 1998 release of our memoir, *Dance on the Wild Side*, I simply didn't know which project to tackle next.

Writers are, of course, notoriously plagued by writer's block, but in my case the problem was the opposite—too many ideas. I proposed three to my editor, Bob Elman, and asked him which one he thought was the strongest. Those outlines included: (1) another book on bears; (2) another memoir, sequel to the *Dance* book, this time focusing on the writing career; (3) a collection of my stories, adapted from newspaper columns and radio scripts. The collection was Bob's hands-down recommendation. Thus I grudgingly agreed to a year of writer's hell.

Manuscripts for books, you see, require a style and length far different from newspaper columns and certainly radio scripts. Newspaper space is tight and radio times are even tighter. I made those original columns and scripts fit their allotments, even if the stories could've been better presented by lengthening them. Thus, each script or column included herein was laboriously rewritten specifically for this book. Some also needed to be re-researched and updated for current authenticity.

I expected that rewriting would afford little opportunity for creativity, so I began the process flat-out bored. It was as much of a surprise to me as to others involved when the book began to seize my attention.

As we worked, a pattern of chapter selections focusing primarily on inspiration and humor emerged. We turned ruthless, Bob and I, in rejecting pieces that failed to fit the mold. We also ferreted out and discarded topics that had been presented in the four previous books. This work, as a result, developed purpose and style, yet retained much of its brief, easy-to-read chapter format. With the project finally completed, that year of writer's hell doesn't seem, in retrospect, so awful. Turning out a book is a little like raising a child: often scary while the work is in progress, but leaving warm memories as soon as it's over.

And what about those other book ideas that were shelved while I worked on this one? Well, time will tell.

In the interim, we who worked on the publishing and production of *My Best Work is Done at the Office* are proud of it. We trust you'll not think our pride misplaced. ∎

Roland Cheek

I really enjoy your radio spots so much. Nice way to wake up each day.
Sunny Amundson • Bozeman, MT

In your newspaper column, you say that if we don't see goats at Hidden Lake, we could send you a nasty letter. Has anyone ever sent you a nasty letter? I'd be curious about them if they did.
Lorie Dulemba • Naperville, IL

Keen Way to Recapture Youth

There was this boy, see? He pedaled out on a broken-down bicycle to ask what was up. It was while me and one of the hands moved a bunch of tailed-up horses along a graveled county road to a pasture south of the home place.

The boy's sandy hair needed trimming and his hands could have stood a dash more soap and water than they'd seen since the Ides of March. He'd blown one knee on his britches and elbows played hide and seek through holes in the sleeves of his shirt. As he pedaled, the boy jerked up on the bike's loose handlebars to keep 'em in reach.

Staring down from the saddle, I could see his head would only top out about my belt buckle, even though he must be heading toward his teens.

He wasn't shy, this kid. He pedaled right along with us, and after I'd explained what we were doing with the ponies, he asked about individual ones. Was that pinto a good riding mare? Could any of 'em singlefoot? Did all of 'em pack and ride? That's how I knew the lad was no novice about horses. So I asked him about his own self.

The kid had to brake the bicycle by holding the toe of a worn-out tennis shoe against the front tire. I could see he wore no socks because his right pantleg was rolled up to keep the unguarded bicycle chain from snagging it—just like I did at his age. Sometimes I didn't wear shoes, neither. But, then, my bicycle's brakes worked.

The boy said there was a whole bunch of kids in his family, including a twin sister. And when I asked what his father did, he told me, "Nothing right now. He got hurt at work."

I gazed down at the top of the kid's head bobbing as he pumped his bike alongside and he glanced up about that time, telling me without saying so that he'd rather be riding along-side this string of horses than doing anything else. "You like horses?" I asked.

"Yep. I got one."

"You don't say. Tell me about it."

The boy's horse was a gelding. A little long in the tooth now, but willing. He also told how a couple of his older brothers were trying to make the big rodeo circuit and how he was rid-ing bucking stock in whatever "Little Britches" rodeos they held around the country.

I twisted in the saddle to check out Dan and our plodding horse string. Little puffs of dust were kicked up by the ponies' hooves and a couple shook off horseflies.

The boy wheeled his bike in a u-turn and drifted to the rear to ride alongside Dan. But he was back by my side in a couple of minutes—I could've told him the taciturn wrangler wasn't strong on conversation.

I got troubled as our horse string plodded farther and far-ther from the boy's home. "Hadn't you better ride on back?" I said. "Your momma will be out looking for you."

"Naw. I'm going with you to your pasture. Won't nobody miss me."

When we got to the lower pasture, the boy helped Dan and me untie our ponies and put 'em in the gate. Then when Jane got there with the pickup truck, we threw our saddles and the boy's clattletrap bicycle in the back and took the lad home.

It's fair to say I took a liking to that kid. When school started, I learned from his teacher that the boy's mother had died the winter before, victim of the big C, and that he'd had a few problems adjusting. I tried interesting the lad in reading, starting him out with *Smokey* and *Shane*, books about horses and the West; subjects of more than a little interest to him.

And we took him along on a couple of trips to the Bob Marshall Wilderness when we packed hay and cut firewood in preparation for the fall hunts. And when spring came....

⚜

When I stepped away to straighten and knead my back, the boy stretched to his tiptoes and peered through the spotting scope. His eyelids fluttered while his pupils adjusted; then he gasped. Centered within his field of view were twenty-seven bighorn rams, most of them lying about, contentedly chewing their cuds.

"Wow! Did you see that big one up at the top? And there's two of 'em butting heads and playing! They're all over the place!"

I grinned and glanced at Jane. She swept distant ledges above the rams, searching through binoculars for mountain goats.

"And ... and there's some over to the side with smaller horns!" the boy continued.

"They're mommas," Jane said. She turned her glasses to peer again at the sheep. "Horns of ewes are always smaller."

It'd been quite a day—and with lunchtime still to come. We'd left home after an early breakfast, with the objective of spotting wildlife and maybe doing a little crosscountry skiing. As luck and experience would have it, we'd already counted nearly two hundred elk along Glacier National Park's southern and eastern mountain fronts, including a couple of dandy bulls still carrying their six-point antlers. And we found over a dozen shaggy, snow-colored mountain goats gamboling on cliff faces and rock ledges of a natural mineral lick near Essex and U.S. Highway 2: blocky billies, razor-horned nannies, and half-grown kids tucked against their mothers' sides.

There'd been deer we ignored as being too common, and a fox posturing in a meadow near East Glacier. Then we headed for Many Glacier, where we hoped to spot bighorn sheep. While we waited for a green light in downtown Browning, the boy had said, "I've never seen a wild sheep. Do you think we'll see some?"

I glanced at Jane over the top of the lad's head and

winked—bighorn viewing is as near to a cinch as any wildlife viewing could be in this part of Glacier. The light blinked green and I cranked the station wagon onto the straight, fast, and featureless Duck Lake Road. "Well, let's try to find you a couple."

Now the lad was looking at his first wild sheep. "Enough there to tickle your interest?" I asked when he finally allowed Jane a peek through the scope. His grin was so wide I thought his ears might topple into the toothy mouth.

Jane moved away from the scope and the boy leaped again to the eyepiece. The sheep were lounging across a steep, south-facing hillside where only scattered snowdrifts lay, burned down by melting sun and chinook winds. The valley where we stood was still shrouded in white, however—still weeks away from green grass and sunburned tourists.

"Well," Jane said, "do you want to hike up there where there's no snow and try to get closer to those sheep? Or would you rather stay down here and go skiing?"

The boy shrugged. "I don't care." Then he considered what he'd just said, mulling over the possibility that we might do the unthinkable. "I … I guess I'd rather hike up to the sheep."

There must be something about good-looking older women, stove-up mountain stompers, and wide-eyed and freckled 12-year-old boys that is comforting to a band of bighorn rams because they never seemed to spot us during our hour-long approach. Stranger still, none took alarm during our stomach-slithering short stalk. And strangest of all, they even seemed indifferent after we'd snapped all our film, clambered to our feet, and strolled among them.

"Gee," the boy said as he paused to stare at one cud-chewing ram that sported broomed-off horn tips and a near-white muzzle, "how far away is he?"

"Twenty feet. Why?"

"I've got a horse at home that's wilder than these."

<hr />

As attractive as the thought might be, few of us chronologically inconvenienced folk would agree to return to our youth unless first guaranteed we could retain our present level of intelligence. Yet we who are experienced seem to lose the joy of youth's exuberance. How can we retain discovery's sense of wonder when we've already been there and done that? Where's the challenge? The anticipation? The thrill?

I've learned a great deal about returning to youth's enthusiasm. The return came through the eyes and the exclamations of a twelve-year-old boy stretching to his tiptoes to peer through a spotting scope at his first bighorn ram. It came via that same boy pedaling a rattletrap bicycle for five miles alongside a plodding string of horses so he could rap with the lead cowboy.

It comes through giving and sharing, instead of getting and keeping. ■

Laudable, Not Laughable

There are some as would say the Indians got the better of the deal when they traded Manhattan Island for $26 worth of beads and other foofaraw. I'm inclined to agree.

Others await with baited breath southern California's sliding into the sea. And there are those who want to shaft Mexico again—this time by *returning* Texas.

Still others ask where's Mrs. O'Leary and her cow when they're really needed to purify northern Illinois. And some wonder—but make no attempt to find out—if there's any truth to the rumor that a metropolis bustles under the mile-high smog blanketing east-central Colorado.

Do the Redcoats still want Boston? Can the Mississippi yet swallow New Orleans? How long do we wait before Niagara's relentless upstream erosion strands Buffalo high and dry? Will the day arrive when the weight of burgeoning Miami high-rises drowns Florida in saltwater?

We're talking about people here. Crass insensitive volumes of people who seem programmed to look down their collective, cultured noses at their underprivileged country kin. Do we care? Only if folks wearing those uplifted noses stop feeling superior long enough to see what keeps us bumpkins content—which is that they keep their human feedlots concentrated while we graze at peace amid our rural pastures.

As a result of the 1990 census, my state *lost* one of our two Congressmen because our population was growing more slowly than that of Seattle and St. Louis. Were we upset? Not on your yahootie—we don't even need as many politicians as we have left.

There may have been a time when Detroit and Pittsburgh were nice little towns, just like our prairie communities of Geraldine and Winifred. But see what having an abundance of politicos has done to Motown and Steeltown? And the more city councilmen and state representatives they get, the worse *it* gets.

So we're left out in the pasture when the hogs rustle to the trough. So what? Maybe by being left out when the slop buckets are emptied, our rivers won't wind up with so much industrial pollution that they'll catch fire—as happened to Cleveland's Cuyahoga a few years back.

Do we really want breadlines and street people and subway crimes? Do we really want our farms paved with asphalt and our lakes gridlocked with the modern versions of Yangtze junks?

Maybe we'd rather go on our sleepy way, leaving it to other places to modernize and demoralize. Let them "advance" with the times while we "stagnate." To tell the truth, we're not all that enamored with politicians or those folks who'd like to Atlanta-ize our living room.

Operettas? We still have the wind soughing through our trees. Great art galleries? How can man's art compare with the Beartooth Plateau? Central Park? It's laughable alongside Glacier Park. Disneyland? I'd rather have farmland.

Some folks think hell is living rural: low wages, few cultural advantages, less educational options, relatively little industry, backward neighbors, not enough government relief and governmental "guidance." But I submit that hell is strolling the streets of metropolitan America.

No, we're not laughable, but laudable. We're not stagnating, but appreciating. May God grant that when another hundred years have passed, we're still behind; still a place dear to the hearts of folks who live by names, not numbers.

Let other folks have theirs, and may God help us keep ours. ∎

*I'd like to thank you for your very interesting radio pro-gram, **Trails to Outdoor Adventure**. As a lifelong outdoor enthusiast, I can easily identify with your tales. Your down-home folksy presentation is most assuredly accurate as you speak of your experiences, but is also "listener friendly."*

*You do a wonderful job of including **me** in your setting, wherever it may be on that given day. Keep up the great work and may God bless you and your family.*

Monte Jenkins • Ronan, MT

Dutch Cooking the Honest Way

Domestic abuse!" my wife cried when she discovered I'd let both aluminum Dutch ovens go during the transfer of our Skyline Outfit to its new owners. I had no choice but to agree. Those Dutch ovens were the focal point for decades of tasty outdoor meals: coffee cakes and casseroles, stuffed hens and souffles, puddings and pot roasts and French breads, meat loaf, biscuits and turnovers. MmmMmm!

There was no way to make amends but by taking profits from the sale and investing in replacements. Aluminum Dutch ovens of the ten- and twelve-inch variety weren't read-ily available in northwest Montana five-and-dimes, however. So when we visited Jane's parents in Oregon, I dropped into one of the big whitewater-rafting equipment stores typical there. Yes, they had aluminum ovens in stock. Yes, they had the sizes we needed.

Suspecting they'd usher me to the door if I offered an out-of-state check, and desperate for the Dutch cookery in order to mollify a miffed wife, I peeled off cash—a fifty, a twenty, and some lesser bills. I also handed a business card to the salesperson in order to expedite his preparation of my for-tax-purposes receipt.

A week later, Jane and I returned home to a mountain of

mail—mostly window envelopes, catalogues, and sensational-ized announcements that I was nearing the winner's circle in the latest *Reader's Digest* sweepstakes awards. There were also upwards of twenty messages on our telephone recorder. One of the messages was a request to return a call to Cascade Outfitters in Springfield, Oregon. They left a 1-800 number.

Did they undercharge us for the ovens? I wondered. So I called a couple of days later—at my convenience.

The receptionist sounded cheerful until I identified myself. "Were you into our store a week or two ago?" she then asked.

"Yes, ma'am."

"Did you make a purchase?"

"Yes, ma'am."

"Aluminum cookery—Dutch ovens?"

"Yes, ma'am," I replied. "Mind telling me what this is about?"

"Did you pay in cash? With a fifty-dollar bill?"

Caution lights flashed! *Was it counterfeit?* "Y-e-e-e-s."

"At last!" she exclaimed. "It must be you!"

"Huh?"

She laughed aloud. "Were you short of money?"

"Always," I said. "But I'm surprised at your interest in that fact."

"There were two fifties stuck together. They had consecutive serial numbers. And our till was fifty dollars over for the day. We just knew it was you!"

I clutched the phone, dumfounded. There *are* honest folks in this world.

Cascade Outfitters have since moved from Springfield, Oregon, to Boise, Idaho. The move of such an honorable firm to the Gem State had to be a loss for Oregon. But the good news is they're still in the outdoor supply business.

Incidentally, that phone number is the same: 1-800-223-7238. ∎

Wanted: Men of Action

Has anyone considered how impossible it would've been to mount the Lewis & Clark Expedition if Europeans had already settled out West? With only unbridled rivers, the furies of winter and mosquitoes of summer, three-thousand-mile supply lines, and restless Indians, Meriwether and William led a pushover compared to what it'd be like if they tried their trek today.

First off, the problem would be barge traffic on the lower Missouri—that's if they could catch the right bus to the St. Louis waterfront. If they managed to wriggle their pirogues through the barge lanes and fend off being swamped by the big scows' bow waves, then they'd bump into the first dam. After that it'd be one portage after another, all the way up the Missouri—not to mention the slack water and mud flats represented by those dams.

If the mud flats behind Fort Peck's huge dam are a fair sample, likely there'd be no antelope, bighorn sheep, elk, or buffalo within sight of the no-longer-mighty Missouri.

Above Fort Peck, of course, the Voyage of Discovery would finally strike an unfettered stretch of river where they could get back to bona-fide exploration. However, if the party was deemed to be an outfitted group, they'd be required to obtain a permit from the local Bureau of Land Management office. And it might be questionable whether new management regulations would allow them to paddle upstream against oncoming downstream traffic.

Chances are, when they arrived near the Missouri headwaters, Messrs. Meriwether and William and their men would find little water to float canoes because of giant pumps and hay meadow irrigation. And with the threat of giardiasis, cattle grazing riparian areas, and chemical fertilizers washing from the land, they'd probably have to be regularly supplied with Perrier for safety's sake.

Merely crossing the maze of Interstate highways might be all a man's life was worth, especially when encumbered with trade beads and shiny medallions to hang around tribal chiefs' necks. And if they tried traveling up the Bitterroot Valley during morning or evening rush-hour traffic, they'd no doubt pen a resignation to Marse Tom, back in Washington.

Barbed wire—think of that! Mile after mile after mile of snagging their hinders as they crawled under, squeezed through, or clambered over.

And how about camp sites? What chance would those Presidential emissaries have at competing with the locals for suitable campsites on busy July weekends? And even if the Lewis & Clark gang stumbled onto a Fish, Wildlife & Parks' campground with an empty picnic table, think what a ruckus it'd cause when somebody happened by to collect a fee for using the outhouse toilet.

Or consider their trading for horses: Various and sundry Indian tribes treated the strangers reasonably well, though no mention was made by Messrs. Meriwether and William about Appaloosa horses, despite the fact that the explorers traded with the Nez Perce—the canny tribe of horse breeders who developed the ugly cayuses. (There are some horsemen and women who claim the Nez Perce failure to trade Appaloosas to Lewis and Clark constituted a favor to the newcomers.)

At any rate, can you imagine what kinds of busted up, wind-broke, spavined livestock the expedition would wind up with had they dealt with modern throwbacks to yesterday's slick-talking Yankee horse traders—today's used car salesmen?

It's possible the expedition couldn't cross National Forest land, either—no special-use permit. Neither would they get one without an EIS, EAR, or approval from the EPA. Besides, the party was too large. To travel through any portion of the Bob Marshall, Scapegoat, or Absoraka-Beartooth Wildernesses, there can be no more than fifteen persons using not more than twenty-five horses—which would be a distinct hardship for the explorers, who sometimes ate a superfluous horse during the journey.

Of course, such National Forest, Bureau of Land Management, National Park Service, U.S. Fish & Wildlife Service, and various state Fish & Game agency limitations would be academic since the party could hardly have worked their way through all the no-hunting and no-trespassing signs on private lands along their way.

Shooting wild game out of season would bring the wrath of game wardens down upon them, not to mention that of private groups dedicated to requiring everyone to eat rutabaga sprouts.

And think of the furor that would erupt every time those Lewis & Clarkers even so much as frowned at an "endangered" grizzly bear, even in self-defense.

They came down to the sea in ships, sturdy little vessels hewn from cedars. And they subsisted on salmon along the way. Wouldn't the laugh be on them if they tried to do that today? More dams, more government, less water, fewer trees, no salmon. Corps of Engineers, Bureau of Reclamation, Bonneville Power Administration, Department of Marine Fisheries—such obstacles would be overwhelming even for those intrepid explorers.

A corps of "men of action" was what we needed at the beginning of the nineteenth century, and men of action was what we got. By great good fortune, it was a time before red tape, before governmental forms in triplicate, before unfathomable legal systems requiring barristers in depth and politicians in pocket to properly interpret what we can't do.

Maybe men of action are also what's needed at the beginning of the twenty-first century! ■

Hi, my name is Trevor Alton. I'm 11 years old and live in Montana City. I love to go camping and hiking. We don't get the paper so it was by accident I saw your column. I would like to learn more about how to "survive" in the "wild." I was wondering if you could please write back and tell me some things I should know. This is of course if it is convenient for you.
Trevor Alton • Montana City, MT

A Match Trumps Baseboard Electric

I was ensconced in my easy chair, feet propped up, staring dreamily at a crackling blaze when the thought flitted through my head that I was thinking of nothing. That, of course, is cause to ponder. Why was I so content sitting there doing absolutely nothing except staring at the flames? Was I mesmerized by the blaze? Somehow comforted by it? Was it something in my subconscious tugging me toward primeval roots? Certainly there's something hypnotic about a fire. It attracts us collectively and holds us individually.

A campfire was the center of aboriginal life, the gathering place where important tribal decisions were rendered, the day's gossip exchanged, coups recounted, and children entertained.

And it's still that way, even in the modern world, as witness any traveling group in any wilderness, anywhere. They can be scattered to their separate tents, reading, writing, sleeping, or engaged in countless other pursuits. But build a campfire and all are drawn like moths to surround and stare into the dancing flames with no apparent purpose. Soon the stories begin.

A campfire brings out tale-telling even in the most shy people, invoking again the image of primitive heritage. Without a fire, storytelling could not have taken root. Where else could the entire group gather for such inspiration? Certainly not during the hunt. Certainly not while bucketing water, washing clothes, or seining fish.

Without fire, we'd not be the beneficiaries of Homer's *Iliad*, Shakespeare's *Hamlet*, Twain's *Huckleberry Finn*, Steinbeck's *The Red Pony*, or Mitchell's *Gone with the Wind*. Without fire and its contemplative invitation, there would be no written language, no technology, no advanced standard of living. Aside from its intellectual stimulus, fire played a most important functional role. It provided warmth and light, cooked food, and helped fend off predators. Later, fire was utilized to bake vessels for storage and melt metals in order to shape them into weapons and implements. Fire was harnessed to clear land for agriculture and to provide better forage for domestic and wild animals upon which primitive man depended for sustenance.

Aside from its intellectual and functional purposes, fire played an important spiritual role in the development of early man. It has at least some significance in most religions, even today. Incense is burned, candles are lit, eternal flames tended. Keepers of the fire in primitive societies were almost always considered holy—especially before man learned effective methods of fire ignition.

Fire, then, and the ability to harness it was undoubtedly man's greatest discovery. With fire came a quantum leap forward, ultimately leading to the written word, agriculture, animal husbandry, the wheel, mathematics, science, rocket ships to the moon. Without fire, little would distinguish us from the beasts of field and forest.

Why modern fireplaces? After all, in today's world, only a few homes are dependent upon them for heat, thus they serve little functional purpose. Our own fireplace provides peace of mind, however. Once last winter, during a four-hour electrical outage, we were dependent upon it for both heat and cooking. For us, the electrical inconvenience provided adventure rather than hardship.

When we torch a fire in our fireplace most winter evenings, our objective is aesthetic rather than practical. As an intellectual and spiritual force, it beats baseboard-electric all hollow. ∎

Why Grandpas Lap Up Attention

Most of our friends consider me something of a masculine enigma. I know the shortest distance along mountain trails between Mortimer Gulch and Meadow Creek Gorge, but I've never understood the connection between fingertip switch and overhead light. I can pack a wheelbarrow, half an elk, and nine-foot bridge planks across the Chinese Wall, but can't shove a Skillsaw along a straight line or drive a nail without it dodging before my eyes.

So when Jane and our grandson suggested I hang a swing from a backyard tree limb, the idea met with resistance. A wife of multi-decades I can usually resist with ease, but how does a rough ex-outfitter resist a three-year-old who crawls into his lap, turns oversized blue eyes upon him, and says, "Will you, grampa?"

Scene 1.

I pick out a stout limb, prop an aluminum extension ladder against it, climb the ladder, adjust a rope to the correct height, and secure both ends. Then I cut and notch a plank seat, place it firmly, and with wife and grandson applauding, sit and test it by beginning to pump just like in childhood.

On the second pump, the *dead* limb broke.

Fortunately, the limb missed—but ensnared in several coils

of rope, the aluminum ladder didn't!

Cut to Scene 2.

Yesterday, I moved dozens of boxes of our *Montana's Bob Marshall Wilderness* book from a storage room to another shed—with the boy "helping," of course. Twice I snarled at him to get out of my way as I wheeled a laden dolly into the back of a pickup truck. Another time I gave him a stern tongue-lashing as he sought to clamber into the storage-shed door while I backed the truck toward it.

Cut to Scene 3.

He's a non-stop noise-maker, that kid. Though he starts slowly when first awakening, he's wound as tight as a new drum when bedtime rolls around. And grandpa is like an old dog around a mean-spirited pup: hiding behind the door, under the bed—any place where he can't be found.

So why does the kid stagger from bed in the morning and crawl into my lap to be sheltered and cuddled and loved? Why does he choose doddering, inept, cranky grandpa over a grandmother who has always won the heart of any soul lucky enough to spend five minutes around her? One of life's mysteries, that.

But grandpa laps up the boy's loving attachment. Anytime that kid wants, he'll have a horse to ride, a game to play, a swing to swing, cartoons to watch. When he gets old enough, he can look forward to wilderness packtrips and fishing excursions to whichever river or lake he chooses.

You see, we grandpas so seldom get tender loving care that whenever a little dribbles our way, we'll knock ourselves out to prove we're worth every bit of it. ■

Crackbrained Answers to Cockeyed Questions

One of the more enlightening bits of wisdom to come my way during my two decades as a Bob Marshall Wilderness guide was how little I knew at the outset. Success at the world's *second* oldest profession, as I quickly discovered, requires an unusual blend of traits and skills, none of which I possessed from the outset.

When I went into outfitting, I thought one must know how to ear down an outlaw bronc, find his way across the Continental Divide in a raging blizzard, and find where every three-pound cutthroat, six-point bull elk, and thirty-five-inch mulie buck lurked in the northern Rocky Mountains. I expected, too, that it was all-important to be able to top pack with a diamond hitch on a balky mule, torch a fire in a cloudburst, and locate a tent above flood-stage during spring run-off.

How stupid.

Instead, I quickly discovered an unforeseen need for a diagnostic truck mechanic capable of setting distributor points in a fog at midnight, and using a ball-peen hammer as my only tool.

It helped, too, to be a graduate dietician with a minor in

prophecy in order to develop a tasty, balanced menu that appealed to everyone, no matter their religion, ethnic origin, or medical history.

To be an outfitter, one must have more patience than Job. You must be able to shrug it off while hanging around an airport for an hour or two waiting for a guest who failed to arrive when scheduled because he failed to show up for his departure on time. Then, after he does arrive it's necessary for an outfitter to be able to explain to the distraught hunter or fisherman from Poughkeepsie how Tallahassee Air lost a fishing rod or rifle in an airline change at Pittsburgh or Dallas or Dulles or O'Hare International.

So an outfitter must be an amateur psychologist, too. And *that*, folks, is the single most important skill the poor sucker must acquire. Without it, he's doomed....

<hr />

"Can I shoot from the backs of your horses?"

I stared at the man for only a couple of seconds before answering, "Yes—once."

He'd crowded up to our Pennsylvania sport-show booth to ask what he thought was an important question relating to elk hunting. I sighed and repeated my stock reply to that stock question. The guy looked puzzled for a moment, then the logic of what was said washed over him and he grinned.

Most folks with a modicum of experience find it difficult to believe the kinds of questions an outfitter is obliged to field from folks who haven't had too many outdoors clues. Early on, some of those questions dumfounded me, but one soon learns to employ sardonic wit in defense.

"What do you guarantee?"

"That you'll get back. If you don't get back, we'll refund your money."

"What's your success rate?"

"Depends. Physically able, experienced hunters have better success rates than couch potatoes."

"How much do I have to walk during a trip with you?"

"None. 'Course, if you wish to hunt ..."

"What rifle do you recommend?"

"The one you're familiar with."

Then there are the others: the lady who comes to the booth demanding to know about campgrounds in Idaho. The guy who wants to know about lodge accommodations in Yellowstone. There've actually been folks who became angry because I didn't have Montana highway maps to give them.

Perhaps I'm leaving the wrong impression. Most of the folks who came with our outfit during the decades I served as a Bob Marshall Wilderness guide and outfitter were more perceptive than those I've portrayed here. Still, for some reason, we sometimes drew the other kind.

"When's the best time to hunt?"

"Whenever you have the time."

"Is your country steep?"

"No, it's flat. But danged little of it is on the level—it's either flat up or flat down."

"What's the weather going to be like during hunting season?"

Sigh. ∎

I enjoy your show and listen each chance I get.
                    Mark Koroshetz • Cedaredge, CO

I love your radio program.
                    Ann Bresson • Challis, ID

I just heard your program. Nice!
                    Grace DeSaye • Prescott, AZ

Clean as an All-Day
Sucker in Kindergarten

This getting ready for a Cabinet appointment is not an easy task. It's not enough to slop the hogs, feed the chickens, carry in wood, pack out garbage, dust the furniture, and vacuum floors. Now it's shine shoes, press boiled shirts, and practice my four-in-hand in case the President calls.

Why would the nation's President consider a fat, bald, ugly, White Anglo Saxon Protestant with a track record of know-nothing and do-nothing indolence?

Because he's gone through most everyone else, and I may be the only guy left who's relatively unknown to the Religious Right and who never failed to withhold Social Security on domestic help.

The fact that Jane and I are faceless to Jerry Falwell is because we're unknown to Archie Bunker and Henry Kissinger, too. And it helps our Soc/Sec record that we've never failed our withholding obligations on domestic help because we've never employed domestic help. But it makes no difference how we got there, only that we're as clean as an all-day sucker in kindergarten.

As far as qualifications go, I'm available for most any Cabinet post. Take agriculture, for instance....

Though I know very little about price supports and per-bushel breakdowns on grain prices, nothing at all about pork bellies and angora futures, and couldn't even raise a row with my wife on the best cropland in the lower 48, I'm confident I could do at least as well as the last twelve Secretaries of Agriculture who spent a lifetime learning about Washington politics and Russian glad-handing.

I'd be strong with Interior, too, because I know even less about public land grazing than anybody west of Plymouth Rock. But I do believe a farmer or rancher ought to be able to drink water flowing from his land and ought to be willing to eat produce he crop-dusted last week.

How about the subdivisions within those agencies? Well, I'll admit to being weak—or even distrusted—with the U.S. Forest Service. I'd probably be weak with the Fish & Wildlife Service, too, but for a different reason. My trouble with the Forest Service, you see, is that I know something about forests, having felled, skidded, and hauled logs in my youth. Then I've hiked, rode, smelled and swelled amid much of the wildlands of the Northwest almost since Grover Cleveland's mommy was a baby. So maybe I know too much about forests to be effective at overseeing folks who spent a lifetime studying engineering and wood technology. On the other hand, maybe I'd be a breath of fresh air.

Fish & Wildlife, now, that's a different show. You see, I've recently come to understand that I don't know nearly as much about other creatures carving their niche out of the same land I love—elk, bear, ground squirrels—as I once thought. Thirty years ago, things were a bunch clearer. I had a barn full of antlers to prove I knew as much about elk as any man ever needed to know. Bears? They rob bee trees and can be cranky if surprised. Ground squirrels pilfer grain if they get half a chance.

Then I hit a few dry years elk hunting, and bears turned out to be far more puzzling than a guy could guess, and darned if watching ground squirrels at work or play didn't wind up turning my crank.

No doubt I could do well in other Cabinet posts, too, though the striped-pants boys leave me cold. The reason why the diplomatic corps is somewhat lower than ground squirrels to me is because all this "inferring" and "insinuating" and beating around the bush like a Secretary of State has to do with both enemies and allies is the pits to a boy who grew up among men. Back where I come from, we tell it like it is, and the devil take the hindmost.

I'd do okay in Housing and Urban Development, even though I believe part of the title is oxymoronic.

I'm in favor of Interstate Commerce, too, even though I've been unsuccessful throughout a lifetime in trying to develop some.

Although I'd be proud to serve as Secretary of Defense, I'd have to tell Congress and the President up front that I'd find it difficult to spend as much money as the job requires.

Labor? Maybe, though Jane would handle the job better—she's been overworked and underpaid most of her adult life.

Transportation? I suppose some eggheads might believe all those years spent a-horseback would serve no useful purpose in a modern world, but nothing could be farther from the truth. Hours in the saddle provide perception and depth, something lacking in Cabinet appointments since Marshall was charged with European relief.

Nope, the longer one thinks on it, the more likely it is that I'm your guy. That's why I'm going inside now—to sit by the telephone. ■

Color-Coding Union Suits

How many of you know wool underwear used to be color-coded so the proud owner of longhandles would know what he was donning before the sweat popped out: white was the lightest weight, red for medium, and black for heaviest.

When someone slipped into the scratchy "long-black" you knew he figured on exposure to the elements at their rawest. Or else he didn't want folks telling at a glance whether he'd changed since the winter's first norther blew in from the Canadian prairies.

Lighter-weight white, of course, was more suitable for evening wear or all-season use. White was the hands-down choice of early Montana range men—which seems odd until one learns that they simply donned a second suit when the winter turned bitter.

Wearing two suits of long underwear must have been unhandy for early-day cowboys, however, considering the button-up flaps of yesteryear. Let's see ... unbuckle the six-gun and heavy batwing chaps, unbuckle and unbutton and then jiggle loose the tight-fitting Levis, fumble hurriedly with the flap of the first set of underwear and fold it down, then rip off them bloody #$&@# buttons from the second—aw rats! Too late!

Loggers wore the long black beneath suspender-supported wool trousers tucked into lace-up, high-topped, caulk-soled leather boots. Most wore wool shirts beneath heavy, double-layered-over-the-shoulders wool coats except when they were engaged in the hard work of crosscut sawing. Then they stripped down to the long black on their upper torsos, even unbuttoning to the belt if we can go by early-day photographs. Utilizing such stripped-down attire must have facilitated flap-unbuttoning in emergency situations for those canny woodcutters.

However, most ordinary folks chose medium-weight red: miners, railroaders, farmers, and the like. I presume it was because they were either undecided in the mercantile check-out lines or they chose to add a little class to otherwise humdrum existences.

Whatever their reasons, it was the red that went down as the "union suit" of history, and it's the red that's still lampooned in cartoon and verse. But that's a bum rap, the red served a useful purpose despite the satire. It offered occasional splashes of color to the early-day landscapes, especially across the bleak western plains. It had body to it, and character—something lacking in yesterday's blacks and whites, as well as today's fashionable two-piece synthetics.

No matter that today you can buy those imitation-fiber longhandles in leopard-skin print or passionate pink or blaze orange, the character of the attire has gone straight to hell. After all, who's to see? Today there's no scratching in relief while fumbling for buttons with these blasted two-piecers. Today, folks do their thing in the privacy of their own bathrooms, or behind locked doors at truck stops, service stations, or Interstate rest areas. Why should anyone care what color is someone else's chosen apparel?

So let's give another cheer for those "next-year" homesteaders who dotted the western plains, breaking prairie sod behind a span of mules. From time to time, they must have been colorful specks on the distant horizons, mooning their Norwegian neighbors on the next half-section. The red added color and class to what might otherwise have been a dreary life.

Two-piece leopard-skin, even in chartreuse, could not have contributed half so much. ∎

My father-in-law and I both enjoy listening to your stories on KDTA Delta, CO. Patty Tharp • Austin, CO

I really like your program—I would like it longer, though. Rick Gill • Provo, UT

Where All God's Creatures Are Out to Get You

In all my life, I've never gone without water. Oh, I've been inconvenienced a time or two. But gone without when I was desperate for it? Huh-uh. That's why it's a revelation for me to visit places where worry over water is the traveler's most constant companion.

Raised in the Oregon Cascades and with half a lifetime spent among the wildest peaks in the northern Rockies, my concerns have usually been to locate adequate firewood, shelter from bugs or wind or snow, perhaps to find forage for my horses. Seldom has an adequate water source been a problem.

Yes, I know there are sections along Montana's Hi-Line where early homesteaders hitched teams to wagons to haul water for miles for their livestock and themselves. Yes, I know water is at a premium amid the mesas and buttes of the Powder River country, and down in Oregon's High Desert, or Wyoming's Purple Sage plateaus. But in most cases, even in those places, it's inconvenience we're talking about, not a life-threatening situation.

Little puffs of dust squirted from the soles of our hiking boots as we trudged across the sun-baked Utah mesa, heading for vehicles parked earlier in the week. The climb out of the canyon had been grueling under a relentless sun. Two of our party wore bandannas draped over their heads, Arab fashion. Skins glistened with suntan lotion. All wore sunglasses, save one who'd left his lying on a rock two days before.

Ruth mentioned she'd recently read of a turn-of-the-century expedition that had left the San Juan River to visit the area now known as Natural Bridges National Monument. She spoke of the weeks it took them to make the journey. She told of the party's horses, dogs, and people.

As Ruth outlined what she'd read, I thought about the sheer logistics of such an undertaking before highways, automobiles, refrigeration. *My God!* the thought struck—*water alone!*

We'd left water in our parked vehicles, now less than two miles distant. Mirages of the vehicles were already shimmering in the distance. As careful travelers, we'd dutifully filtered and filled two extra water bottles each from the canyon bottom's intermittent pools before beginning our ascent. By the time we'd reached this plateau, our water was largely gone. The vehicles' re-supply beckoned. But what about a party that must be self-supporting for weeks while crossing this land before roads and automobiles? What about water for their stock?

Up in the country where I dwell, even on the dry side of the Rocky Mountains, one seldom finds land that is farther than a day's hike or horseback ride from stream to stream. But in that scorched Utah country, canyons containing water are treasured. More to the point, in that plateau country of giant earth cracks, canyons with water accessible to livestock are rare or entirely absent.

My hat is off to those early desert travelers. For them, other concerns had to be put on hold until they solved the ever constant need for water. Theirs is a tough land where sidehills are vertical, where every single type of vegetation claws, scratches, pokes, or scrapes. All moving objects sting, snap, strike, or slither. The sun blisters, shade freezes. There are no in-betweens.

That's why I found it amusing when a veteran desert traveler seemed awestruck to discover I'm from Montana. "I don't know how you do it," he said.

"Huh? Do what?"

"Get around up there in the north country where a man can freeze to death in a blizzard or get ate by a grizzly bear." ∎

Airborne Face Plant
vs Flying Buttocks Arrest

Ski slopes are fine. They bring visitors, who also bring money. Ski slopes contribute to community cash flows at a time of year when most residents with disposable income huddle around a fire and contemplate their navels.

Ski slopes also contribute to bizarre behavior, especially amongst country folks more accustomed to slopping hogs for their recreation. Most locals can't stand to see others having fun without sampling same, but a problem arises when they discover it's essential to pay the cost of a candlelight dinner for two in order to stand in a lift line that ultimately allows them to careen down Mount Everest with both eyes clinched.

Us saner bumpkins, therefore, migrate into crosscountry skiing. The crosscountry variety is supposedly better for your body and has the added advantage of no lift tickets.

Still, though relatively inexpensive and good for its adherents, crosscountry skiing is an art form requiring skill, dexterity, and a certain flair. Having engaged in the activity before the age of smart bombs and guided missiles, I have the whiskers to warrant your believing I'm a qualified instructor. Take technique, for instance: I've prepared a cursory list of challenging and accomplished ski maneuvers that can enable novice and intermediate alike to blend with any veteran ski crowd.

The very first technique to be mastered is the *Uphill Pant*. This consists of sliding each foot forward ahead of the other, always toward the highest spot on any distant skyline. The chief requirement for accomplishing the *Uphill Pant* is no discernible physical weakness.

Successful conclusion of the *Uphill Pant* usually leads to the *Peek-at-the-Peak Shriek*. This impromptu maneuver is usually accomplished near the halfway point of the *Uphill Pant*. It should always be employed as a prelude to a course change.

There is little to be gained by continuing the *Pant* past the *Shriek* because one might incur *Grand Canyon Quiver*. *Grand Canyon Quiver* is a phenomenon akin to sighting a flying saucer or becoming snared in the Bermuda Triangle. Proceed beyond the *Shriek* at your own risk.

Instead, my advice is turn around and return to the valley floor. Any valley floor. Immediately. Your quickest method of return is via *Maxi-Glide/Mini-Guide*. Besides being far and away the swiftest method down any hill, *Maxi-Glide/Mini-Guide* is also the one most likely to provide supine transportation in a heated custom van with crimson crosses painted left and right.

Should you be reluctant to employ the *Maxi-Glide/Mini-Guide* technique, try either the *Horizontal Shuffle* or the *Teeter-Totter Flounce*. Of the two, the *Teeter-Totter Flounce* is more likely to be successfully concluded. Though the *Horizontal Shuffle* sounds cosmopolitan, it has a bad reputation because its practitioners are usually tardy for supper. The *Teeter-Totter Flounce*, incidentally, obscures your tracks, in case process servers are in hot pursuit.

Most novice crosscountry skiers seem obsessed with descent control. They should not be so focused on the rigors of downslope travel. Here's why:

There are several effective methods for descent control while skiing. Two stand out. Each is recommended if you must make a bathroom break in the middle of a *Maxi-Glide/Mini-Guide* maneuver. First, of course, is the time-tested *Flying Buttocks Arrest*; the other is the more aesthetic—and spectacular—*Airborne Face Plant.*

Sophisticated practitioners of artful crosscountry skiing have usually mastered all of the above techniques.

Me? I can do them in combination.

⟡

Jokes aside, travel through mountain country can be dangerous—especially spring travel.

We'd glided down the stream just a couple of weeks before, and the only danger was our skis' failure to grip the wind-blown glare ice. Now, however, water gurgled ominously beneath the rotting ice surface, and open leads of riffles were common. Perhaps most to be feared were the collapsing snow bridges we'd depended upon to cross what we'd expected to be a winter-locked stream.

Two weeks of unseasonably warm days accompanied by chinook winds foretold change. Spring rode those winds. There was "feel" to the air that should trigger an unconscious—but automatic—"traveler's advisory" in the mind of every backcountry adventurer, for dangers are myriad.

We tested a couple of the remaining snow bridges, and when they collapsed with probes from our ski poles, we turned and headed back the way we'd come.

Spring beguiles. It caresses with soft winds and warm sun. There's promise of new life in tree buds, greening fields, and old bones. Yet for the backcountry traveler, a multitude of dangers lurk behind spring's beckoning wave.

We could have crossed that stream on our ski trip. Perhaps someone would've fallen in as a snow bridge or ice bridge collapsed, but the day was so warm, the weather so mild, that such a mishap would've been more inconvenience than threat to life.

Not so two weeks before or two weeks after. Anyone who slipped through the ice two weeks before would have done so amid chilling temperatures and a thirty-mile-wind. Two weeks after, and one would have to attempt crossing a raging torrent at spring flood.

Spring travel through mountain country harbors other dangers as well:

Avalanche-prone hillsides should be avoided or, if you must, cross rapidly, with an ear cocked for the slightest strange and unidentifiable sound—the beginning avalanche.

Stay off snow cornices, the wind-blown drift's roll-over on the lee side of ridges. They are certain to collapse, shatter at cliff bottom, then melt sometime before midsummer. It's the collapse that eats the unwary traveler. As a general rule, I make sure that's not me.

Pre-planned routes can be hard to follow during spring's turmoil on the way to summer's relaxation. Low-country trails can be blocked by winter's accumulated blowdowns or by mud slides, and mountain passes are often locked tight by snowdrifts higher than a tall man astride a tall horse.

Even vehicle travel can be chancy along off-highway roads gripped by breakup.

Emergency rations should be standard equipment just in case your F250 winds up stuck in a boghole. Or in case you must retrace your last twenty miles with your packstring. Or in case your backpacking journey is held up by avalanching snows or rampaging rivers.

All the foregoing doesn't mean you should cower at home, under your bed, during the "traveler's advisory" period. No indeed. But if you choose to venture into the backcountry during spring, you should be aware of potential dangers, keep your options open, never tempt fate, and prepare for contingencies. That's all.

If you prepare and are prepared, spring is a most delightful time of year. I know. I've been in the middle of the Bob Marshall Wilderness on May Day—*very* early spring to that high country land. And you know what?

I had the place *all* to myself.

———

I exploded when I glanced back and saw my wife on her rump, sliding down a near-perpendicular chute packed with drifted snow. "Get off there," I roared.

It was late June. Our group was strung out on a thousand-foot descent from Mount Aeneas to Birch Lake. Jane was uppermost. I stood on safe ground at the chute's bottom. The other couple were between us, picking their careful way down.

Marilyn, too, was on snow. But she was just fifty feet up the slope and appeared safe enough. Doug was off to the side on bare ground, tromping down through leafless tag alders and snow brush. It was Jane, 150 yards up the steep chute, who frightened me. If she lost control and rocketed down the mountain she must surely crash against one or more of the scattered boulders littering the chute's bottom.

As the woman crawled sulkily from the snowfield, I turned to study the rest of our route down to the Alpine Trail. Then I heard a gasp and a throaty giggle, and I spun back to see Marilyn sliding down slope. Gravity pulled her toward the chute's trough, sweeping her toward a melted-out chasm in the drift where a swift whitewater stream roared.

It all happened so quickly! Marilyn's eyes widened and she lost her hiking staff and backpack as she picked up speed. Then she tumbled over the chasm lip onto stones and into the run-off torrent.

I reached the crevice in time to give Marilyn a hand out. She clambered up soaked and bruised and shaken. Fortunately, her careening run was brief and the drop onto the rocks resulted in no broken bones.

Doug picked up his wife's hiking staff and backpack, then helped her to a log where she could rest and take stock. Jane arrived moments later. She'd watched from up-slope as her friend had careened down the chute, out of control. Her eyes met mine. "Thanks," she silently mouthed.

There are few folks from my part of the world who've not cavorted on spring drifts by fanny-bumping down a slope of packed snow. Sure, they scream in mock terror, laughing all the way. And if such experiences turned out well, they were either lucky or careful.

All too often, snowfield fanny-bumping turns into a runaway express. There've been many times when revelers crashed into rocks or trees. Injuries have occurred—even death.

Although Jane had begun sliding at the top of a perilous drift, she had not progressed so far that she was unable to stop and scramble from danger. It was her friend, almost at the bottom, who lost her footing and slid out of control. Even at that, Marilyn was lucky. Jane was luckier.

Pick your fanny-bumping snowdrifts with caution. Stay off the steep stuff. Avoid drifts with exposed rocks or trees. Be sure there's a glide-out at the bottom, where you can slide to a stop while still on snow.

One might wonder why we were on that mountainside in the first place, but each of us knew. The view was fantastic from Aeneas that day—east, west, south, and north lay mountain range after mountain range, all standing in bold relief in the crisp, clear air. After gazing our fill, we headed to Birch Lake for a swim.

What's a thousand-foot descent over crumbling cliffs and down avalanche tracks if it provides such experiences? ■

With Health, Who Needs Swiss Bank Accounts?

I'd reckon that in the whole world there's nobody with more obligation to be thankful than the guy writing this.

First of all, there's the accident of birth—that I was born in America, not Somalia; brought into the world by poor but honest parents, not drug addicts; parents who owned their own tiny hardscrabble farm instead of occupying a squalid hut in a displaced persons' camp.

Second, I grew up amid plenty. Not money, mind you, but the important stuff: food, water, wild country, opportunity. And good access to the three "R"s. That I never took proper advantage of educational possibilities is my fault alone. Yet, the fact that I didn't has never been a stigma; has never been held against me. Thus, the life our family has is of our own doing and not dependent on the charity of others, nor beholding to government dole.

Third, not only do we live in America, but in rural, down-home America where our neighbors are the best people in all the world: honest, thrifty, hardworking, wise beyond their province; just like my own long-gone father and mother.

Fourth, I could have done no better in marriage if I'd searched the whole world for a stand-out woman instead of grabbing the neat one growing up next door. And our children are honest, hard-working adults who contribute to society and are tributes to their mother and father.

Fifth, we're enjoying top-notch health. True, money seems to be most illusive throughout life, but both Jane and I are superbly healthy for a couple of old duffers. We still enjoy the exhilaration of standing on a mountaintop, or the thrill of whizzing down a remote forest road on crosscountry skis. Others can shake their heads in distaste, wondering what makes us tick, but nothing can keep us from hiking or riding or floating or fishing or hunting or skiing or driving someplace at least once every week. Alongside the benefits of superb health, who needs Swiss bank accounts?

Sixth, life is fascinating. There've been several careers: working my way up through the wood-products industry, wilderness guiding and outfitting, becoming a free-lance journalist and radio commentator. I can't remember not wanting to get out of bed; not believing each day that something important waited to be done.

Seventh, I love to learn. I read newspapers, magazines, and books about subjects of national and international interest. I savor good writing wherever it's found. In addition, my interests are broad: geology, botany, biology. That can be interpreted to mean the land, plants, and animals found in God's creation. And most of all, I'm fascinated by people—all people, everywhere. Each has opinions, special insight, knowledge, skills. Most are willing to share with others who demonstrate a genuine interest.

Eighth, my woodpile is full, hay barn stocked, horses fat, and storm windows up. Our skis are waxed, vehicles winterized, wool clothing laid out, and coffee pot on. Let the seasons do what they will.

Where to from here? Who knows? But that's part of life's charm, isn't it? Life isn't a destination, it's a journey. Achieving goals is not nearly so important as striving for them. Success should in no way be measured by material possessions, but by personal satisfaction. My own search for the Holy Grail is not the normal quest for a hereafter. Instead, it's how I'm thought of here, after I'm gone.

I wrote this in November, as Thanksgiving Day approached. Thanksgiving seems an appropriate day to recollect all the above. But it seems to me there are abundant reasons to be thankful every day. ∎

Extending a Hand for a Job Well Done

He paused before our Skyline Outfit's wilderness adventure booth, hands thrust deep into trouser pockets. Someone bumped him, but he seemed not to notice, continuing to stare. It was at the Pennsylvania Sport Show, in Harrisburg. Aisles were especially crowded that day, with attendance well over the hundred-thousand mark as Easterners jostled one another to view the hundreds upon hundreds of outdoor displays ranging from Bechuanaland safaris to fishing for arctic char in Canada's Northwest Territories.

He moved a step closer to read a small sign propped on our counter, then peered down at the sheet of paper and its wilderness proposal. No expression crossed his face as he began reading the petition. He looked to be maybe thirteen years old.

We watched in silence as the boy read. But when he'd finished, Mike, our former trip guest who helped me in the booth that day, asked, "Do you know what that is?"

The boy nodded. "It's a petition."

"Do you know who it's addressed to?"

"It's to the Congress of the United States of America."

"Do you know what it's for?"

"It's to make a wilderness out there in Montana."

"Do you know why?" Mike persisted.

"I sure do," the boy said. "It's to keep them from tearing up the land and cutting all the trees."

Mike's voice softened. "You could sign that petition, too, you know. Every signature will help."

The boy smiled as he reached for a nearby pen and filled out a petition blank. Then, without another word, hands again thrust into corduroy pockets, he strolled away into the jostling crowd.

"That was well done," I said to my friend.

Mike nodded, seemingly lost in thought. "You know, there's something special about that kid—don't you think? He didn't sign because it was something cool to do. He really did think it all out—don't you believe?"

I shrugged as I turned to answer a question from one of our customers.

It was thirty minutes later when a mob surrounded our booth. One minute the crowd flowed past, the next minute there must have been a dozen of 'em crowding right up to the counter where the petition blanks lay, reaching for pens. I looked blankly at Mike. He seemed bewildered, too.

The first lady to the counter wore a well-tailored wool suit and appeared to be in her late thirties. She carried a big plastic bag stuffed with God-knows-what under one arm, but she used the other to quickly sign a form asking Congress to help save a beautiful piece of land spreading along the northern Rockies.

A stately, elderly gentleman read the petition thoroughly, then signed it with a flourish. He handed his pen on and it was passed from hand to hand as others crowded to sign. There must have been three generations in that large family group: grandparents, fathers and mothers, sisters and brothers. The youngest? Perhaps ten. The eldest? Lord knows.

Then Mike spied him. Standing amid them all was a maybe thirteen-year-old boy with hands thrust deep into corduroy pockets. He made no attempt to move to the counter and he said nothing to anyone while we watched. Neither did any expression cross his face as each member of the group added another name to the petition to save a piece of wildland crucial to wildlife.

When the last of the people had signed our petitions and melted away to examine other displays, Mike walked around the counter and extended his hand for a job well done to a quiet kid in corduroy trousers. ∎

New Things Under the Sun

A fellow once told me, "You can't miss what you can't measure."

I suppose there's truth in it. Do I miss not being able to hunt buffalo on the western prairies, riding pell-mell through the sage after a band of the shaggy brutes bursting from a hidden draw?

No. Neither do I miss the feathered tempest of passenger pigeons or the singular cry of the heath hen. How can I—having arrived on the scene a century late?

Do I miss not being permitted to hunt mountain goats or fish for bull trout? Yes. You see, having done both, I'm able to measure yesterday's privilege against today's constraint.

Does the western rancher resent not being able to take destiny in his own hands when his sheep pasture is invaded by grizzly or wolf? Probably.

Is today's average weekend hunter satisfied with shrinking opportunity to pursue his or her sport on private lands? Not a heavyweight question, that. Everyone remembers the time just past when neighbors were welcome on neighbors' land.

Are we who remember abundant free-flowing streams, prairie potholes and teeming waterfowl, happy with the proliferation of pumps lowering stream flows and emptying lakes and marshes and potholes? Absolutely not, for we have yesterday's memories against which to measure today's realities.

What about our grandchildren? Will they miss being able to hunt buffalo? Shoot passenger pigeons? Stalk heath hens? Unlikely. But more to the point, will they miss hunting mountain goats or fishing for bull trout? Will they remember how ranchers and farmers once welcomed average folks to hunt and fish on their property? Or how a flock of mallards once rose like a cloud from the marsh that presently grows alfalfa?

I find it sad to think my children's children will probably not miss things we once took for granted because they'll no longer be able to measure their loss.

Not having a full range of outdoor options is tragic enough, but let's think beyond even that—would they miss not being able to fish at all if they'd never had the opportunity? Will the fever and excitement inherent in opening of hunting season some day be relegated to the musty pages of history texts or the faulty memories of antiquarians?

Aldo Leopold had this to say on the subject:

> For one species to mourn the death of another is a new thing under the sun. The Cro-Magnon who slew the last mammoth thought only of steaks. The sportsman who shot the last pigeon thought only of his prowess. The sailor who clubbed the last auk thought of nothing at all. But we, who have lost our pigeons, mourn the loss. Had the funeral been ours, the pigeons would hardly have mourned us. In this fact, rather than Mr. DuPont's nylons… lies objective evidence of our superiority over the beasts."

Mourning a lost species, as Leopold perhaps fails to note, is triggered first by those who feel the loss. It's questionable whether our kids who never fished for bull trout will properly rue their loss, just as I cannot in any way comprehend the cataclysmic natural disaster that was the demise of the passenger pigeon.

Although I'm following Leopold's lead, I find the mere mourning of a lost species is not enough. Our goal should be to sense a species' decline in a timely enough manner that we need never mourn its disappearance. That's where the Endangered Species Act comes into play. With bull trout at least, we're not mourning a lost species, but only mourning lost opportunity to fish for them.

We're doing much more than even Leopold sensed—we're intent on *saving* species in trouble, not content to mourn them. That is *really* something new under the sun.

Teeming millions of chinook salmon fade into the sunset like once-teeming millions of bison. Salmon are at risk not from the discharge of .50-caliber rifles, but from the discharge of 600 megawatt generators. Grizzly bears are threatened not so much by the infamous "shoot, shovel, and shut up" fraternity as by the roads, row houses, and wreckage of unbridled growth.

I've fished for salmon and watched grizzlies at work and play. Whether we'll not have to miss what we *can* measure will depend on our continuing to do "new things under the sun. ∎

Ways to Better a Torch

I go back before flashlights. No, that's not exactly true. But I do go back before *reliable* flashlights were available for backcountry travel; when moonlight and starlight on a clear night were more comforting than a dim beam from a cumbersome flashlight with a short in its switch.

Back in the year 1948 B.P. (before plastic), flashlights were constructed of metal that shorted, rusted, and weighed enough to anchor your backpack in a cyclone. And if you wanted a beam stout enough to reflect a cougar's eyes on the dark side of your tent flap, its batteries weighed almost as much as the F250 housing my current Die-Hard. To make matters worse, those heavyweight flashlight batteries usually lasted only long enough for the user to scamper to the privy, brighten the immediate surrounds while there, then hot-foot it back to a warm sleeping bag.

With today's lightweight plastics, and batteries so tiny I pitched two into Sunday's collection plate by mistake, a man could take a midnight stroll through Central Park and feel comfortable that he could spot incoming muggers in time to begin reciting the rosary.

What did canny outdoors folk do for night-lights before the age of reliable flashlights? I used miner's carbide lamps. One of my buddies who'd worked in the mines at Butte came up with the idea. Pretty clever, these innovations—probably been used for centuries before I tumbled on the trick.

The trick actually was simple. Buy carbide flakes—in those days, hardware stores sold the Union Carbide flakes in small metal cans. Fill the bottom portion of the lamp, then add water to the storage tank on top. When you want light, turn the cock to let water drip into the flakes, creating acetylene gas. Ignite.

Each carbide lamp had a flint and steel striker where the gas jet exited onto a reflector shield. Simply strike a spark and presto! Let there be light. Be careful with your water, however. Don't drown your flakes or starve them. Let just enough water drip to produce gas—no more, no less.

Aside from a crying need for careful water regulation, carbide lamps were nearly trouble-free. Occasionally the jet plugged, and a wise miner always packed a piece of fine wire for reaming out the jet hole. But how in the world he found it in the inky blackness of two thousand feet below ground boggles my mind!

A single carbide charge in my lamps lasted for several hours. And one could buy larger reflectors that would actually throw a beam for a couple hundred feet. The lamps, of course, were designed for fitting onto a belt or headband or into a socket on a miner's hard hat. I simply reversed my baseball cap and slipped the clip over the backstrap in order to free my hands.

A simpler, more ingenious lighting device was the "Palouse lantern" used by the Brash family from Spangle, Washington. A bright and shiny three-pound coffee can was the reflector, and a candle produced the light. Turned sideways, with a bailing-wire handle and a four-corner hole punched in the coffee can to hold the candle, the Palouse lantern was near windproof, threw a remarkable light beam, and was as long-lasting as the candle you used.

Today's lightweight flashlights and long-lasting batteries retired my old carbide lamps and, I presume, Brash's Palouse lanterns. Today I use a lightweight but sturdy headlamp that is almost indestructible. The components are so well-protected and the housing so solidly constructed that I've never had a loose wire or faulty switch. It's virtually foolproof. In addition, there's a place inside for an extra bulb, and I always carry four AA backup batteries.

These headlamp flashlights sell for somewhere in the neighborhood of twenty bucks. Less expensive ones are on the market, but we tried 'em and didn't like 'em—here's a real case where you get what you pay for.

And what you pay for is a comforting, easy to handle, reliable reading light, cooking light, trail light. During the years I led others to wilderness adventure, I equipped each of my guides with a headlamp for emergency use and for saddling and unsaddling horses before daylight or after dark.

A blazing torch beats nothing at all. But all of the above beats a blazing torch. ∎

Fending Off Really Dangerous Animals

L ord knows, I saw enough dangerous animals during my
years as a guide and outfitter in the Bob Marshall
Wilderness. That's to be expected, I suppose, when one
spends the better part of each year sleeping under stars and
traveling upwards of fifteen hundred miles over long and
lonesome trails.

One of my most savage adventures was running into the
llama at Pentagon Guard Station. Odds are this experience
wouldn't have been so traumatic except that I was responsible
for a group of hunters. We were on our way back to camp
after an exhausting and fruitless day of elk hunting. Unknown
to us, another group had camped near the station and turned
their single pack animal—a llama named, as I recall, Isaac—
loose to graze.

Our horses were in a hurry, walking or trotting. They were
bunched up, eager to get back to their oatbags at camp. We
riders were tired, lallygagging in the saddles, chattering about
the elk we'd jumped and nearly got a crack at. That's when
Isaac galloped in amongst the ponies.

I'm sure the aberrational cross between puppy and pachy-
derm was merely trying to be friendly, but in those long-ago
days my horses had never seen a llama. On top of that, Isaac

was decked out in blaze-orange ribbons fluttering from ears, tail, back, and nose, apparently to keep some errant hunter from mistaking him for an elk. (Of course, after it was all over, I had to talk like a Dutch uncle to keep *my* hunters from going llama hunting.)

Isaac caught us all by surprise. The first I knew, horses exploded everywhere. There were horses with yelling, clinging hunters jumping over hitchracks, dashing through hawthorn thickets, under low-hanging spruce limbs. Riders grappled with saddlehorns, saddlebags, stirrups—whatever chanced to fly near.

The only thing that saved us was speed. Curious llamas, as it turned out, are no match for spooked ponies in a flat-out foot race.

Another dangerous encounter occurred on that same Spotted Bear River Trail, some miles below Dean Falls. At the time, I was walking, leading my saddlehorse. Ten packhorses loaded with hay trailed behind. The first I knew of impending horror was when the packhorses dynamited through the lodgepole, and my saddlehorse jerked me, legs dragging like travois poles, back the way we'd come.

He was huge.

He must have been a cross between a Newfoundland and a Black Angus cow. He acted as though he was no more than six months old, and he seemed deadly intent on placing a front paw on each of my shoulders and licking me to death. Before my horses scattered their packs and departed for nether regions, they saw only this giant bundle of black death hurtling around a trail bend, red tongue lolling, charging into their midst.

The dog's mistress saved me. She did this by calling off the savage beast before he licked all the skin off my face. The dog then galloped back to dance around what I discovered was a not-in-the-least contrite woman. As I regained my feet and dusted off, the lady looked down her nose at me, then eyed the packstring's destructive wake. "I think it's terrible," she said, "that hikers and horses must use the same trails in this godforsaken country."

I've been bitten by horses and kicked by mules. Wet dogs have either lounged upon my sleeping bag or just inside the tent flap for me to stumble over.

Bears? Lions? Wolves? Naah. They're not so bad. Not nearly as dangerous as the really frightening animals I've faced during my two dozen odd years working vast wildernesses stretching along the northern Rockies. ■

No Room Up the Tree for Me, Too

There was a time in my earlier days when I hunted grizzly bears. My reasons, I told myself, were myriad: I wanted a grizzly rug for a trophy. Or maybe I wanted the thrill of challenge and danger. It's certain I viewed the effort as the ultimate in hunting adventure, its successful conclusion as the number one credential for a consummate outdoorsman.

I've never killed a grizzly bear. As a matter of fact, I've never even flung a rifle ball after the brutes. Oh, sure, I've seen my share—quit counting after seventy (some with cubs at their sides).

But somewhere along the line, just seeing them was enough. Somewhere, sometime, I made the transition to watching brer bruin feeding on huckleberries, tearing up rotted logs in search of grubs, excavating beargrass-covered slopes and rolling over boulders in pursuit of marmots or ground squirrels. Somehow, just viewing those sights became more important than proving I was Jim Bridger incarnate.

I haven't any quarrel with those who legally hunt grizzlies, or with anyone defending himself or herself against a marauding bear. If there's a sustainable, huntable population of the big carnivores out there, I'll come down on the side of carefully regulated hunting as an appropriate management tool.

The key, of course, is the word *sustainable*. And that word has much broader implications than meet the eye. Sustainable population means a viable bunch of the big bruins interacting in an acceptable fashion with their human contemporaries. It doesn't mean catering to marauding bears that wantonly destroy cattle or sheep or pretty maidens helplessly straitjacketed in their sleeping bags.

I guess I subscribe to a long-ago rule of bear researcher Dr. Charles Jonkel that removal of problem grizzly bears—perhaps by hunting—is necessary to gain public acceptance of a viable population of the big bears. But even Dr. Jonkel's perception changed as the renowned researcher participated in litigation to block a Montana hunting season. Why?

Because today the ball park is threatened. It makes little sense to argue the rules for playing if there's no place to play. Jonkel believes there's too much logging and too many miles of roads being constructed into prime grizzly habitat. There are too many second homes going up in *Ursus horribilis'* feeding grounds. And there are too many active participants in the "shoot, shovel and shut up club."

There are trade-offs, you see. And hunting suffers. Is the big bear really in deep trouble, as animal-rights organizations maintain? Or is he on the way to recovery, as federal and state wildlife agencies claim? And most puzzling of all, how is the average Joe American supposed to know who is right? Is it even important that we who live with the bears have an opinion about something that just might matter more to school children in Connecticut?

All I know is that only a few days ago, four hikers sat and ate lunch while watching an enormous grizzly sow and her two-year-old cub feed on huckleberries a hundred yards below. I was one of those hikers. That day was one of the highlights of my entire year.

<hr/>

I've had other highlight-days during my outdoors career. Some involved bears. Some involved bears and people. One such day began with my drinking from a full Jewel Basin cup.

I've many times sniffed the fragrant air, drunk from mountain freshets, and gazed upon the gem-like lakes of Jewel Basin. Most often, during the early years, I traveled into the Basin by horseback—which gives you some idea how long ago that was, since Jewel Basin has been a hiking area closed to horses for the better party of thirty years.

Jane and I no longer have our summers tied to leading guests into the Bob Marshall Wilderness and are free again to visit Jewel Basin. Doing so brought back memories of my last visit, decades before. It was during a combination day hike/fishing trip with a couple of buddies to Birch Lake. (For reasons that'll become clear later on, my buddies will remain unnamed.)

I quickly tire of angling when the fish aren't clamoring for a place in my creel, so I told my companions to continue fishing while I climbed Mount Aeneas to glass for mountain goats. The last thing I said was, "I'll meet you guys back at the rig at six."

They nodded.

The day was gorgeous as I struggled to the mountaintop, the view spectacular. All my internal vibes were in sync. I fell asleep. Upon waking, I flicked a look at my Timex and realized time had danced away. Surely my buddies were waiting. To save time, I plunged from the summit of Aeneas, bushwhacking in a straight line to intersect the trail back to my Jeep station wagon.

My buddies, of course, had already started their hike back along the precipitous Birch Lake Trail—the one that affords such spectacular views into the upper Flathead Valley. They were perhaps halfway to the roadhead when they rounded a trail bend and spotted a huge grizzly bear lumbering along their trail toward them!

Prudently, they decided discretion was the better part of valor and retreated. After rounding a couple of additional bends, they peeked back. The grizzly, grazing on huckleberries, continued to advance. My friends went into a caucus. Neither had previously hiked in Jewel Basin and they were unfamiliar with the country. All they knew was if that bear continued herding them south, they'd never make it to the Jeep before dark. Thus they decided to climb a tree and let the bear pass beneath. Flaws existed in their plan, however.

The first flaw involved tree quality. Near the crest of the Swan Range, the scattered forest is made up of mostly alpine fir and limber pine. Neither is noted for growing to spectacular heights. The second flaw lay in both of them shinnying up the same tree.

Who could blame them? Their chosen refuge was the tallest tree around, and each wanted to scale the tallest one. In addition, this tallest tree sprouted twenty feet from the trail on the uphill side, which, of course, would provide them with additional height over the bear. Up they went.

The fifty-foot alpine fir was supple, though. And with the weight both men added to its top....

I broke from the brush on my bushwhacking plunge, and skidded to a stop in the trail only a few feet from my two buddies, who clung to the top of an alpine fir that bent like a horseshoe, almost into the trail!

"What in God's name!" I exclaimed.

"A bear!" one of them cried. "Right up ahead! Coming this way!"

I walked to where I could see farther along the trail. "There's no bear up here."

They looked sheepish when they dropped from their treetop. "It's just as well," one of them said. "There wasn't room for you up that tree, too." ■

I really enjoy your radio show—you have had fun times (like us), haven't you?
Bette K. Smith • Helena, MT

I listen to your program each morning on my way to work. I was disappointed I could not make it to the Farm Forum when you spoke. I enjoy your humor and style of writing. Your support and praise of your working partner, companion, wife is refreshing and leads me to respect you both. **Mrs. Ron Prewett • Conrad, MT**

Shriveled Like a 1952 Prune

She was in there a long time—clear to her armpits in the frigid waters of a high mountain lake. She'd waded out earlier, farther and farther from the brush-lined shore, until she had enough room to work her flyrod. Her first cast landed (bad word choice since terra firma lay fifty feet behind) a fat ten-inch rainbow, which she released. She whipped her line again, just head and arms thrusting above the lake surface. Another strike. A whoop of delight!

I grinned and sat upon a buckskin log to watch my beginning fisherperson-wife engage in the first great fly fishing she'd experienced. My eyes wandered. Our teen-aged son stood in water to his knees a quarter of the way around the lake. By the looks of it he was having trouble with his backcasts snagging brush. Apparently, the boy lacked enough savoir faire to emulate his mother and wade out to his neck.

I leaned down to stick my finger into the icy water, then shook my head.

Jane hooked another trout. And another. And another.

I yawned and ambled along the lakeshore to watch Marc. "Why don't you wade on out like your mother?" I said when he snagged another spruce limb.

He peered at me as if I had a toad hanging from an ear.

"Why don't you come on out and show me how?"

I smiled again and wandered on, heading for the lake's far end. This was the first time we'd been to Lena Lake, and my passion is more for exploring new country than for catching fish. I climbed a low ridge from the lake's west end, then sprawled, propping elbows on the ground in order to glass the surrounding country. No wild animals were out in this noon-day sun. I dozed.

After a while, an ant tickled my nose. I flipped it off, glanced at the sun, and clambered to my feet. Marc was gone and so was Jane. No—wait a minute. There! Sunbeams glistened from a thousand flashing water drops as Jane whipped her flyline. I raised my binoculars.

She hadn't moved—except for her arms lifting the rod aloft, waving it magically. Even as I watched, the rod tip darted to the lake surface, then started jitterbugging. I worked my way around the lake to the log I'd perched on an hour and a half earlier. "Have you been in the water all this time?" I called.

"Uh-huh." She fed line to her rhythmically pumping rod.

"You're going to be as shriveled as a 1952 prune."

"I don't care. *I'm catching fish!*"

"You sure as heck are. You're also catching cold, chilblains, the hoof part of hoof and mouth disease, and your arms and hands and face are beginning to light up like a Manhattan stoplight."

Her line fell into the water as she paused to look for the first time at her sunburning arms.

The waterlogged line sank immediately.

A plump rainbow brought it back to the lake surface with the speed of a submarine's missile launch. ∎

To Lose a Shoe, or Find One?

We led a family group from New Jersey on a week-long, mid-August packtrip through the Bob Marshall Wilderness. They came notably unprepared, ignoring the recommended clothing list I'd mailed them some months before, showing up without rain gear and with only light jackets. It was an opportunity not to be ignored by the malign weather gods of the northern Rockies, first sending rain, then snow.

Jane made rain ponchos out of plastic garbage sacks, and we loaned the poor folks our spare clothing. Actually, they took their discomfort as good-naturedly as anyone could expect of someone caught riding in a rainstorm that was mixed with numbing, intermittent snow.

Four inches of wet fluff lay across the high land when we broke camp to begin our two-day run for home. Because of their general misery, the folks asked me to take them over the shortest route to civilization. It happens that, in this case, the shortest route is not the best one—full of mud, rocks, roots, blown-down trees, overhanging brush, and sometimes landslides. But this shorter route *is* the fastest. And that's what was wanted.

We were into the thigh-deep mud of Wall Creek when I first noticed signs of someone hiking ahead of us. Was that a bare footprint? No, there's a shoe print. Another bare footprint? What's going on here?

We caught and passed the hiker only a short distance from where we planned to spend the night. He stepped from the trail to let our horses pass. I nodded and said something cheerful, but the man only bobbed his head. I glanced at his feet. He was wearing a worn tennis shoe on his right foot. The left was bare.

Jane, following behind, paused and asked how long he'd been out.

"A month," the man said.

"I'll bet it's been a while since you had fresh fruit." She offered him an orange. He snatched it, mumbling, "Thanks," while gobbling rind and all.

Jane said he appeared so ravenous she would have given him more, but she had nothing else left from her lunch.

We pulled into our campsite amid more rain and snow and busied ourselves setting up camp, building a big warming fire. We never saw the shoeless backpacker again until the following day. He sat on a log, off to the side of the trail, glumly watching us pass. Jane gave him her lunch. He told her he'd planned to live off the land, but rain had ruined fishing, as well as the berry crop he'd counted on for survival.

We met a former guide and his family as we neared the road and our waiting vehicles. They were on their way into the wilderness for a few days of sightseeing. Ed later said they'd encountered the hiker. "The guy had his arms wrapped around a tree to help him stand." Ed laughed. "He asked for food and we gave him something. Never did hear how he came out. Did you?"

I shook my head. But I've thought of that backpacker often. Where did he come from? Why did he undergo such an ordeal? Was he on some sort of vision quest? Or did he simply underestimate either his skills or the ability of the land to sustain him?

But of all my questions, the foremost has always been: Did he lose a shoe? Or find one? ∎

*I read with interest your article entitled "Generation Challenged Nature's Way," in the **Great Falls Tribune** November 3rd edition. It's too bad it was not published on the front page instead of section D.... Would you consider allowing us to run your article in our hospital newsletter? We would like to use it to support our theme for beginning the New Year with our futures in mind.*

Lori Thackeray RN,
Northern Montana Hospital • Havre, MT

Blueprint for Disaster Avoidance

I'd like to share with you a couple of environmental essays that appear to be contradictory. Perhaps I'm still groping for the truth. Or maybe I fell from bed and landed on my head. The first of the two was drafted, according to my notes, in August, 1991; the second in November, 1994.

Are they, in fact, contradictions? Here's the first of the two.

───────

A bright young eco-warrior with a degree in sociology and clear ideas about what constitutes black and white tried to force me into a guilt trip. This young lady, God love her, is long on theory but short on experience. She was polite, her smile infectious, and her wide and shining eyes sincere and uncomplicated. She thinks deeply and has command of a plethora of buzzwords. But she depends too much on rote.

The second time she mentioned how rapacious my generation had been toward the earth and its environs I quit nodding and smiling. And when she allowed it was true a third time, I commenced to tastefully demur.

It's amazing how a bashful, blushing, timid young thing could turn so adept at shouting and table-thumping, requiring me to call on my deepest reservoirs of grace and humility to finally send her stumbling from the room in tears.

After she left, I began meditating on her premise—which is a popular one held by those too young to have spent much time in the trenches:

My generation runs from 1935 until the present, but we can hardly be considered responsible for what might have occurred prior to adulthood—say prior to 1960. So let's consider the three decades since 1960 in order to learn just how grasping we Depression-era babies have been. It's my contention that within those three decades, much environmental degradation has been slowed, stopped, or is in the process of being reversed.

~ Rachel Carson exposed insecticide pollution, and laws were enacted for pesticide control.

~ *The Wilderness Act* was passed to protect certain portions of our public land resources for perpetuity, and subsequent additions to the protected lands continue the process.

Legislation protecting free-flowing rivers was instrumental in saving thousands of miles of America's streams for tomorrow, meaning wholesale construction of dams is largely a thing of the past.

~ *The National Environmental Protection Act* was a great and significant roadblock to uncontrolled and deleterious development of public land.

~ *The Endangered Species Act* has not only been instrumental in halting the decline of certain wild plants and animals, but has been invaluable to species recovery in some cases.

~ Strip-mine reclamation, forest planning, the *Clean Air Act*, water purification, highway beautification, old-growth forest protection, superfund waste cleanup, hazardous-materials disposal, the *Conservation Reserve Program*. All have been important tools for slowing, halting, or reversing previous degradation. All contribute to the quality of life we presently enjoy.

True, there have been and will continue to be reversals of this noble process. But on balance, the generation I'm lucky enough to have been born into has an admirable track record of trying to make our country and our world a livable place for generations to come. Here's a challenge, young lady: see if your generation can do as well—or better.

<hr />

Then there's this:

It's possible no generation's expectations have soared so high or crashed so low as those of mine. Mine is the generation that decided we could improve on God's creation and developed the means to do so. While others may have dreamed it, we're the ones who did it.

We harnessed rivers to better serve mankind's needs. We dammed and dredged and straightened their meanderings. But we've destroyed salmon and steelhead runs, perhaps forever. And that's only for starters. Flood control? Turns out it may be an illusion that sets us up for even greater disasters when God returns control to nature.

We're the ones who learned how to drain marshes and swamps and convert that rich land into agricultural cornucopias. Belatedly, we're discovering those wetlands might be God's filtration systems to purify the water we drink.

We're the ones who developed giant pumps to irrigate cropland in arid desert—and have so dangerously lowered aquifers that we may have doomed vast regions for tomorrow. And we increase the land's salinity while doing so.

We're the generation that decided God was doing a lousy job of growing trees. So we unilaterally took over the task of producing wood fiber—and destroyed forests thousands of years in the making.

We're the ones who strip off tons of rock, crush it, and pour cyanide over it to recover a single ounce of gold.

We're the generation to develop farm machines so huge they're impractical to use on less than a section of land and so expensive few farmers can afford to meet the interest payments. Yet we learn that Amish farmers who use only horse-drawn equipment are competing with Pennsylvania mall developers for cropland purchase.

We're the ones learning to fertilize for greater yields, but discovering to our dismay that we're depleting soils for tomorrow. We're the medical generation that learned to extend life—but not its quality. We're the ones who make babies in test tubes, but can't seem to lessen the flood of babies in the projects, barrios, and poverty-stricken shantytowns.

We're the ones who send rocket ships to the moon, and the ones who deplete the ozone layer.

We can easily transform mountains into molehills, but have learned God has a franchise on doing it the other way around.

We've learned to convert fossil fuels into shopping-mall lights and discovered we're trashing downwind landscapes with acid rain.

We can send fishing fleets around the world, turn rain forests into sugar-cane plantations, make deserts bloom, predict earthquakes and volcanic eruptions, move vast numbers of people in short amounts of time. But we pollute rivers so they burn, lakes so no fish can live in them, and we even have a start on poisoning the oceans.

I was born in 1935. It was the decade of the Great Depression, but also of Grand Coulee Dam. I've watched mankind's great leap forward with interest, and observed our confusion as we discover we have much more to learn before God shuts down His system and lets us play with all the switches.

We began with unlimited egos and learned a little about humility along the way.

So where's the lesson in the two essays? I'm not sure. Perhaps it lies in the premise that to escape the calamity of the second, my generation needed benefits accruing from the first. Taken together, there's ego here, as well as a certain humility. Contradiction? Certainly. But under the circumstances, perhaps we did the best we could.

At the least, we can take some pride that we provided a blueprint for staving off total disaster. Whether that disaster is to be long avoided might lie in how adept our kids are at reading that blueprint. ■

We enjoy your program and news articles. Your wife Jane sounds like a very special person.
Joedy Foster • Kalispell, MT

I have been enjoying your radio programs. What a good life you and your brave wife have lived.
Iris Jean Scott • Plains, MT

Atonement or Servitude?

It's heavy work, maintaining a practical compromise between man's twin cravings for outdoors adventure and matrimonial harmony. There are some pedants, of course, who claim those primary masculine drives to be irreconcilable. Cataclysmic crashes, they say, are inevitable for the simple outdoorsman who strives for wedded bliss.

I'm not one of the doomsayers. In fact, I vehemently refute their premise of mutual exclusion. So listen up and I'll give you some insight on the why and how:

First of all, I work quite hard at mending matrimonial fences in the off season. By great good fortune, my off season extends from December to May (the time of year when horses aren't practical for travel in the northern Rockies), so I have plenty of time to expedite any spouse-pacification plans.

There are benefits and liabilities to my strategic compromise. One major liability is the duration of the wilderness siren's song that so captivates me for seven months. But the benefit is that it's the only siren to which I harken. And it means there are five consecutive months when I'm usually around to carry out the garbage—toting up credits only the meanest of fishwives could ignore.

Even so, five long months are barely enough. Pity the poor

ice fishermen and trappers and houndsmen who tramp the winter's snows. Marital survival for them dictates domestic atonement during summer or fall—unthinkable when cut-throats rise or elk bugle.

Why is marital atonement necessary for the outdoorsman at all? Only those who've recently staggered over the nuptial threshold would ask. In my case, it's because I regularly forget both my wife's birthday and our wedding anniversary. After all, the first comes in July and the second falls during elk season. But I usually make up for the lapses by purchasing her a nice card for Christmas and by picking a handful of daffodils for Mother's Day.

And I never forget Valentine's.

Remembering Jane on Valentine's Day is a good way to reinvigorate a love affair that may have flagged since I left a bloody elk liver in the kitchen sink or forgot to scrape my boots after wading through corral mud.

There's something about February hearts, and impish urchins in diapers shooting arrows into 'em, that causes Jane to overlook a lot of summer dust and fall mud and an absent husband who gives her only an absentminded peck every ten days during my most active time of year.

Atonement, you see, need not necessarily mean servitude. There's nothing wrong with carrying out garbage, mind you, but it is somewhat menial work for a big, tough, outdoor-bred mountain stomper. Thoughtful surprises are far better because they keep the helpmeet off balance enough to put a benign face on your next string of kitchen-sink perch.

Tell you what—why don't you really surprise her next Valentine's Day? Call her from work and invite her to a candlelight dinner at some quiet, romantic place—just you and her.

It might help achieve forgiveness for past adventure—and a leg up on a pardon for future transgressions. ■

The Masochism of Keeping Horses

L et's talk about genetic engineering—which may seem a
trifle off target for a book focused primarily on the outdoors. I don't plan to discuss test-tube babies, however, or
cloning. Nor is breed development for the production of
more Porterhouse steaks of paramount interest. Nope, it's just
about dogs and horses—the foundations of two American
Indian cultures that wound up on a collision course.

What got me on this subject was wondering if Indian pack-
dogs were developed from wolves. I suppose all dogs
originated from a common ancestor of the wolf, although it
takes a quantum leap of faith to believe a chihuahua or
wiener-dog has any commonality with a wolfpack strung out
over the Arctic tundra.

Indian dogs were not so far removed from wolfish ancestors, but they were domesticated, which must have been the
first Native American trick of genetic engineering. Before the
horse, Indian dogs were selectively bred for size—for packing
big loads and dragging loaded travois—although given the
chaos of village dog packs running at large, achieving packdog
status might be more a matter of surviving stewpot demand
rather than the quality of ancestors standing at stud.

Then came horses. They began as mustang progeny of

Spanish Barb ponies, and they upstaged the dog, reducing his role to sentry duty and the occasional K-ration supplement for desperate tribespeople. Not only could a horse take the place of eight to ten dogs when it came time to move camp, but more importantly, the pony didn't compete for food with his master, preferring bunchgrass to spareribs. And a brave could ride him to war! Or on a buffalo hunt! Infatuation became total. Native American genetic engineering became solely devoted to the horse.

How much so? Well, I'm intrigued by the Appaloosa. Most everyone knows Appaloosa horses were a Nez Perce Indian development, but nobody knows how they did it. We've all read of Chief Joseph and the desperate attempt of his people to reach Canada. We know how they fled for over a thousand miles and how, though outnumbered and out-armed, they fought several pursuing U.S. Army detachments to a stand-still. In reading this tale, we learn the Nez Perce's relatively unknown breed of spotted horses were their "secret weapon," carrying the tribe tirelessly, with little feed and less rest, almost to their Canadian goal.

As a consequence, all America became intrigued by these tough mountain ponies that stayed fat on scant grass, were docile to handle, and proved tireless on the trail.

The Nez Perce war was in 1877.

Now consider this: The Nez Perce could not have acquired the horse until about 1750. No mention was made of the Appaloosa in the meticulous journals of Meriwether Lewis or William Clark during their visits to Nez Perce country in 1805-06. Do you find it strange those two explorers saw no unusually spotted horses, even though they traded for dozens of ponies with the Nez Perce and described several large horse herds belonging to these Indians? How, then, was it that seventy years later the breed was fully developed?

I'm told the feat would be near-impossible to duplicate today, despite our advanced understanding of genetic engineering, controlled-breeding stations, and unlimited financial commitments.

How did the Nez Perce accomplish it?

Few horses kept on today's farms and ranchettes justify their existence. Most equine types, even those of gentle persuasion, will, given enough time, become pests instead of pets. They're not cuddly like a rabbit, not loyal like a dog; don't gambol like a lamb, won't walk softly like a cat.

They're persistent to the point of being obnoxious at feeding time, slow to leave the barn at riding time, and dangerous to head for home at anything faster than a walk.

They'll come from the far end of their pasture at a gallop if you have so much as a sugar cube hidden in your pocket. But hold a halter behind your back and it'll take the Philadelphia Marching Band to drive them into a corner so you can slip it over their ears.

They'll swell their bellies if you try to tighten a cinch, then exhale to loosen the saddle when you're clinging in fear on a perilous trail.

They bite when your back is turned and stare innocently at a distant horizon when you jerk around in anger. They'll kick when you're at your most awkward and shift to the end of their halter rope in apparent dismay when you bellow in distress at the horseshoe print on your left knee.

They'll stand on your toe and shift three other feet as you curse and pound and turn red around the collar. They're uncivil, disobedient, lazy, and a bother. Why man attempted domesticating the creatures, I haven't a clue.

We keep four.

I use them occasionally to carry me up a distant mountain peak or ride to wilderness meadows. They haven't packed a bull elk hindquarter since I retired from outfitting several years ago, but there's still a packsaddle or two in the barn, game bags in a closet, and know-how enough for me and the ponies to do so if push comes to shove.

They work well as riding lawnmowers to hold down weeds around the house, add class to the place while standing atop a mid-pasture knoll at sunset, keep me from growing sedentary, and offer a sort of neat switch from the shank's mare of day hikes.

Yes, I know they cost a bundle to buy, another bundle to feed and are a pain at tax time, shoeing time, veterinarying time. I know one must maintain a truck or stock trailer to haul them and a barn for hay storage.

I know I could easily pay for a horseback packtrip or two with an outfitter for what it costs each year to maintain enough horses for Jane and me to ride out on our own pack-trips. I know an outfitter's ponies would probably not be barn-soured, would be better conditioned, more docile, working animals.

I know if I went with the outfitter at the same price it cost me to go on my own, he would supply all the food, set up the camp, saddle my horse in the morning, and brush him down in the evening. I know the outfitter would chop firewood, cook meals, wash dishes, and handle all worries about whether the ponies ran off during the night, ran into a bear during the day, or lost a rider on the way back to camp.

So why do we keep four horses?

Just masochists, I guess. ■

My husband listens to your program, usually in the tractor cab while feeding livestock. I listen each morning in the car on my way to work. We both have only one criticism—it isn't long enough.   Joan Brock • St. Ignatius, MT

Trail User's Dictionary

I've often been bewildered that otherwise intelligent folks don't always comprehend an ordinary trail traveler's nomenclature. Therefore I have, at considerable effort, put together this simple dictionary of common language. This first section is devoted to trail *riders*:

Bareback: Horseback-riding method not involving use of saddle; often utilized briefly. Not recommended for riding at a trot.

Blanket: Paraphernalia placed between a horse's back and saddle. Sometimes used to cover traumatized beginning riders who tried riding bareback at a trot.

Bone: Prominent protrusion along back of trotting horse ridden by bareback rider. Also, formerly rigid skeletal members of human who tried riding bareback on trotting horse with prominent protrusion along back.

Boot: Uncomfortable, high-heeled, pointy-toed invention from a sadistic cobbler's last.

Chaps: Leather (or vinyl) leg protectors; also called chaparajos. Most often worn by city slickers imitating boob-tube cowboys. Usually purchased at considerable expense and worn only once. Perhaps the single most expensive and least functional wardrobe piece ever invented. Popularized by fashion-conscious professional rodeo riders emulating a rhinestone cowboy.

Cowboy: Bull Durham-rolling, spittoon-spitting, ten gallon-hatted, Levi-trousered practitioner of Western cattle herding. Most often found with spurred bootheel draped over nearest bar rail. Easily importuned by offer to buy beer. Sometimes difficult to dissuade from drinking until bar closes for night.

Hoof: Ultimate extension of quadruple equine appendage. Sometimes used to stamp at snakes or discourage bothersome and unwary humans. Always firmly planted in a jarring manner calculated to wring utmost discomfort to bareback rider.

Horse: Devilish development of sadistic, misguided creative process, probably engineered while God was on coffee break. Cute, cuddly, frolicsome when colt. Sucker for sugar cubes or grain until a person tries to catch one. Then Patton's 3rd Army couldn't corner. Evil-tempered when haltered. Known to kick, bite, or buck without provocation. Chameleon-type personality with endearing moments calculated to make one forget the evil side. Undoubtedly the most expensive pet ever obtained. See Rodeo.

Rodeo: Performance trial which every horse feels compelled to practice each time he's saddled. See saddle.

Saddle: Inadequate tool utilized by would-be riders to smooth their chances during rodeo performances. Also laughingly used for "comfort" during long rides.

Singlefoot: Name for a particularly smooth pace used by well-bred horses during ancient times. Bred out of modern horses in order to develop more character in modern riders.

Spurs: Tools strapped to bootheels and used for encouraging a cowboy's horse to greater effort. Also handy training wheels when one must roll a cowboy from bar at closing time.

Stirrups: Fiendish device to "enhance" a rider's stability. Actually, most often used by horse to ensnare victims.

Whoa: Term of endearment a person should use for a loved one who is thinking of horseback riding. Also, term frequently used by novices when mounting their first horse. Thereafter utilized more frequently and stridently and with rising crescendo through each riding stage: walk (whoa), trot (Whoa!), canter (WHOA!), rodeo (*WHOA!!!*).

There are two main types of trail travel in America—by horse and by foot. In order to provide proper nomenclature for both types, I've included a beginning backpacker's dictionary:

Backpack: Medieval torture device popularized during the Spanish Inquisition. Used sparingly, hurts only a little. Confined within maze of sadistic straps, loaded with overnight rations and all other accouterments necessary for immediate survival in inclement weather, and faced with a three-mile hike or a thousand-foot climb, broken prisoners have been known to recant, gasp out locations of buried heirlooms, or babble endlessly about frosted glasses of cold beer.

Beer: Delectable, delightful, deliciously cool, thirst-quenching beverage one must swear to forgo forever when backpacking; or until the end of the present trip.

Campfire: An exhausting rite of return to mystic origins. There is, however, a slight chance it could be a functional camping accessory when facilitated by dry wood and a match for ignition.

Dehydrated Food: Smells good, tastes bad. Supplies minimum daily requirements to lie in a torpor on an emergency-room operating table.

Hiking Boots: Pleasingly comfortable sheaths to encircle lower appendages. Used to absorb shock and fend off abrasions, scratches, and blisters. See Moleskin.

Moleskin: Emergency adhesive repair material if hiking boots are *not* pleasingly comfortable, and if they fail to absorb shock or fend off abrasions, scratches, and blisters.

Mountaintop: Mythical summit, viewed by modern man only amid a haze of induced dreams or from the porthole of a 737. An ancient named Moses was once supposed to have ascended to a summit but there's little hard evidence to substantiate the legend.

Poncho: Ludicrous portable tent to be used during a rainstorm. As if anyone smart enough to read this book would be caught outside in a rainstorm!

River Ford: Unlike mountaintops, river fords are common

locations for backpackers caught outside in a rainstorm. One must exercise considerable caution when traversing a ford. Always know the stream bottom, stream depth, stream speed, etc. And how can anyone dumb enough to be caught outside in a rainstorm know that stuff?

Sleeping Bag: A silky envelope of nylon and goose down or synthetic insulation; too hot in August and too cold in March and October. Much too bulky to fit into the stuffbag that came with it.

Sleeping Pad: Oriental torture device akin to dripping water. Lie on it and try to sleep—I dare you!

Space Blanket: A handy, tightly folded, eight-foot square of super-thin foil. I've yet to find it useful.

Switchback: A trail reversal. You're staggering along under your loaded backpack—suddenly there's no trail. Rule number one: Look around. Likely it's a switchback, but it could be a washout or end along a clifftop. Avoid switchbacks like the plague—they mean you're climbing!

Trail: Part of our American transportation system. Largely constructed during the Great Depression, then continued during the century's second half. Later construction known as the Interstate Highway System. Latter half more expensive. ∎

*I am writing to tell you that I thoroughly approve of your article in the **Shelby Promoter** last week regarding our flag—and hope that many more folks do, too. I hope your ideas will be shared by many.*

Agnes Crocker • Shelby, MT

Go Ahead and Wave the Flag

My eyes sometimes wet up when our National Anthem is sung and I see the country's flag snapping in a brisk breeze. And if folks cry "Play ball!" before the last notes fade, it somehow seems bad manners. Yet I don't spend a lot of time flying or waving the Stars and Stripes, maybe because I don't think it necessary for a man to demonstrate to others how patriotic he is in order to truly believe in the principles for which that flag flies.

If those principles weren't in place, I wouldn't likely be writing this. Couldn't, in fact, because chances are a free press would be one of the first cherished American rights to be curtailed, along with free speech, freedom of assembly, and freedom of dissent.

Maybe that's why I get a lump in my throat when I hear the Star Spangled Banner, watch our flag raised, see it flap in the wind. Maybe that's why I tend to think the 4th of July is the most important single holiday celebration of the year, more important than Memorial Day, Thanksgiving, or even Christmas.

Christmas, of course, has little to do with the birth of Christ since that date is actually unknown. The earliest evidence for celebration of Christ's feast day hails from Egypt in about the year 200 A.D., spreading from there primarily to the Spanish-, English-, and German-speaking regions of the world. In any case, today's customs of Santa Claus and Christmas trees and exchanging gifts have more relationship to Madison Avenue hype than to any religious significance.

Thanksgiving Day serves a useful purpose, reminding us how grateful early Pilgrims were for their survival and how tenuous were their efforts to escape religious persecution and temporal bondage. But Thanksgiving celebrates freedom's roots, not its full flower, as represented by Independence Day. And Memorial Day is a particular reminder of those millions who went to their graves defending the principles for which our flag flies.

July 4th represents a new world order that is even yet emerging and evolving; an order that burst upon the earth's community in a declaration that "… all men are created equal, that they are endowed by their Creator with certain inalienable Rights, that among these are Life, Liberty and the pursuit of Happiness. That to secure these rights, Governments are instituted among Men, deriving their powers from the consent of the governed…."

Since that day more than two hundred years ago, the tide of freedom has washed inexorably on from the New World to the Old. Much blood has been shed as men and women in other lands seek an order to their lives that we Americans sometimes take too much for granted.

Our eyes should turn misty every time we open a newspaper, sign a petition, or attend a political rally or the church of our choice. The 4th of July stands for all that and more. Without the things it stands for, there would likely be no hunting or fishing for common folks, no public land for them to visit, little or no education for their children, no chance to live in dignity as they age.

It's the *why* behind the Berlin Wall's collapse, the *why* for the ignominious retreat of communism, the *why* dictators are running scared all over the globe. We may celebrate many feast days, but there is only one 4th of July. ∎

Good Folks-10, Bad Ones-0

It was mid-May. We headed for an early trip into the Bob Marshall Wilderness's Sun River country. We'd planned to pull our horse trailer to Benchmark, stay overnight, then make a short first-day pack to Pretty Prairie. Info on road status was sparse, even at Forest Service stations along the way, but I was sure we could make road's end.

We couldn't. A couple of miles past Ford Creek, the roadway dipped under three-foot snowdrifts. I rammed the pickup into four-wheel-drive low-under and busted through a couple, then thought better of the plan as we ran smack-dab against a drift that had no end in sight. After floundering by foot and still finding no end in sight around the next bend, we stampeded back to plan B.

Plan B meant finding a place to camp. It also meant a disgusted wife, tired friends, hungry horses, and turning a 23-foot horse trailer around on a 19-foot road.

But a couple of hours later, with camp set up, horses contentedly munching alfalfa hay, and Jane and friends mollified by my specialty—concocting mollifying aperitifs—we settled down over a set of maps to decide on a fall-back maneuver.

A pickup motored by and we waved, nodding knowingly to ourselves that the guy would be back as soon as he nosed head-on into the endless drift.

He returned as expected, parked, and ambled our way. "Couldn't make it, huh?" he said.

I shook my head.

"Too bad. It's only a couple more miles to Benchmark."

I nodded.

"Soon as you break through the canyon, road'll be free of snow."

I nodded again.

"You folks have horses. Should be able to do it easy."

"We're not anxious to set up camp again," Jane said.

"Heck, if that's your problem," the man said, "you can stay in my cabin."

When we looked blank, he said, "I have a cabin up there at Benchmark. Plenty of wood, stove, dishes, cooking equipment. I'll leave you my key, and you can stay as long as you want." Then he added, "Just leave it clean is all I ask."

Jane and our friends stared at the stranger who was offering use of his cabin to people he didn't know. Finally I said, "Do I know you?"

"Dunno. Thought you looked familiar, but I can't get a grip on you, either."

"Down in Helena," I said, "couple of years ago." I told him my name and said, "You were representing the Montana Graingrowers in the legislative session. Right?"

He nodded and smiled, holding out the key. We all grinned and shook our heads, then Jane handed him a cocktail.

We didn't take Bob Stephens' key, having already made up our minds to backtrack and try the trailhead at Mortimer Gulch, the main jumping-off place into the North Fork of the Sun. But his offer flabbergasted us.

We talked about it after Bob left for his home in Great Falls. We decided we like living and recreating in a part of the country where folks are trusting and kind.

All too often we hear in the media about the other kind. But it's been our experience that *good folks* outnumber *bad ones* everywhere you go. ∎

*At the time, the Luhr-Jensen Company sponsored "**Trails to Outdoor Adventure**" and my favorite advertising technique was to disparage my own propensity to fish dry flies while talking about their lures. -RC*

San Juan Worms to the Rescue

It was September of a low-water year. Cutthroats had apparently fled the riffles into deeper water and weren't rising to what we offered. By shading our eyes, we could see down into the deep water where trout schooled, and it galled us that they showed no inclination to feed.

"Looks to me like it's time to try a San Juan Worm," one of my fishermen said. Not being the type who stifles opinion, it was all I could do not to laugh when he held up a hook that had a bit of brightly colored material wrapped around the shank. No wings. No body. No hackles. No bristles. I'd not seen anything like it during a couple of decades of guiding.

"You catch a fish on that," I said, "and I'll eat your rod, handle first."

He grinned. "That, now, I'd love to see. But I don't want to lose a good flyrod." He clinched a tiny white bobber eight feet up his leader and flicked the contraption into the water as we drifted slowly along the surface of a deep pool. "How about settling on you cooking the fish for me?"

I cackled. "Anything you'd catch on that set-up would be too ugly to pull into the raft. Not to mention too tough to cook and too bony to eat."

Just then his rod tip dipped to the pool's surface and his

eyes lit up. Ten minutes later, we both admired a fat sixteen-inch cutthroat. He released it. "Ugly, wasn't it?" he said.

His partner changed from a Spruce Fly to a San Juan Worm. Both men began catching fish. Another of our rafts drifted up, and John passed along the word, "Try a San Juan Worm, boys. They're hitting on 'em."

"What color?" one asked.

"I don't think it'll make any difference. Put a 'marshmallow' up the line and watch for 'em to strike."

Our third raft drifted up. Soon everyone was catching fish. And everyone was using San Juan Worms. It was my first experience with what, at that time, was a new development in fly fishing.

"Fly fishing!" one of my purist friends spat. "That's not fly fishing. No one but a social misfit would think of using such abominable contraptions in pristine water."

Mine was a thin grin. I'd taken a beating on that trip. The guys were on their third adventure with me and we'd become friends. As a consequence, their taunting was merciless. "You don't think these San Juan Worms will work, eh, Roland?"

If only they'd unlocked the San Juan secret toward the end of our trip, it might have been tolerable. Unfortunately for me, John tried the scantily clad hook on day two of a seven-day float.

But I learned. And so should you. San Juans can be deadly when stream flows decline and fish school up. Don't ask me why, just believe it works. After my guys got bored with catching so many fish with San Juans, they tried wet flies deep. Wet flies failed—all wet flies.

You can argue whether it's a proper fly, but if you fish trout streams flowing from the northern Rockies in late August or September, lay in a dozen or so San Juan Worms before you disappear upriver. Take along a few tiny split shots to drop the line down in the current and some fingernail-size bobbers or strike indicators to tell you when a cutthroat noses the hook.

Take the San Juans even if you're a purist. Think how good you'll feel if you don't use them. Think how good the trout will taste if you do. ■

Watching Life's Backtrail

Under certain conditions, no one—no matter how experienced the person may be—is immune to becoming lost in forest and mountains. Thinking about the possibility beforehand is perhaps the most important single tool for survival. Thinking about it means preparing for it.

Have I ever become lost? Yes, once in a dense fog that settled into a Pacific Coast rain forest, and once while guiding hunters in a white-out snowstorm in the Bob Marshall Wilderness. In both cases I knew the area intimately, having hiked the land many times before. In both cases, after a time, the weather eased, allowing me to take better bearings. But only in one of those instances did a warming fire cheerfully blaze.

The first time, an inventory of the materials I carried in packsack or jacket pocket went like this: Matches (wet from sweat and rain), knife, two pieces of hard candy, a few feet of nylon cord, a pair of woolen mittens, handkerchief, comb, extra ammunition, pocket change, watch, pad and pencil, a rubber band, small vial of aspirin, the nub of a candle.

Notice there were several important items missing: No compass, no suitable matches, no fire starter (except for the candle nub), no Space Blanket, no extra clothes, no raincoat.

And, except for the aspirins, no emergency first-aid supplies.

Did I learn anything that would be useful the second time? Absolutely. By then I'd taken time to think about survival and what it meant for a guy responsible for the welfare of others. In addition to all the things listed above, I carried matches in a watertight case, extra food, extra gloves, a down jacket, change of socks, wool cap, topo map, and a keen sense of humor. The last was indispensable when my two hunters discovered their guide couldn't, in the middle of a raging blizzard, find elk, deer, the way back to camp, or the horses we'd left tied to trees an hour earlier.

More important than the extra survival gear packed for emergencies was something I'd learned—the importance of the acronym S.T.O.P. (Stop, Think, Observe, Plan). We stopped near a small stream and built a roaring fire. My guys were advised not to eat all their lunch—to hold some in reserve in case the unthinkable occurred—but to drink all the water they could take on. We gathered extra wood. We kicked snow away from grass and ground beneath the overhanging limbs of a big Douglas fir "wolf tree." And finally we discussed what our course of action might be if the snow didn't let up before darkness fell.

Just a half-hour before night, the snow slowed and stopped. I gazed across the white world and took my bearings. Our horses were but two hundred yards and a single low ridge away. Tracks of two elk, half-blanketed by the last flakes, meandered between horses and humans.

We kissed our horses hello and waved goodbye to those will-o'-the-wisp elk.

Even as a young buck, my homing instincts were pretty good. Of course I grew up in mountain country where, if a man or boy kept his eyes open and occasionally checked his back trail, it was easy enough to return home in time for supper.

Not so easy, I suppose, is direction-finding in the north woods of Minnesota or Michigan. There, hills to climb for taking your bearing are few and far between. There, too, swamps frequent the flatlands, turning a wanderer off course. A compass, I'm told, is a must for anyone abroad in that land—and I believe it. But amid the mountains and valleys I call home, such an instrument is, to me, merely excess weight.

Yet many folks who hike and hunt the northern Rockies each year cannot find their way back to camp or car. Search and rescue units, sheriff's posses, and forest and park rangers are often called out to find them. Bloodhounds are sometimes used, and even search planes and helicopters are employed.

Happy endings are the norm for most of the lost, but even those happy endings are not without embarrassment for the cold and bedraggled; and not without considerable expense for volunteers and organizations.

Some endings are tragic. Most of those tragedies, if researchers are able to piece together an accurate account of what transpired, occurred because someone lost his sense of judgment and ultimately died from exhaustion or exposure. And therein lies the real cause of such tragedies—not that someone became confused, but that he panicked.

Lost hunters are the single most haunting specter to outfitters and their guides. Fortunately, we never lost anyone during our two decades at the trade, but the fear was there nevertheless. True, there've been folks we've guided who couldn't follow a knife-edged ridge on their own; others who had to hang out flagging ribbon merely to find their way back and forth between cooktent and camp privy. But we always returned them home to their loved ones.

Most prospective hunters are amused at my stock approach to the subject of someone becoming lost: "We've never yet lost anyone. But ours is a money-back guarantee—if you don't come back, you get your money back."

Some, of course, fail to see the humor. But we operated on the theory that we'd just as soon not spend a week or two in the big lonesome with humorless people. Being able to look on the bright side of marginal situations helps when the thermometer bottoms out, or it rains for ten solid days.

Does self-deprecating humor play a consequential role for a poor soul who wanders for days on the way to the privy?

Search me. I do know, however, that game trails have a habit of looking like Sunset Boulevard until you try to follow one back the way you came. Only then do you notice all the feeder trails peeling off, many of which also look like they might boulevard into the sunset. Let's see, which one did I follow this morning?

Look over your shoulder on the way out, for crying out loud! Turn full around and study your back trail. See that leaning tree? How about the elk rub in the tag alders?

Studying your backtrail is a good formula for finding your way through life, too. ■

Wood Selection Mastery Means Great Campfire Cuisine

There is nothing—nothing at all!—as critical to successful campfire cooking as proper wood selection.

You will note I didn't say wood *supply*. I said *selection*. Proper wood supply may be vital for comfort, desirable for confidence, and important for camaraderie—none of which will help you steam corn or brown the cobbler. Proper wood *selection*, however, makes cooking to perfection a snap.

The most common mistakes made by novice campfire cooks are: (1) they try to use a warming fire for cooking; (2) they think they need lots of wood to cook an outdoor meal; (3) they allow someone else to feed *their* cooking fire.

Actually it takes very little wood to cook an entire gourmet meal over a campfire. But it takes *dry* wood. And it requires careful and systematic replenishing in controlled amounts. Small limbs—even twigs—best lend themselves to a controlled cooking fire that will surprise you with its heat.

Was it just yesterday when Jane first cooked Cornish game hens, halved and threaded onto willow sticks? The sticks were green, about the size of a woman's ring finger, cut three feet long and with one end sharpened and thrust into the ground so that the hens were four to six inches from a tiny blaze. The fire was fed frequently, but never more than enough to keep it barely going.

Once, the blaze died and I was pressed into service to feed it twigs and blow on the coals to bring back the flames. But you get the picture—just the tiniest blaze is enough.

The hens were turned frequently to brown on all sides. They required, as you'd expect, about a half-hour to roast thoroughly.

Jane baked au gratin potatoes in a Dutch oven, starting them before roasting the Cornish hens—and that's another matter entirely. Dutch-oven cooking requires lots of coals. Proper coals require larger wood. We used wrist-sized aspen, but dead lodgepole or fir limbs work as well. Get a good hot fire going. Let it burn down to coals and use a shovel to scoop them mostly onto the oven's lid. Save only a few to place beneath the pot.

(Proper wood selection, one should note, is a *regional* thing. There are no hardwoods, for instance, in the country where we presently dwell; but oak and madrone and maple were common woods in the forests of my youth. Hardwood coals burn much hotter and require only half as many to cook to a fare-thee-well.)

With proper coals, au gratin potatoes take approximately twenty to thirty minutes to bake. While they cooked, Jane prepared her hens for roasting. Meanwhile, her fire tender (me) fussed the fire into a tiny controlled blaze.

Once the game hens were cooking, Jane began slicing, dicing, and tossing the salad.

My other duty, besides tending the fire, was to have cocktails ready for the ten minutes between salad preparation and dinner bell.

Sound easy?

It is—provided you don't try cooking over a fire that's blazing high for warmth. And provided a pack of other folks aren't crowding around the cooking fire, tripping over roasting sticks, turning over the coffee pot, and kicking sand and ashes into everything.

How does one prevent that?

Let them mix their own cocktails and build their *own* fire. Let them gather and pack their own wood. They won't love you for making them do their own thing, but they loved Jane for doing her thing to perfection. ∎

Mountain Lions and Rib Steaks

According to news accounts, it was the first day of July, 1990, when Skip Goerner, armed only with a fishing rod, fought a mountain lion to a standstill at Glacier National Park's Quartz Lake.

"I caught a movement," Goerner said, "and then there was this lion running right up the path at me. He didn't make a sound. I shouted 'mountain lion!' and started whipping at him with the fishing rod. He'd back up and come at me, and I just kept slapping at him."

The news report told how the embattled man backed away step by step until he reached his companions. At that point, the lion simply walked away.

According to information gleaned from a recent mountain lion workshop held in Denver and attended by most of America's cougar research and management experts, Skip Goerner is a lucky guy. Had he utilized defensive tactics common in bear encounters, he might well be dead!

In response to a rash of mountain lion incidents, an advisory published by the Colorado Division of Wildlife tells you what *not* to do if you suddenly discover a mountain lion in close proximity: the key strategy is never play dead. Don't so much as crouch. Instead, stand tall. Spread your jacket or shirt to appear larger—cougars can be intimidated by size.

Intimidation is not so likely to work on grizzly bears. Threaten a grizzly and you risk triggering a violent response. That's why playing dead has worked for folks who've rounded a trail bend and bumped into one of the mighty bruins—he already knows threats aren't common from the prostrate dead. Playing dead with a mountain lion, however, can be tantamount to inviting him to the dinner table—with your tenderloins as the main course.

Do not jog alone in cougar habitat. There is evidence that the big cat's predatory instincts can be triggered by running humans who unwittingly mimic actions of the felines' normal prey. Joggers have been attacked in Colorado, California, and British Columbia—each while jogging alone on isolated foothill trails.

Never turn your back on a mountain lion. That, too, may trigger a disastrous reaction. If you encounter a lion, so say the advisories, don't panic and don't make quick movements. Talk calmly to the cougar and back away slowly. Don't make direct eye contact; mountain lions may perceive eye contact as a threat.

Here's a recommendation from the British Columbia Ministry of Environment: If a cougar is advancing toward you, make a lot of noise by yelling and screaming. Use a club or stout stick to poke at him while continuing to make noise. Back away.

So everyone says *don't panic*. One state advises you to *talk calmly*, while one province advises *yelling and screaming*. Of course, telling a person not to panic while a mountain lion is advancing with visions of pot roast is akin to saying, "Don't get pimples." And advising one to talk calmly is probably appropriate advice for lion tamers, but hardly a cinch for a computer programmer transplanted from New Jersey to Silicon Valley who's presently hiking the foothills of Glacier Park.

Yelling and screaming seems better advice to me; that's a pearl of wisdom I would find easy to follow. With luck, it would even come out something more than a whimper.

Besides, yelling and screaming is what Skip Goerner did. And along with using his fishing rod as a lion tamer's whip and backing slowly away, *he* did everything right!

Actually, I'd druther not be confronted by a mountain lion at all, so let's talk about techniques to avoid contact with a hungry cat. The state of Colorado (where folks have had considerable experience interacting with mountain lions) offers advice in two documents—*What To Do If You Live In Lion Country* and *Tips On Living In Lion Country:*

Do not allow pets to run at large. Roaming pets are easy prey and can be an attraction to lions.

Do not leave food remnants in outside pet dishes.

Children should not play alone outdoors in areas where mountain lions live.

Consider escorting your children to the school bus stop in early morning. Clear an area around the bus stop of shrubs (30 foot radius). Have a light installed there. Parents can take turns staying at the bus stop with the children.

Landscape or remove vegetation so that you don't provide hiding places for lions, especially around children's play areas. You might even want to fence play areas and keep a radio playing.

Make sure your children are inside before dusk.

Install floodlights that you can turn on and off to light those places you must travel during the times lions are most active.

Make a lot of noise if you come and go during the times mountain lions are most active—dusk to dawn.

Consider getting a dog as a companion for your children. Dogs can see, smell and hear a lion sooner than humans can.

Protect your dog by constructing a kennel with a closed top.

Do not encourage deer to come into your yard.

Protect livestock in corrals or stalls.

Never feed mountain lions (or any other wild mammals).

Keep an axe or a club in the yard where you can get to it if you need it to fend off a mountain lion attacking someone.

Discuss lion safety with your children. Show them how they can protect and prepare themselves in the unlikely event they encounter a lion.

Colorado's Division of Wildlife put the question in perspective:

"This is a habitat issue. The very core of this situation is based in the decisions our communities have made regarding current land uses. People have chosen to live in an area of abundant wildlife and have taken steps (low-density housing, abundant open-space areas, no hunting around suburban developments) to ensure these animals flourish.... With increased numbers of lions and more people around, the chances of lions encountering people have increased. With each encounter that has ended in no harm or fear to the lion, they have begun to learn not to fear people...." ■

I am the fourth generation of a Montana ranch family and am very close to the land, and greatly concerned about what happens to it. Your columns take me that much closer to the land and certainly echo my sentiments.
                              Jim Milos • Great Falls, MT

Remember Yesterday
(While Heading for Tomorrow)

Just for a few moments, let's pretend that Glacier National Park is *not* a park in today's world, that a proposal has just been brought before Congress for its creation. Now let's consider the current political and economic climate in my home state and try to reconstruct some of the rhetoric that might be inherent to such a scenario. Bear with me while I experiment with reconstructing some of the rhetoric through a newspaper editorial:

> *The bill for the creation of Glacier National Park is again before Congress. We do not know whether we favor the bill or oppose it as we are not conversant with its provisions. Generally speaking, it could be a good thing for this community if it does not rob us of more rights than it is worth. In the first place, the North Fork Valley, containing as it does, large areas of agricultural land as well as coal and oil land and some magnificent meadows, should not be included in the park.*

> *The copper mines of Java and the prospects in other parts of that country ought not to be shut up in a national park. The proposed park is covered with a fine growth of saw timber and this should be placed under*

regulations similar to the forest reserves, so that the timber could be cut from time to time as it matures. Provisions should be made to allow mineral prospectors to go into the park grounds in search of minerals.

In short, the natural resources of that magnificent region should not be tied up and inaccessible to the wants of man. All this can be done and not detract from the value of the tract as a national park....

Well, yeah. Glacier, as it presently stands, was established precisely to protect those magnificent resources the above fictitious editorial portrays as unimportant to the integrity of a future park. Pretty ridiculous stuff isn't it? Something that would be dismissed out of hand by an enlightened public grappling with land-allocation problems.

Certainly we're smarter today. After all, everybody knows how rich are the ore bodies, hydrocarbon reserves, and timber volumes within areas being proposed for wilderness areas as we approach the second millennium; how they'd be "locked up" forever for the benefit of a handful of rich and idle easterners.

Besides, how could anyone even think of comparing those magnificent scenic, scientific, and recreational values of Glacier with today's poor-second proposed wilderness areas? Glacier Park's economic value to Montana and the nation is enormous and would be apparent to even the most obtuse observer of any age. Besides, the scenario used in the example is absolutely unbelievable, isn't it?

That so? The above editorial is fictitious only in referencing it to the current era. You see, the editorial, edited slightly into more modern language, *was lifted verbatim from a February 3, 1910, copy of The Columbian—a Columbia Falls weekly newspaper of that day.*

Columbia Falls is the community near where I live. Today, its economic well-being is largely dependent upon Glacier Park and the people who visit there. Yet, in 1910, people dwelling around the area were willing to sell tomorrow's birthright for a little short-term gain.

Has anything *really* changed? Is there anyone out there who believes northwest Montana would not be engaged in "the mother of all conservation battles" over the future of the land that is currently Glacier National Park if that decision had not already been rendered?

Isn't there something instructive about all this? Why shouldn't we compare current conservation engagements—no matter in what region they occur—with those that preceded them? The Everglades, Grand Canyon, Boundary Waters, Great Smokey Mountains, Yosemite, Yellowstone—all came at a price in blood, sweat, and tears.

Yesterday's battles were every bit as hard-fought and bitter as those occurring in the current era—nothing worthwhile ever comes without a price. But isn't it a tad ridiculous for those who hope to tear riches from our national splendors to accuse little old ladies in tennis shoes (who are trying to save those national splendors) of being selfish elitists.

Best we remember yesterday when working today to benefit tomorrow. ■

I have appreciated your program for many months since my retirement, and as I was sitting in front of my fireplace this morning listening to you tell of building a fire while guiding a group of hunters at five below, I stoked mine up a little more.   **Robert M. Waits • Helena, MT**

Survival of the Fittest

The winter of 1886-87 will always stand out as the worst in western history. It was the one that catapulted a young cowboy holed up in a Judith Basin bunkhouse to fame via his outstanding pen-and-ink drawing of a starving steer. Charlie Russell's sketch, "Waiting For A Chinook," was sent in response to a cattleman who wrote inquiring about his herds.

Winter blew in during November of '86 in the form of blizzards from the Canadian prairies. A chinook in December softened the snow, then another freeze-up turned it to ice.

More blizzards hit, one after another. Cattle froze to death where they stood; weakened ones were occasionally blown over by gale-force winds. Stock losses mounted to ninety percent in northeastern Montana, and sixty percent throughout what would shortly become the Treasure State.

But was 1886-87 *really* that bad? Can we expect another such devastating winter?

Yes on both counts. In fact, we've already had one similar to that memorable late-1800s winter—1977-78. And we're sure to have more. But times change. So do needs, and ability to cope.

Just as occurred during Charlie Russell's experience, blizzards roared down from the Arctic during 1977-78. Snow piled and kept coming. Temperatures plummeted to fifty below, and hard winds piled drifts against fences and buildings and in gully bottoms. Cattle died in '77-78, too, for it was a long winter. Losses during that hard winter ran up to ten percent.

Ten percent you say? How can you claim the winter of 1977-78 was as severe as the ordeal that occurred during Russell's day?

For one thing, little supplemental feeding was done in 1887. Most stock foraged year-round, and it was *expected* that winter losses would occur. In fact, ten percent was deemed acceptable in the 1880s.

In addition, ranges were overstocked in the mid-1880s. Low beef prices the preceding fall had caused many ranchers to hold over steers they'd planned to market. Forage was, as a consequence, depleted even before winter began, contributing to the die-off disaster.

Conversely, in 1977-78 most ranchers wintered cattle from haystacks stored for that purpose. Herds were confined to limited pastures, often protected from the worst elements.

Crawler tractors with dozer blades plowed through snowdrifts and cleared feed and bed grounds for the herds in 1977-78, whereas a century earlier, cowboys simply couldn't have reached the cattle with hay had any been available.

It's interesting to note attitude changes. None are more dramatic than the attitude of today's cattlemen compared with those of yesteryear. Nineteenth-century ranchers prayed for an open winter. Not so today. Today's cattlemen pray for snow—lots of it. They need it to replenish oversubscribed streams and groundwater for irrigation. Ranchers have learned to cope with severe cold, blizzards, and mounting snow.

We *all* still have to learn how to comport ourselves when water is no longer abundant.

There are some things I grew to dislike during my two decades as a Bob Marshall Wilderness outfitter. Of those, dwelling in canvas tents during prolonged periods of deep snow and bitter cold became the most nauseating. The energy-sapping battle to heat tents, keep supplies from freezing, provide the horses with adequate feed and grain, and the never-ending struggle to cross ice-bound streams and chop water holes for stock turned my way of life from fun to drudgery.

Returning home to a warm fire, comfortable recliner, and hot drink after packing out that last camp became an obsession. Never mind that after a couple of months of lounging in lassitude, I was charged up and ready to charge out; the specter of coming bitter weather still left me looking over my shoulder.

Consider then the plight of the early sodbusters dwelling on the high plains. Arctic blizzards are commonplace to high-plains folks who can wave into Canada from their doorstep. Keening winds have more force on the prairies than in the forested mountain valleys where I've faced the elements. Most of those homesteaders' homes were as drafty as my canvas tents, and unlike my two months of cold-weather travail, that drafty place was where they spent an entire winter.

Wood was never plentiful on the prairies, and water could be a big problem, too. In fact, many were the homesteaders who had to haul water for miles just for household use. Keeping stock water open was an all-winter chore. And their struggle with the elements was so strenuous that the mere feeding of draft animals often took up most of their winter's daylight hours.

It's a wonder to me that any of those homesteaders survived, let alone prospered. But a few did—today's plains are dotted with their descendants.

None of those descendants survive on the quarter section originally deeded to an ancestor. Instead, the acreages of those who failed, who fled the harsh land and fierce weather, have been combined through attrition into the working farms of those who stayed. Those huge farms are tilled with massive tractors that can plow and harrow and cultivate more soil between Sunday afternoon football games than a four-horse hitch could work in a month.

In a sense, we're all beneficiaries of our fathers and mothers—but few so much as those folks who live in what was once called, "next year country." ■

Missing Hop Toads and Lost Sparrows

Articles of legislation—laws to guide us—are supposed to resolve questions, provide direction, settle arguments. But seldom has legislation engendered as much controversy as Public Law 97-304: the Endangered Species Act.

From its passage in 1973, the Endangered Species Act ran into difficulties. Intended as a moral and physical commitment to the creatures with which we share space, the Endangered Species Act instead has degenerated into an ill-funded political squabble between developers, environmentalists, bureaucrats, politicians, scientists, educators, news media, and lay folk like myself who really don't understand but want to hear a wolf howl.

Perhaps we expected too much. What we really wanted was to avoid needless extermination of furry, finny and feathery creatures, such as happened to the passenger pigeon. We figured sea turtles and peregrine falcons and California condors were worth saving. And in order to ensure their survival, we were willing to change the way we did things. We were also willing to put up a few bucks to give the idea a kick along the road.

But something went wrong. Nobody, I expect, imagined that *thousands*—not dozens—of our country's wild animals were in deep trouble. Ever hear of the Wyoming toad or the Henslow sparrow? No? You'll never see one, either, for their species have become extinct since passage of the Endangered Species Act.

Sure, we know all about condors and whooping cranes, and something about sea turtles. We all applaud the Act's most conspicuous success: the recovery of the peregrine falcon. And we're cheering the bald eagle's revival from the brink. But few of us dreamed that several thousands of additional species of birds, mammals, fish, reptiles, amphibians, and plants await analysis to see if they should be listed as protected species. Or that almost a thousand of those species are perilously close to the brink!

So what happened? And what's still happening?

The Act became a political football, kicked by opponents and misused by proponents.

Most of the available budgeted dollars are spent on a dozen high-profile species: grizzly bears, timber wolves, alligators (for a while), and the aforementioned peregrines and turtles. Meanwhile, environmentalists twist the purpose of the Act, using obscure endangered creatures to thwart development projects that perhaps should have been thwarted—but without weakening a desirable and beneficial law: i.e. Public Law 97-304.

The Endangered Species Act is also beset from another quarter. Delisting is, in itself, a political football, particularly with species that are in direct competition with man: grizzlies and wolves. The Act, it seems, provides ideal protection for animals that folks might shoot in self-defense or property defense, so some conservationists vigorously oppose delisting even where appropriate.

Yet that's precisely the goal—to get species *off* the list. To recover them. Delisting wolves in Minnesota, alligators in Florida, and grizzly bears in Montana, where possible and appropriate, might have allowed enough dollars to save the Henslow sparrow or some hop toad in Wyoming. ■

Road-Kill Policy Smells

7:00 a.m. - Climbed from bed. Still dark. Gratefully accepted a cup of coffee from my honey. "A truck must have hit a deer in front of our house," Jane said. "I heard his brakes, then a thud."

8:30 a.m. - Daylight now. Jane started to drive away for the day, then returned to say, "There's a buck lying in the ditch near our driveway. I'm afraid Tess [our Brittany spaniel] will find it."

"Okay, honey, I'll call Marc [our son] and get him to help me load the deer so I can haul it to a garbage dumpster."

9:30 a.m. - Still hadn't called Marc. Happened to look out the window as a man walked toward our house from where I presumed the buck to be. He knocked and I opened the door. "There's a deer out in your ditch that looks as though he'd just been hit and ... well ... I never got a deer this year," he said. "I wonder, can I take it?"

"Search me," I replied. The idea struck me that this was my easy way out. "But if you want, I'll help you load it in your rig."

"Maybe I'd better call Fish & Game," he muttered. So I dialed the agency's Region I office number and handed him my phone. When he hung up, he said, "It's no go." He'd been told it was against the law to take a road-killed deer. He was also told the deer had been reported and someone was already on the way to get it.

"Gee," the man said, "it's a nice five-point, too."

9:40 a.m. - The man left.

9:45 a.m. - I wandered out to look at the five-point. Its head had been cut off and was gone.

10 a.m. - The deer was still lying in the ditch. I drove to town on business. Two more fresh-killed deer were in ditches within two miles of our home.

11:30 a.m. - When I returned home, neighborhood dogs had chewed on one fresh-killed carcass near the Little League ball field, across the highway from the neighbor's place. The headless buck was still in the ditch by our driveway.

1:30 p.m. - I called Fish & Game and asked what had happened to the person who was supposed to salvage the meat. They wondered about his absence themselves. I told them the buck's meat was going to waste. They said it was illegal for anyone to pick up road-kills without permission. They said they only gave permission to charitable institutions. They said two people had called their office wanting to know if they could pick up the buck, adding that I'd be in violation of the law if I hauled the buck carcass to a dumpster.

4:30 p.m. - Jane returned home. She was upset because the buck carcass was still in the ditch after I'd agreed to dispose of it.

4:35 p.m. - Duly chastened, I began making other phone calls to find out why perfectly good venison that folks wanted was wasted because of stupid laws. I couldn't follow the chain from Fish & Game to the proper people from the charitable institution. Finally gave up and asked the agency's Warden Captain for a copy of the law.

8:00 p.m. - An agency employee hand-delivered considerable pertinent information, including copies of the law. The buck carcass was still in ditch. Jane was still mad. I was growling, myself.

7:00 a.m. (the following morning) - The buck carcass is still in the ditch. My honey does not hand me a cup of coffee. Neither is she speaking. So I pour my own coffee and sit down to read the information packet delivered by Fish & Game. I do not believe the law that was written to discourage poaching necessarily applies to road-killed deer. Today is *not* turning into a nice day. Yesterday was not a nice day.

10:00 a.m. - I haul the buck to the dumpster in violation of the law. I am thoroughly convinced that my state's road-killed deer policy—like rotting venison itself—stinks. ∎

I really enjoy your show, Roland, and I look forward to reading your book. Hunting has received a lot of negative public-relations blows in the press.... Shows like yours are telling the story about the thoughtful side of hunting. Keep up the good work. **Scott Swenson • Billings, MT**

Who Cares About "Non-Game"

A decade or so ago, folks criticized Montana's Fish, Wildlife & Parks Department because non-game creatures were getting short shrift when dollars were allocated for wildlife management. I'd like to examine whether that charge was (or is) valid.

Most of the wildlife treasure, it is true, goes for bucks and bulls, and for scrappy trout that do a topwater jig whenever they're hooked.

To hell with pine squirrels and whiskey jacks that chirp or chatter each time a careful hunter creeps up to a slumbering elk. Who cares about snail darters or blackfooted ferrets or peregrine falcons, anyway?

Who indeed, one might ask as my state's non-game program struggles in the wake of declining revenue.

The charge was that Montana's Fish, Wildlife & Parks was putting disproportionate money into high-profile finny, furry, and feathery things for which rod and gun toters were willing to shell out the long green. The charge was true, of course. But the ugly implication was swiftly dispatched by rational residents who simply pointed out "them as pays gets."

"Okay, if you won't let us into hunting and fishing license money," the bluebird and mollusk enthusiasts said, "we'll raise revenue for our first loves some other way. So they bounced a non-game tax check-off proposal past my state's legislature.

The idea was to provide a space at the bottom of residents' state income tax form where an individual receiving a refund could choose to check off a portion of that refund as a donation to non-game fish and wildlife management.

Legislators bought into the proposal when non-game advocates assured them the check-off would support the entire non-game effort.

Has it?

No. The last time I checked, well over half of the $85,000 non-game management budget comes from hunting and fishing license sales, or from federal excise taxes on sporting equipment, while only forty percent comes from the check-off. So hunters and fisherfolk still wind up paying for the bulk of little-critter management after all.

You don't know the half! Can you guess what kind of hobbies folks who actually do contribute through the tax check-off participate in?

Seven out of every ten hunt and fish, that's what. The same folks annoyed by that chattering whiskey jack are, in the final analysis, the ones who care most about him. They're the ones who pay the freight not only for elk and deer and trout and paddlefish, but for reptiles and amphibians and loons and cormorants.

Where are Cleveland Amory and his ilk—the ones who profess such intense regard for all God's creatures that they'd disarm America and outlaw sport hunting? Where are they when it comes time to divvy up for an inventory of eagle nesting sites?

Tromping the rotunda in Dee Cee, that's where—lobbying against the very folks who pay the bills to insure that any furry, feathery, or finny creatures are left in America at all.

But Cleveland Amory and other such lobbyists in Washington may not be the only forces working against pine squirrels and barn swallows. Your accountant may be an unwitting part of an unholy triumvirate.

The last time I checked, my state was one of thirty-seven implementing non-game wildlife management programs. Like others, we offer some support through a check-off space on our state tax forms. But despite assurances from advocates that it would support the entire cost of the management program, revenue for non-game wildlife management has steadily declined since the check-off inception.

Why do revenues decline? Because the number of donors dwindled from over 6,600 in 1984 to a mere 3,000 today. Why?

Are my state's residents growing more callous about the so called non-game creatures? Do we no longer care about wildlife if we cannot hang their heads on a wall or tuck their backstraps into our freezers?

The answer may be a lot simpler than burgeoning cynicism among the populace; we simply no longer prepare our own income taxes.

In this age of applied calculus and trigonometry, home computers and electronic calculators, space ships to the moon and supposedly simplified tax forms, we seek out others for help in interpreting income-tax tables. I know I do. I can't understand the #@$%&° thing! *And so do seventy-two out of every one hundred of us.*

It's likely that few have told their accountants to check off $2 or $5 or $10 for a non-game donation, and it's not something he's likely to call you about, either. So the little creatures receive short shrift because of some bureaucrat's confusing tax design.

What is meant by non-game management? What is the non-game program? How much does it cost?

The last time I checked, my state's annual non-game budget was somewhere just short of $100,000 dollars. In addition to one non-game biologist, that money was used to:

Support a symposium on non-game wildlife.

Determine distribution and status of fifty species of special interest.

Print and distribute non-game information pieces.

Implement a bluebird project along the Yellowstone River.

Survey bald eagle nesting sites.

Conduct non-game inventories in Wildlife Management Areas.

Establish a challenge grant for non-game research.

Support the Montana Loon Survey.

Is non-game money being squandered? No. Neither is it wasted on controversial creatures like coyotes or gophers or prairie dogs.

Is the program worth having? I think so. I'm in favor of knowing a little more about herons and cormorants and eagles. And I'd be more likely to follow Highway 200 across the Treasure State if I thought the journey would be flavored by an occasional vivid-blue feathery thing fluttering along a roadside.

So, tell you what I'm going to do: I'm going to drop a note in the mess I send my accountant. I'm going to tell him to check off ten bucks for non-game wildlife. Why don't you do the same. ■

Just a short note from a flatlander who really enjoys your columns and radio shows. As I read or listen to your stories, it strikes me that many times your clients don't always limit out or take a trophy, but they always gain a valuable memory and enjoy Mother Nature. As one who enjoys most forms of outdoor activities and as a Hunter Safety Instructor, I think there is an important message there. Keep talkin' and writin'.   Dave Tweet • Conrad, MT

A Few Good Things About Nimrodding

One important point that is often overlooked in the debate about hunting is how much healthier the meat of wild game is than that of pen-raised, force-fed, flavor-subtracted, feed-lot creatures. In an era when practically everything that tastes good is supposed to be bad for you, doesn't it seem strange there are few health columns advocating elk burgers or deer ribs?

Couple wild game's nutritional benefits with the peace of mind inherent in sitting on a distant ridgetop on a frosty morning, then consider the physical effort of getting there, and I find it darned strange our nation's Surgeon General isn't promoting the real values of sport hunting: its win/win health bounty.

No medical doctor will claim man can exist on rutabagas and Brussels sprouts. And if there were any quacks who did, few folks who've snuggled up to a banquet table would pay the slightest bit of attention.

Meat—fresh if its available; or canned, smoked, salted, or raw if not—is one thing most of us must have, at least occasionally. Certainly meat isn't illegal, and Cleveland Amory aside, neither is it immoral. But most of it *is* fattening. And it's the fattening that's frightening. High blood pressure, cholesterol, blocked arteries, excess weight—all are endemic to habitual fatty meat consumption.

The American Medical Society doesn't tell us *not* to eat meat. Though they tell us to eat more vegetables and grains and fruit, they don't tell us (or expect us) to become vegetarians. Instead, they tell us to eat lean meat. Cut off the fat. Feed it to the dog.

But how much really lean meat do you find at the market? Lean claims are made, of course. No marbling in this cut, no excess fat in that steak; an extra dollar per pound. But is it free of fat? Huh-uh. Not like an antelope hind quarter or the backstrap out of a mule deer.

But deer and antelope and elk taste "wild," you say? Ha! Ten times out of ten, that's because the animal was shabbily cared for in the field. How often do you see a feedlot beef chased wildly over a half-section, then (when finally dropped) cleaned improperly and skinned not at all until a week later? How often do you see a prime beef draped over the fender of an automobile and transported five hundred miles through all kinds of weather, then unceremoniously dropped to lie on a garage floor until hung the following day? Tastes wild? You bet.

The key word is *tastes*. Cared for properly, it'll still taste, but not "wild." If it's quickly cleaned in the field and skinned within the hour, cured with care, cut skillfully, and wrapped to preserve it the way good beef is handled, wild meat will be a hit on any dining-room table.

And it'll be lean—as will be the hunter who spent time afield and is eating the meat he worked for and earned. Even if the wild animal was in top shape—plump and heavy bodied—its meat is still lean. And there's precious little marbling—ever—in an animal that made its living toodling around the outback.

Few folks can trust everything they read (my writings excepted). For instance, anti-hunters would have us believe nothing positive comes from sport hunting. According to naysayers, hunting is a "blood sport" that brings out the most "base" instincts of mankind. To hunt for and kill animals is a throwback to ancestral savagery and should have no place in a kinder, gentler, more enlightened society.

I don't agree. You see, I can think of a plethora of good stemming from the sport of hunting.

There are lots and lots of folks who, except for their enthusiasm for the sport, would fail to allocate time from busy schedules to get the kind of exercise afforded during their annual hunting trips. While it might be possible to duplicate the physical élan gained from standing atop a distant ridge at daylight, it's probable that many participants simply wouldn't take the necessary time without being driven by autumnal echoes from remote wild country.

And how about the mental restoration that comes from standing atop those far-off ridges? Most folks need to recharge their psychological batteries in peace and serenity; others need the challenge afforded by coping with the elements.

So far, we've been talking about benefits to us. But how about our kids?

<hr />

I recollect the days I spent afield hunting when I was a youth. Though there weren't nearly the options for getting into trouble for youth of my day, at least compared to temptations beckoning today's kids, we could still find plenty of mischief in which to indulge. But because hunting and fishing provided alternative outlets, I had limited time for mischief.

And it's refreshing to see that today's eager youngsters can still engage in healthy and educational outdoor pursuits; to know they can tell druggies to get lost. I sleep more soundly at night knowing my kids and grandkids have someplace besides street corners to hang around.

Perhaps crusades against drugs and alcohol and teen pregnancies should devote a modicum of their efforts to promoting healthy outdoor consciousness among today's youth; toward promoting alternatives to insidious, degenerate, and corrupting influences.

Kids need challenge. High-school sports provide such challenge, but not all kids are athletic. Likewise, not all kids are academic giants. But that's another nice thing about the outdoors—there are many levels for involvement. And just maybe kids who discover the enchantment of frost on a spiderweb, or match wits with a lunker trout or a whitetail buck, will come a tad closer to telling a drug dealer what to shove and where to shove it.

Hunting and involvement in outdoors adventure is a healthier and more enlightened alternative than hanging around a street corner waiting to get a knife between the third and fourth, don't you think? ■

Although I am not a hunter or fisherman I enjoy your program.   Terri Snyder • Colville, WA

We listen to your radio program every morning—it is enjoyed by our whole family.
Patty Vanden Bos • Valier, MT

I have enjoyed listening to your program on our local country western station, KVLE.
Ruth Moody Maguire • Gunnison, CO

The Hunger Moon

March was the Hunger Moon to the Indians. It was a time of hardship and want, not only for themselves but for most of the creatures sharing the land with them.

Yet March also brings the first stirrings of spring. Accumulated winter snows melt in the low country, and spring breakup inevitably occurs. The first buttercups peep forth toward the end of the month, to be followed soon after by spring beauties, shooting stars, and a host of other wildflowers. Soon, buds will be forming on the willow and serviceberry, and greening grasses will burst forth. It's ironic that the Indians' hungriest time came amid such promise.

But so it was. Before the advent of the horse and gun, the Hunger Moon meant the ragged end of a long winter. By the time of the Hunger Moon, their scant provisions—the smoked buffalo rib strips and carefully pounded pemmican saturated with rendered fat and flavored by dried berries—had long since been consumed. By then, foraging game animals had been driven far from the snowbound encampment and were themselves gaunt and stringy and never enough to feed the village. Even surplus dogs had disappeared into stew pots, while the canine survivors were no more than wild scarecrows.

The bitter cold and deep snows of December, January, and February had so taken their toll that hunters lacked either the strength or the will to ferret out small bands of life-sustaining, wintering wildlife. Nor did they have the energy reserve to enable them to make a buffalo "surround," or the stamina to drive the animals to a "jump." As a result, they sometimes resorted to peeling the outer layers of tree bark to reach the softer cambium layer—not real tasty, but life-saving.

Theirs was a subsistence of snared rabbits or beaver or other small game. The eating of carrion was not unknown. Lucky was the hunter who frightened a mountain lion from a fresh-killed deer, or did battle with a pack of wolves for a ham-strung buffalo calf.

There's irony that the Indian faced down the depths of winter only to face the unrelenting Hunger Moon just when salvation was at hand. This is also true for most big-game inhabiting the northern Rockies. The critical time for elk and deer is when? March. Always March.

March is when the last of wild ungulates' reserves are expended; when the easy-to-reach forage is gone. They've easily withstood howling gales in November, shrugged off the bitter cold of December, struggled against the blizzards of January, and barely survived a last reckoning of all three in February. If only March lives up to its promise of renewal, they'll make it. But if it doesn't … if more cold and more snow and more wind come in March….

It's March when the creatures die huddled in the deep-packed snow of narrow canyon bottoms, unable to beat their way back up a south-facing hillside to life-sustaining nourishment that's about to burst forth with spring's first blush.

That's why Indians named March the *Hunger Moon.* ∎

Airborne Attack!

The osprey sailed from its nest of sticks precariously perched atop a fire-killed tamarack snag. A few powerful thrusts from its wide swept-back wings and the bird was out of sight.

I shrugged and glanced back at the six packhorses toiling behind. Hmm, inflatable rafts riding fine. Ditto with the long oars, their ends criss-crossed above the horses' packs.

I twisted forward again, then stared toward the stick nest. *Babies up there,* I thought. *But she's one shy momma.*

We'd packed past this nest for several days running, carrying a couple of "drop" parties to Black Bear and hauling hay for this horseback-in, float-out fishing trip. Though each day the osprey was somewhere around her nest, I had yet to get a good look at the reclusive bird.

Once I even spotted her fishing in the river off Black Bear Flats—saw her dive to the water in a mighty splash and come up with what looked to be a foot-long trout. But she'd dropped the fish and winged away the moment she saw me and my horses.

Now she was winging away once again.

Then, here she comes! Wheeling in at treetop level, pumping her wings for all she was worth, the huge bird swept past her nest, angling to cross the trail. I stared, mouth agape, admiring her flight mastery. Then, apparently to thrill me even more, she executed a sharp turn directly over the trail, about two hundred feet away, and sailed a path to bring her directly overhead.

I stared up at her with mouth and eyes and arms spread wide. Then she released her load.

The bird must have been constipated for a week—I know so little about the internal working organs of predator birds. But all she had was released (squirted would be more accurate) in one long blob ... with my red hat bobbing defenseless below.

I've seen borate bombers drop retardant on blazing wildfires with less accuracy.

Journalistic honesty compels me to tell you that was the only airborne attack suffered by this outfitter during that summer, although I passed the nest many more times. Honesty also compels me to admit her—uh—movement over my head might have been accidental. But the result was that I lost interest in things osprey. And I never saw her babies.

The reason I never saw her babies, even after they'd grown older, was that every time I passed the birds' nest after the mother's—uh—accident, my head was down inside my denim jacket's collar like a turtle's in his shell. And the newly cleaned and blocked red hat was concealed beneath that same jacket. ∎

Wild Cows for Wild Country

Shifting his battered old pickup down rather than trust its brakes, the driver slowed and swung off into the over-grazed pasture. Dust fogged behind.

"I gotta move 'em, Claude," the driver said. "What with no rain this spring and none in sight, I'm plumb out of grass up here on the flats. That's why I thought of your place over in the breaks." He blew his horn at a cow and calf that stood amid the wheel tracks, fighting flies. When they moved aside, another cow lay behind, placidly chewing her cud. The men finally drove around her.

"You think they can handle the breaks?" Claude asked. "They look pretty soft and tame to me. That's wild country, y' know."

His uncle nodded. "Have to. Be a shame to sell 'em off now, just when I got a good bunch of blooded Herefords goin'." Claude's uncle stopped the pickup and reached out the window to scratch the nose of another cow.

The two men checked on the cows and calves several times that summer, driving out to the edge of the Missouri Breaks and glassing for them; or walking out to the first hill or two.

Sometimes they wandered among the contented animals.

Came fall and time to pull the herd. "Tame as they are, won't take us a half-day to round 'em up and head home," the uncle said as they backed their two saddlehorses out of the trailer. That was before they cantered over the first rise and surprised a small bunch grazing below. The lead cow threw up her head and tail and headed for distant pastures, followed close on her heels by the other six.

"What the hell!" Claude shouted and spurred his pony after the cattle. The two riders topped another ridge and a second bunch of cows and calves took off like frightened jackrabbits.

Another ridge and another stampede. Another. And another. The two men tried to herd the cattle, but nothing doing. The wild-eyed, ring-tailed cows outran mule deer they jumped at the same time; ran through drift fences and property fences. They started in a section-sized pasture and by the time they'd plowed through all the fences within miles, ran loose over five thousand acres.

The men ran for their pickup and managed to turn one bunch that oddly became docile. But as soon as those cows rejoined a larger herd down in the breaks and the men tried to herd them via horseback, the entire bunch threw up their tails and bolted for the next county.

More riders joined them the following day, but to little avail. The cows tore through more fences until their tongues hung out. Flesh melted from their frames. Finally, the cowboys gave up and began roping the wild-eyed animals one by one, dragging them to load into trailers.

"Why, Claude?" the uncle asked as the last cow was loaded. "What turned them so wild?"

"They weren't wild," Claude growled. "It's just that they'd always been herded with a pickup truck." The man shook out his lariat, then coiled it before looping it over his saddlehorn. He leaned forward to stroke his sweating gelding.

"And I'll tell you another damned thing," Claude said, pausing to spit to the side, "there'll never be another cow on my place that never saw a horse before roundup time!" ■

Modern Mountain Men

The kitchen door opened, then closed with a whisper. Since Jane was already in the house, and since both our kids are wont to enter like a Panzer Corps breasting the Maginot Line, a whispering door should've been my first clue.

"Well, Marc, did you catch anything?"

The boy's reply to his mother's question was unintelligible to me, perched as I was in a living-room easy chair, feet propped before a crackling fire. But then, I wasn't trying to eavesdrop. I turned to the editorial page, scanned that, then headed for the comics to see what insight "Hagar the Horrible" provided today. Gradually, it seeped in that I wasn't alone.

The boy was there when I peeped over the newspaper. He stood just before my chair, wearing his heavy school jacket and a wool cap with flaps pulled low over his ears. And he stared at the toes of his felt-lined boots. Oh, clues were abundant had I only had eyes to see, ears to listen.

"How's the trapping going?" I asked.

The boy had set his first traps two weeks before, digging out a couple of rusty no. 4's from a box of discarded odds and ends in our garage. The kid already knew a bunch about hunting and fishing, handling his Daisy BB gun with confidence and care, and getting along famously with his Christmas fly-

111

tying kit. So neither Jane nor I was surprised when our son wanted to branch into different outdoor adventures.

"What are you planning to trap?" I'd asked when, lugging the no. 4's, the lad had started for the woods near our home.

"I dunno," he said. Ordinarily, "I dunno" wouldn't be good enough since even an eight-year-old must have a license to trap for Montana furbearers. But I let him go, reasoning that the boy was so young and inept he'd be lucky to get the traps set without snaring himself. Too, as far as I knew, no furbearing creatures of value lurked in our small wood plot.

Marc took his trapping seriously, however, checking his sets faithfully after every schoolday. And his interest never waned, though fortune seemed always to elude him.

"Well?" I said, folding the paper neatly and laying it on my lap with Hagar on top. "I didn't get an answer—how's the trapping?"

"Okay," he mumbled, meeting my eyes for a brief second, then dropping his gaze back to the floor.

I suppose my forehead crinkled into a puzzled frown, but I shrugged and picked up Hagar. I finished that strip and was just getting into "Beetle Bailey" when Marc said, "Dad?"

"Huh? What?"

His voice sounded far away, but he stood there in front, same as before, still staring shyly at the floor.

"What is it, son?"

"What ... what if I was to catch a skunk?"

I laughed. "Then you'd have a big problem, wouldn't you? Ha, ha. Best not to set the traps around skunk holes. Ha, ha. Be a real mess. Your mother would have to soak you in tomato ..." I trailed off. "Marc! You didn't catch a skunk! Did you?"

He looked up, the tip of an index finger in a corner of his mouth. The reply was almost inaudible.

Jane laid in a big stock of tomato juice. It was added to our bathwaters for the next several days.... ∎

Mystic Men, Marten Magic

It was a pine marten, all right. I'd strolled from the cooktent just at good daylight. The marten scampered from a pile of new-split wood to a big Douglas fir overhanging a steep embankment. He was no more than thirty feet away.

The saucer-eyed, round-eared, triangular face peered around the tree's rough bark. Cute. I stepped nearer. The marten darted up the tree, onto its first limb, running along it until the limb would no longer bear his weight. A pine marten, I knew, could leap from tree to tree. But this fir was a solitary one, more than thirty feet from its nearest neighbor.

The outsized relative to the weasel ran back along his limb, stopped to stare, ran another few feet, stopped to stare, then started down the tree trunk. I took another step nearer. He retreated around the tree, and I could hear him descending. But the animal's escape could only be down the steep bank and across the broad, exposed gravel bars of a river bottom. He peeked around the tree again, almost at ground level. I took another step and the marten ran back up the tree.

It was a stand-off. Each time he made a move to descend, I stepped nearer. I'd never been so close for so long to a free-ranging marten. At the end, we were no more than eight feet apart as he scampered out on his limb, then darted back, circled the tree, and stopped every few steps to peer at this strange human who made no overt move. I began talking to the marten in a soothing tone. It worked. He sat up on his limb to stare for the longest time through his saucer eyes.

The creature was darkish-reddish and at least twice the size of a pine squirrel. I resisted an irrational urge to reach out to stroke him.

Finally tiring of the game, the marten descended the tree on my side, hesitant step after hesitant step. Hitting the ground, he darted for nearby woods, then stopped halfway, turned, sat up, and stared back at me, as if he could hardly believe the odd human he'd just met. Then he was gone.

As strange as it may sound, this was not my closest encounter with a pine marten. One afternoon, over thirty years ago, we were on our way out of hunting camp. I brought up the rear, pulling three laden packhorses. Up the trail ahead, I saw our lead rider point above. The next rider came to the same spot, twisted in the saddle, and pointed up for the next man. So it went, rider after rider, horse after horse. Nearing the spot, I saw something perched on a tree limb, not over eighteen inches from the hat crown of the rider ahead. The man twisted in the saddle, staring up, then grinned back at me.

It was a pine marten sitting upright on the limb, swiveling his head as he stared wide-eyed at each horse and rider to pass beneath. The marten seemed not in the least frightened. His was an apparent attitude of sheer puzzlement.

I watched behind as my last packhorse rumbled beneath the little creature. As it did, the marten spun clear around on his limb to watch us disappear into the sunset.

I missed a great photo opportunity that day. Though I had a camera in one of my saddlebags, I was so amazed at that marten's audacity that I didn't think of it until later. Much later. ■

Last fall you told stories about a family that spent about a month in the wilderness hunting elk when it was way below zero. This was some time ago when they didn't have automobiles. Do you have a book with stories like this?

Iris L. Vergason • Lewistown, MT

Sandpaper Tough or Wet-Clay Soft?

The guy across the river attracted my attention. He carried a fishing rod and, because the morning dew was heavy, wore unbuckled overshoes that flopped loosely upon the calves of his worn trousers. He shouted. I recognized him then—probably the best packer ever to hoist a U.S. Forest Service load onto a mule's back—Gene Brash.

"What say?" I shouted back.

"What are you doing?"

"Going home," I hollered as I swung the last pack atop our packhorse.

"Need help?"

"Tell him no," I grunted to Jane and she waved to him: "He says no."

Undeterred, the big man waded into the South Fork—a puny stream at Big Prairie, far inside the Bob Marshall Wilderness, but still up to the man's knees.

"How come you're going home so soon?" he asked when he waded out on our side, water sloshing from inside his overshoes.

I grinned as I tied the load in place with half-hitches and a slip knot. "Big party going out in a couple of days. A float trip. Should be back up here come Friday."

"What day is it now?" he asked.

I said I thought it was Sunday and he replied, "I'll be in Martin City then."

I lashed an empty cardboard box between the packs at the top of the saddle. Jane and I had packed into Big Prairie for a busman's holiday. We had a week between trips and figured we'd rather spend it in some of the prettiest country God ever made than watching Tom Brokaw or Dan Rather dredging up dirt on Gary Hart or Jimmy Carter or whoever might be this week's whipping boy.

I checked the cinches on our saddlehorses, then Jane handed me the little sore-footed cocker spaniel. I spread a blanket in the cardboard box and set the dog inside. Just the head of the long-eared mutt stuck up above the box sides, soulful eyes turned pitifully upon Jane.

"Well now, ain't that about the cutest thing you ever saw," the old packer muttered.

I glanced at the man, seeing him through different eyes. Here's one of the toughest, crustiest, hardest-working mountain men ever to fork a bronc. The guy's been coming to this country since long before it was called the Bob Marshall Wilderness, accompanying his parents for a month or two every autumn. Likely he was whelped here; certainly the guy was forged here, honed here, became a legend here. Probably Gene Brash will die here. Today he's waded a river just to chat with a friend. And now he's thinking a cocker spaniel perched ungainly in a cardboard box, atop a packhorse, is "cute." Will wonders never cease?

Then I recollected how one of my early-day heroes—a man who guided Zane Grey on fishing trips into the High Cascade country of southern Oregon—once packed a tiny Plymouth Rock chick inside his shirt for several days while herding cows because a weasel had killed the rest of his homestead flock and Perry Wright couldn't bear to leave the chick to die.

Tough, indeed! Crusty, indeed! Perhaps God makes tough, crusty mountain stompers soft inside because otherwise they'd be too sandpapery for us ordinary folks to rub against.

Or is it the other way around? Is it that He makes mountain stompers out of only a few chunks of clay because they're too soft to dwell among civilization's sharks? ∎

All about Mountain Moods and Willful Women

Exasperated, I finally muttered, "Why don't you bitch?"

Her nose lifted airily. "I have every right to bitch," she said. "But I'll hold out this thread of hope: my disposition will improve as the day progresses. What about yours?"

I laughed despite my peevish wife. We were on our way to Turtlehead Mountain, near the crest of the Rockies. The day began with horsebacking along a narrow, perilous trail—not her favorite line of outdoors adventure. Then we'd tied our horses and bushwhacked up a scramble-steep mountainside, through tag alder and huckleberry bush. Though sunbeams broke through a rising fog and gave every promise of a gorgeous day, it'd rained the night before and we were soaked from the waist down by the sopping brush.

"What are you grinning about?" she demanded.

The grin spread as I turned and trudged on up the mountain. Soon, I knew, her "bitching and grumbling" would turn to "whining and sniveling," which would eventually give way to "indifferent acceptance," which—as we worked toward the more open high country—would metamorphose into "grudging approval."

"Just how much are we to climb today?" she asked when we next paused for air. "I'm tiring already." (Whining and sniveling.)

The fog had lifted completely by the time we clambered into the tiny meadow along the crest of a spur ridge. "Feel that sun," I said. "It'll soon dry the bushes and grass."

"I hope so." (Indifferent acceptance.)

Another half-hour and we could see our target mountain crest, ahead and to the left. Pausing to rest once more, I pointed out Big Salmon Lake and Holland Peak in the western distance.

"It is pretty," she murmured. (Grudging approval.)

So far, so good, I thought. But eyeing the cliff ledges we must clamber over to reach the mountain's inclined plateau, I knew Jane had yet other phases through which to pass. The first would be "hesitant fear," which—as we continued to climb—would turn to "absolute terror."

"Are you hurt?" I solicitously inquired after she tumbled on a talus slope.

"No, I'm all right. Just bruised. But this is hard walking." (Hesitant fear.) Then, "Are we going up *there!*"

I helped by offering her a hand, an arm, and placing her feet. Finally we reached the ledge along which we must travel. I could stroll it with my hands in my pockets, but she crept step by hesitant step, hugging the cliff above, staring wide-eyed at the chasm below. "I … I don't think I can do this," she croaked. (Absolute terror.)

But she made it through the notch, and as we plodded on up the grassy, tundra-like slope to Turtlehead's crest I mused that the woman had but two mood swings left: "awestruck wonder" and "enthusiastic advocacy."

At the top, wind blew strands of hair charmingly around her pretty face as she turned in every direction. Mountain peaks thrust up as far as one could see. "Isn't this marvelous?" she shouted into the wind. (Awestruck wonder.) "I just can't wait to get back to camp to tell everyone." (Enthusiastic advocacy.)

She turned to slide her arms around my waist, twisting her face up toward mine. "You've been grinning like a Cheshire cat all day. Now you'd better tell me why."

My grin spread wider, every bit as full as my love for this woman. ■

I first heard your program while driving across mid-Washington a little over a year ago. Was so amazed you live so close to my home in Lakeside. I've since located you on a local station. Thanks much.

Darrell Marshall • Lakeside, MT

*I enjoy listening to your **Trails to Outdoor Adventure** over KUDZ here in central Minnesota. Keep up the good work.*

Norman Galercel • Hector, MN

Tributes to Torch-Carriers

Earth Day comes, I'm told, on April 22, and the day is big to lots of folks; as it should be, since the earth is about the biggest touchy-feely thing with which any of us will ever be associated.

On a local level, kids will ferret out accumulated roadside debris that insufferable pigs have discarded through auto windows during the previous year. And we'll hear a drumbeat roll about recycling—as well we should because when we've once developed both the will and the mechanics, recycling may save us from thoroughly fouling our own nests.

On Earth Day each year, conservation documentaries are trotted out and dusted off and sensationalized. Nationally, politicians posture and students demonstrate for protection of our environment. The news media report both posturing and demonstrations with a straight face, and Americans listen and watch and read about it with a modicum of bored interest. It's inescapable, we're all forced to become aware of our environment for one day—then we go back to doing things the way we always have.

We'll throw orange peels and empty beer cans and disposable diapers out of car windows, pollute telephone poles and barn walls with election posters that eventually blow away in the wind. We dump raw sewage into rivers, erect slag heaps upon hillsides, slash and burn forests, and poison land "in order to save it."

Frankly, I don't see what's the big deal about Earth Day. Sure, it has a certain nuisance value whereby the public's conscience can be piqued and disgraceful polluters can be tweaked. But to my way of thinking, making a big deal about Mother Earth one day each year can easily lead to acceptance of the premise that it's all right to ignore the land during the other 364.

Fortunately, *everything* isn't yet polluted in the country where I live. Sure, they say we shouldn't drink water flowing from Glacier Park. But it's comforting to know that any pollution that might be in such water stems from some natural but obscure giardia snail rather than from a smelter's tailing ponds leaching into McDonald Creek, or from smokestacks pouring out airborne acids.

We who dwell along the Crown of the Continent can be thankful for those folks who, in years past, fought to keep us from Butte-ifying all of our land. Glacier Park and the Bob Marshall Wilderness didn't happen by accident—folks worked hard for 'em. Just as in later years, others worked hard for the Great Bear Wilderness, a Wild Rivers System, clean air, and a big lake still unpolluted by Canadian strip mines.

And the people who made those things happen didn't practice their conservation concerns only one day each year.

George Bird Grinnell campaigned and wrote editorials through his *Field & Forest* (forerunner of *Field & Stream*) magazine for ten years before Glacier National Park became a reality. And even then, it took the muscle of Jim Hill and his Great Northern Railroad to persuade Congress that the park could benefit the people of America, as well as northwest Montana.

Bob Marshall carried the Wilderness system torch for half his life before the wilderness bearing his name came to pass after his untimely early death. And even then, it took the political muscle of the Roosevelt administration to turn dreams into reality as a tribute to one of FDR's strongest political supporters.

Most of us aren't slated to be monumental movers and

shakers. But it's important we bear in mind these words of Helen Keller:

> *The world moves not alone from the mighty shoves of its heroes, but by the aggregate of the tiny pushes of each of us.*

Maybe if we tried exercising Earth Day *twice* each year, we could double the tiny pushes from each of us. ∎

The Art of Whitewater Survival

Running whitewater is an art. It takes a firm hand, yet a deft touch; a keen focus, yet a broad feel. The best whitewater men and women seemingly hold a cavalier attitude toward life, yet share a superb sense of survival. But of all their attributes, when it comes to reading the river, none is as important as experience.

In reading rivers, there's only so much you can get from books; so much you can glean from listening to experts; so much you can grasp from common sense and logic. Actually piloting a raft or canoe or kayak down a torrent is the only way to become really adept. In becoming a veteran whitewater rat it's sometimes necessary to find out what you can't do before finding out what you can.

The techniques for guiding each type of craft are different. Oar strokes differ, not only from oar to paddle, but from oar to oar, depending on the size and shape of your craft. Often inflatable rafts can glide over rocks that would tear the bottom from a canoe. Kayaks and canoes can shoot through narrow channels and gorges where rocks would grip or overturn rafts. Usually, inflatables—especially the large ones—can take wilder whitewater than can canoes or even kayaks.

It's an education for a novice to make a run with an experienced hand. Try it. Try guessing where and how an expert plans to guide his craft—because any skilled whitewater rat will plan far in advance by studying the approaching rapid while still upstream. What may appear to a novice as the best route will often prove to be an invitation to disaster. An experienced pilot will read water flows and adjust with a few deft oar strokes to glide past a dangerous rock. Or he may choose to tick that rock to spin his raft in a manner that will clear another, more dangerous downstream hazard.

You'll never see experienced river runners fighting the water. Instead, they'll go with the flow, using the current to aid their maneuvers. The ability to do so, of course, is directly related to the prior planning that went into their positioning at the head of the rapid, before sweeping on into the maelstrom.

An experienced whitewater rat isn't too proud to pull over and analyze a particularly dangerous piece of whitewater from the shore. He'll usually pause well ahead of the rapid, most always on the inside of the river bend where the current is mildest. The idea is to determine which side of the river he wishes to run, where he'd like to be positioned at the rapid's beginning, and to spot any particular sweepers, rocks, shallows, reversals, or other hazards he needs to know about in advance.

On which side of that rock is the most current flowing? Is there sufficient slack water to pull past those overhanging roots? Given that my strongest oar stroke is pulling, rather than pushing, should I go into this stretch of whitewater with bow or stern forward? These are all questions answered best from experience.

Experience also teaches what's best to do in a catastrophe. All the reading or listening in the world flies out your mind's windows when your raft upsets. Couple the accident trauma with hypothermia from cold water and the hysteria of other survivors, and hell has come a-visiting. That's precisely when there's no longer time to wonder if Mary rebuckled her life jacket after applying sun screen or whether the ice chest was lashed firmly in place. Neither is it a time to discover that safety ropes are missing, or lash ropes dragging so as to ensnare someone who's fighting to the surface.

If the whitewater is really heavy, most experienced rafters

will use two rafts, primarily as safety fall-backs in case of an upset. One raft shoots through each bad spot first, pausing in slack water at the rapid's foot to wait for the next raft.

You say you want to do some whitewater rafting and you want to do it on the cheap? What's that? You bought a Kamikaze raft at the five and ten and you want me to go with you?

Don't call me. If I want to go, I'll call you. ∎

The American Radio Relay League
RADIOGRAM
15 R HXC K95PS 15 Wausau, WI

ENJOYED	YOUR	DANCE	ON	THE
WILD	SIDE	VERY	MUCH	HOW
ABOUT	A	SEQUEL	AFTER	THE
DANCE				

signed: LOU,   K95PS

Trusting Equine Age

Point no. 1. An ancient adage of horsemen is that wet saddle blankets will cure most bad equine habits. This means, of course, that if horses are used enough to keep their saddle blankets wet with sweat, they have neither time nor inclination for gymnastics at inopportune moments.

There's an abundance of truth in that adage. But don't stake your life or the health of your kids on it. Hard work does, indeed, make for more responsible horses, but its calming powers seem to affect the ponies in direct proportion to their age.

Perhaps that's because young horses haven't rounded a trail bend and come eyeball-to-eyeball with a huckleberry-grazing bear. Or kicked over a hornet nest. Maybe they've never stumbled from a mountainside trail after dark, or had kitchenware shake loose inside a packbox they carried, or suffered a saddle that rolled beneath their belly during an impromptu jig because other ponies were acting up.

Most older usin' horses have experienced many of those travails, and more, leading me to advance the idea that wet saddle blankets *and* age will cure most horses' bad habits. Which brings us to the next point:

Point no. 2. Perhaps an experienced older horse is the one upon which your kids should learn to ride, instead of raising a cute and cuddly colt that grows into a rebellious "teenager" so spirited and dangerous the kids wind up fearing all horses.

What age should you look for in a reliable horse?

In my considerable experience, it's a rare pony I would trust with novice riders until the horse has turned eight or ten. And even though we used horses harder in our guiding business than most folks ever would, I never hesitated to buy a good-looking, sound fourteen-year-old; or even one sixteen if he acted eager and was plumb gentle.

You see, most folks fail to realize a fourteen- or sixteen-year-old horse still has many good years left, provided he's used properly. For instance, I tried to retire my old saddle-horse, Buck, when he was in his mid-twenties. But the big buckskin would have nothing to do with retirement.

Each time I dropped the tailgate on our stock truck, there was Buck waiting to crowd in. I said, "Okay, you old fool. You can go one more time." And you know what? He acted so much like an eager kid and was so much pleasure to ride that after resting the old pony for a week, I took him on another, more demanding trip. Again he did well. So I rode him on our season's first hunting trip—a grueling trail across rushing streams, high mountain passes, and deep mud. So what happened? The old fool set a record for the speediest trip ever into our hunting camp, and he was pulling a packstring. I took him for the last time when he was twenty-eight.

We had several horses on the far side of twenty years old in our outfit. All did superb jobs. Sure, we rested them well by rotating their trips. But I never, ever worried about whether or not they'd properly care for their riders.

Even yet, after being retired for several years, Jane and I keep four horses that we've used several times to pack miles into one of the largest wilderness areas in America. All are over twenty. All perform nobly and without the least bit of trouble. They pack well, walk well, never fight with each other, and are delights to have at home in the pasture.

Now—you tell me why an older horse wouldn't be just the ticket to start your children on. Frankly, I'd put my money on a twenty-year-old horse any day if he was carrying my kids or grandkids. ■

I was in a very serious car wreck the 10th of February and spent a month in Billings in the hospital. I'm recovering very well and should be able to ride again on a gentle horse whenever I want to try. Your books were a godsend to me— I needed something that would interest me and give me a sense of direction again. You have helped me open up my past and give it meaning and love. Thank you both.
John Haynes • Bozeman, MT

A Geneology of Wilderness

My kids cannot recollect life before television. They grew up hearing and reading about rocket ships and guided missiles and they predate computers only by a little.

Me? My first memories are of a home without indoor plumbing or electricity. Schools of my early years were small, housing multiple grades in single rooms. Athletic facilities were nearby farm fields where we kept the grass worn to dirt.

My father told of seeing his first automobile when he was eight years old. Another time, he and his brothers and sisters leaped from their farm wagon to hide under a mesquite tree when the first airplane they saw buzzed overhead.

My father's father saw the first railroad laid through Georgia, and his father—my great grandfather—predated steamships.

His father—my great great grandpa Cheek—was 74 years old when his youngest son was born to his third wife. Our records show that third wife—my great great grandmother—applied for a Revolutionary War Widow's pension in 1850, meaning her husband was wearing a uniform when they, as Abraham Lincoln later put it: "… brought forth on this continent a new nation, conceived in liberty and dedicated to the proposition that all men are created equal."

That means my great great grandfather was half-grown when Braddock and his redcoat army were destroyed by the French and Indians in the wilderness of western Pennsylvania. Civilization, as it was then known, consisted of a few settlements scattered along the Atlantic seaboard. Beyond outlying farms were trackless forests, limitless plains, and towering mountains.

My great great grandfather Cheek served several three-month hitches guarding the frontiers of South Carolina while others of his time won independence at a place called Yorktown.

His last child—my great grandfather—was born during an age when American settlement was well established east of the Mississippi, but had only a tenuous foothold farther west. True, a few hardy fur trappers had pushed up the Missouri and the government was busy establishing a meager military presence in the region; but it was surely wilderness beyond the setting sun. My great grandfather died only a few decades later, but by then the first wagons had rolled into Oregon's fertile Willamette Valley to span a continent with settlement.

My grandfather fled Reconstruction Georgia to settle on a lonesome homestead in Texas, where he carved a precarious livelihood from a brush-filled wilderness.

My father left those parched lands to follow earlier pioneers to an Oregon of rushing water and endless forests. There he made a living milling lumber from the country's limitless trees.

Those "endless" forests of my youth had pretty much disappeared when, over three decades ago, I left Oregon for a Montana with more wilderness. *Montana!* The land of unfettered, untouched, untrammeled wilderness. What will later generations think of you?

Just five generations in my family lineage have passed from an America of virtually *all* wilderness until today a concentrated effort is under way to preserve the few scattered wildland remnants left.

And I shed a tear for my great great grandchildren. ∎

*I have just finished **The Phantom Ghost of Harriet Lou**. Wow! It was wonderful! I was transported from my state-room aboard a destroyer to the wilderness I roamed as a teenager. Your tales were well told, enlightening, and dead on the money. The open ocean on a calm, clear night is beautiful, but I'll never hear the hoarse bellow of a rutting bull elk. Driving a warship into heavy seas and tailing green water on the bridge is exulting, but not nearly as much as bucking into a northern blizzard and stumbling across grizzly tracks that haven't begun to fill in with [snow]. Thank you for sharing with me. My dad has sent me the Thursday **Great Falls Tribune** no matter where I am in the world for the past 13 years. I have always enjoyed your writing, but this book was special.*

Joel Stewart • USS Fife Dd 991

White-Knuckling Avalanche Country

On February 4, 25-year-old Kent Biermeister left Cooke City, Montana, for a day of snowmobiling with friends. They were playing "high point" on a nearby slope when Kent's snowmobile stuck. A buddy came up the slope to help, and the combined weight and shock triggered an avalanche. The friend rode out the slide, but it was an hour and twenty minutes before Kent Biermeister's body was recovered.

On March 5, near Montrose, Colorado, highway worker Ed Imel was buried by an avalanche as he plowed out a previous snow slide. Imel was the last of fourteen people killed by avalanches in seven states during a thirty-day period in 1992. Those disasters became known as the "February Massacre," considered to be the worst sequence of Western avalanche activity in recent history. Why did it happen? Two reasons:

1. Widespread unstable snow conditions. Persistent drought throughout the entire West brought little snow in December and January. Much of the unusually light early-winter snowpack was converted to unstable crystal form (known as depth hoar) through heat transfer from warm earth to cold air. Then came February's heavy snows atop the unstable depth hoar—to the point of critical mass.

2. Attitude change. Accepted procedure for traveling in snow country once stressed avoiding slopes steeper than 30 degrees. But today's more adventurous skiers, snowboarders, and snowmobilers tend to accept greater risks to achieve more thrills.

With rising acceptance of inherent risks came an emphasis on risk reduction through recognition of unstable conditions, improved rescue equipment, and certain procedures. Dr. John Montagne of Bozeman, Montana, one of America's leading avalanche experts, lists some of those procedures:

Never ski alone.

Descend initially close to ridgelines, not in the center of gulches.

Avoid skiing above another individual.

Move off slope promptly at end of run.

Select a route that fits the attitude and abilities of your party.

Avoid sudden changes in direction, slope shocks, falling.

The MSU Professor Emeritus of Geology and past President of the American Association of Avalanche Professionals also recommends modern ski equipment to facilitate better skiing techniques, as well as electronic beacons and probes to increase chances for live rescues in the event of avalanche burial.

How can a novice recognize unstable, even dangerous snow conditions? One method I might use is to invert a ski pole and thrust its handle through the snow, to the ground. If there's resistance for most of the distance, and then it's easy to push at the end, you're into unstable depth hoar. If it's a hill you're on, get off.

One of the best ways to recognize avalanche danger, says Dr. Montagne, is to loosen a block of snow, shoveling out from in front, then step on it with one ski. "If it slides, then you're on extremely unstable snow. Even if you jump on it with both skis before it slides, it's still considered dangerous. If you jump once, twice, even three times and the block remains stationary, then you're on reasonably stable snow."

Dr. Montagne asked if I'd ever been on snow that "whomped."

"Huh?"

"Snow that suddenly collapsed a few inches with you—we call it 'whomp'. When it does, it can make your hair stand on end."

I admitted to having experienced "whomps" a couple of times—always on gentle terrain.

"If the snow never started moving [avalanching], you're lucky," he said.

I asked about other methods for recognizing avalanche danger.

"Look for 'flag trees'—scattered trees with limbs growing largely from the downslope side. Farther up-slope, trees will be stunted and of a uniform size and height. Higher still, they'll be more stunted and sometimes scattered—a typical avalanche-prone slope."

I asked whether there's more danger to someone using a snowmobile.

"Of course," the avalanche expert said. He explained that machines are much heavier than people, and the riders have a less tactile "feel" for conditions. They're also traveling faster up-slope and across-slope, and because of their need to con-centrate on machine operation, they can get into danger without realizing it. Then, the machines themselves can injure or kill if they begin rolling with moving snow. "Actually, they can be responsible for as many fatal injuries as the avalanche itself."

During the February Massacre of 1992—the thirty days when avalanches killed fourteen people in seven states—two victims were snowmobilers, two were snowshoers, two were mountain climbers, and one was a highway equipment opera-tor. Seven skiers died; five were skiing backcountry. Surprisingly, one of the backcountry skiers was a contract avalanche forecaster for the Moab, Utah, area.

For people using the backcountry during winter, Dr. Mon-tagne recommends a book entitled *Snow Sense*, by Jill Fredston and Doug Fesler. *Snow Sense* is a handy pocket guide to evaluating snow conditions, slope angle, cornice dan-gers, and a plethora of other stuff. I carry a copy in my daypack.

From all the above, it seems reasonable to conclude that avalanche forecasting is still in its infancy. At least that's the way I figure—about *my* avalanche forecasting.

***

"Listen. It's the best indicator I know that danger is near."

Loren Kreck is a retired Kalispell orthodontist who's an avid outdoorsman and proponent of mountaineer skiing. I'd asked the man about spring avalanche hazards and how novice and intermediate crosscountry skiers might be more alert to danger. I asked, "Listen? Listen for what?"

"Rattles. If you hear rattles on the mountains (meaning small snowslides taking place) while you're skiing, it's a good time to watch out!"

Loren said periodic avalanche chutes aren't the only places of danger. "It depends on the degree of slope," he said. "Snow can break away from above and cascade through trees just as well as down open chutes. A lot of people have found that out."

I thought about what he'd just said as I scribbled furiously during the interview. Presumably some of those who discovered danger amid the trees lived to tell of it. Otherwise how would this avid adventurer know? Then I recalled some years back when this same guy told about skiing near the tree line on Great Northern Mountain. On that occasion the snow he traversed began to move:

"It wasn't moving fast—maybe two or three miles an hour—and the slope was gentle enough that I wasn't alarmed." But Loren said he wanted to get a feel for the power of moving snow, so he grabbed a small tree and clung to it.

"And?"

"The power! The sheer power—unbelievable! It tore me from the tree, so I skied off the shifting snow and watched until it stopped. Awesome."

Loren told me that early mornings, "…before midday air temperatures warm, are better times to cross a danger spot." He paused thoughtfully, then said, "When it's cold all day is a better time to ski those places."

Loren said the most important factor contributing to avalanche danger is the conditions of the slope before the last snow fell. "If it thawed and froze on the old surface, it can create an especially slippery effect."

"When is it most dangerous after a fresh snow?" I asked.

"Within the first three days—if the new snow is heavy."

Another danger in mountain country, Loren said, comes from cornices near the ridgetops, where wind tends to blow snow that builds and builds until a cornice can break away of its own weight. "There's no warning and they'll often roar clear to the bottom because of mass and weight. And the only real way to guard against them is to know what's above you."

Loren's advice continued with an admonition not to trust a chute merely because snow has already avalanched from it into a pile at the bottom. "Some chutes can run two or three times the same year."

"What if skiers must cross a chute?"

"If you must cross," he said, "do it one person at a time. And do it quickly."

The final words of wisdom from this man who has skied through Glacier Park many times were the same as his first:

"Listen! Keep an ear out and listen!" ■

*We enjoy your program on KDIO from Ortonville and
hope you continue it for many years.*
Mary Kampmeier • Graceville, MN

*I enjoy listening to your program on WTYS in Marianna,
Florida.* James Gray Braxton • Cottondale, FL

Listen to you every morning. You are interesting.
Geraldine Hansen • Corona, SD

Platoon Substitution

Wedge after wedge winged north, their distant honking both exhilarating and intruding. I paused to lean against a fence post and stare up at an oncoming flight. Forty-seven in one wing, I counted; thirty-seven in the other.

As I watched, the leader began veering to the right, followed in order by the forty-six other birds of the left wing. The leader veered farther right until he headed east, still followed by the trailing left wing. But the thirty-seven-bird right wing, headed off by their circling flight members from the left, began to bunch and flutter, as if in confusion.

Still, the leader and his trailing wing circled until they were flying south, then southwest. The bunched and apparently confused right wing, nearer the hub of the wheeling flight, finally got their act together and, cutting across the circle, headed to catch up.

But was the apparent confusion, in fact, real? Formed up and flying powerfully and in order, the right wing continued to make tactical adjustments until they formed into a V. By cutting across the left wing's two-mile circle, the newly formed right-wing V emerged in front, neatly on the same flight path, at the point where the circle began. The trailing left wing formed up behind. It was the neatest lineup change I'd ever witnessed, and I stared in admiration at the flock until they disappeared into the distance.

I've watched leadership changes in flights of honkers before—the head goose fluttering to the side and falling back; perhaps another hurrying ahead to spell a flagging leader. But what I'd just witnessed was an entire new platoon taking over. It was unit substitution on a grand scale. And it was so smooth!

How did the leader know it was time for a break? How did the others know to take part in the massive substitution? How did the reserves know to take over? What orders were given? What signal—or signals—did the birds exchange? Was notice provided in the honking? Hup! Two! Three! Four! I'd tuned out their sounds, relegated the insistent noise to the subconscious. Now I wished I'd listened more closely for some change in cadence, some differing tonal quality.

There were eighty-four birds in that flight, yet aside from some initial adjustment among the right wing as they formed for their new mission, no halftime marching band ever performed more flawlessly.

"Honk! Honk!"

Startled, I realized I'd been staring after a flight of honkers that must be somewhere over southern Alberta by now. Night was falling.

"Honk! Honk!"

The rush of their wings came before I saw silhouettes against the evening sky: three local Canadas heading for the river and their island sanctuary for the night.

How about those great northern flights from Sonoran farms to tundra nesting? Do they stay aloft all night? Have they already made another giant circle to replace tiring leaders? Or are they searching even now for a resting place somewhere among alternate strips of Alberta grain stubble? I shrugged and gathered my hammer and fencing pliers.

So much to learn and so little time…. ■

Muddying the Wildlife Waters

There's a knack in spotting wildlife in its natural habitat. One person glimpses the outline of a whitetail buck standing motionless in a willow thicket; another walks past without realizing the deer is there. One person sees a grouse on a tree limb; another doesn't so much as glance up. One person spies a coyote trotting through a herd of cattle; another sees only a bunch of Herefords.

My wife Jane is good at spotting wildlife. I tell her it's because her eyes are twice the size of most folks' peepers. But whether or not it's her Irish-eyes advantage, she's usually first to spot a distant herd of elk, a badger ambling through a meadow, a bald eagle gliding just above a river's surface.

It was not always so. She flubbed her first look at elk—shortly before we married—through confusion and excitement. And it was several years before her skills at spotting wildlife emerged as more developed than mine. Now she's so much better at it that I'm analyzing why. How did she became so skilled?

First off, one must become so familiar with the surroundings that when something is out of place it leaps out at you. For those trained to discern it, the tan rump of an elk poised for flight shines among the deep green of a spruce thicket.

Mule deer blend well with a boulder-strewn hillside, but when you spot one ear twitch or white rump in the shadows, motionless mulies suddenly spring into focus all over the mountain's foreslope.

Another ingredient essential to successful wildlife viewing is concentration. That's where Jane shines. When she's outdoors, the woman's focus is total. I'm disciplined too, but only for a little while. Then I'm drafting a newspaper column or radio program in my head. Let's see (I'm thinking), I'll begin by telling them there's a knack in spotting wildlife in its natural habitat ... what's that? Oh! Were its antlers *BIG?* Most folks find it easy to spot the flashing flag of a whitetail, but what we all would rather do is view the buck before he waves goodby.

Another essential ingredient for wildlife viewing is to watch where they're likely to be abundant. Naturally, national parks and wildlife refuges spring to mind. But mountain goats in Glacier, elk in Yellowstone, and antelope in the Charles M. Russell Refuge are too easy—you expect to spot those animals in those places, and you're disappointed if they fail to show. But think of the excitement of listening spellbound to the hollow laugh of a loon, spying prairie dogs gamboling about their towns, or being surprised by the sudden splat! of a beaver's tail as he tries to frighten you from his domain.

Wildlife-viewing guides are published for many (or even most) states. Defenders of Wildlife has published an excellent series in cooperation with federal and state agencies. Other guides are published in brochure form by various public agencies: U.S. Forest Service, Bureau of Land Management, U.S. Fish & Wildlife Service, and various state agencies.

Some guides, of course, are better than others. But in no case should you consider the guides as an end-all; they're merely starter kits for getting you into wildlife watching. Beyond that, it's up to you.

The best tool, for my money, is simply to practice—by visiting the outdoors often; by being alert while there; by thinking, studying, and filing patterns away in your memory bank. And most of all, by being still and quiet while doing so.

I believe America's interest in our wildlife treasures will grow exponentially throughout coming decades. While it's true Americans have always cherished their wildlife riches, decades of insensitive land and water development and forest overharvests lapped away at those resources until isolated alarms became a groundswell of dismay and demand. Yesterday's muted roar is today's irresistible crescendo, and government administrators, ever sensitive to changing political winds, scramble to respond.

The Endangered Species Act was but a precursor of burgeoning interest in wildlife; an attempt to halt—or at least slow down—further species losses. Now, during this latest period of alarm, resource agencies are allocating more effort and more dollars toward public awareness of existing wildlife-viewing opportunities on public lands.

Pamphlet guides and cooperative booklets are rolling from presses, identifying species concentrations for easier viewing. My state, for instance, publicizes opportunities spanning the gamut from prairie dog towns in Custer County to loons on Seeley Lake.

"Interest in wildlife is the most insistent voice I'm hearing," one Forest Service administrator told me. Other federal agencies, Bureau of Land Management and the Fish & Wildlife Service, concur. But I'm not at all sure that the present emphasis on identifying viewing opportunities will have the desired effect.

Is it possible that mass-produced guides to sage grouse "dancing grounds" or elk wintering sites will result in more human pressure, more habitat disruption, and thus, more pressure on limited and static wildlife populations?

True, most pamphlets and guides are careful to delineate "do's" and "don'ts" for the viewer, cautioning against approaching so close as to jeopardize nesting sites or animals already stressed by short rations and deep snow. Still, concentrations, colonies, rookeries, and roosts *are* identified and one cannot but assume that added stress will occur.

On the other hand, these wildlife habitat guides will enhance public opportunity, and from my perspective, there'll be a beneficial spin-off: a much broader public segment will become interested in wildlife of all sorts, and the surge of enthusiasm will swell to a tidal wave of support. Demand, then, will be to reverse declining population dynamics in order to increase numbers. It seems not at all unrealistic to me that someday in the near future, wildlife enhancement projects on public lands will receive a fair measure of today's emphasis on commodity production such as occurs with timber harvesting, grazing, and mining.

The big question is this: By strongly promoting wildlife viewing, are we getting the cart before the horse? Would not today's limited wildlife budgets better be allocated to reversing wildlife population declines rather than creating additional stress on limited numbers already present? By doing so while we enjoy a stronger resource base, will we in fact spend fewer recovery dollars in the long run?

If we fail to address the problem of reduced wildlife populations, are we making the situation better or worse by identifying concentrations, colonies, rookeries, and roosts?

So there it is. I've taken both sides of the argument during this little essay, and thus far all I've succeeded in doing is confusing myself. I hope a solution to the dilemma is clearer for you. ■

*Thank you for your recent contract to renew KDTA's commitment to the very enjoyable **Trails to Outdoor Adventure**. Your show is well received and fits in perfectly with our programming for the Delta/Montrose area. In these days of declining values it is an honor to know someone such as yourself. Thank you again and may all your trails to outdoor adventure be good ones.*

Brad Link, Station Manager • Delta, CO

Toilet-Use Price Wars

At one misguided fiscal point, the managers of my state's Parks Division were directed to collect fees from anyone using its facilities. This was interpreted broadly by brown-shirted Parks personnel and so zealously enforced that their new rules became painful experiences to anyone trying merely to use a restroom while in transit across the Treasure State. Though the rule for wee-wee collection ran into a firestorm of resistance and was soon abandoned, it did provide fodder for the following newspaper column:

Are you aware that in order to piddle in a state park, you must first pay two dollars? I wasn't either.

It was Friday, May 18, and Jane and I were on our way home from a week of hiking and photography along the Rocky Mountain Front. Luckily, I wasn't the butt of the somewhat painful discovery, so I was able to analyze the entire incident with a detached journalistic air.

Jane was driving—had been since we left Augusta. We'd passed along the scenic Blackfoot River, where an abundance of big yellow pines are available for shy but needy travelers, then headed north on Montana 83—the Seeley-Swan highway—where entire *forests* are handy to roadside piddlers in emergency need.

But no, Jane is fastidious about such things. Intending to borrow their toilet facilities for a few seconds at most, she wheeled into the Department of Fish, Wildlife & Parks Salmon Lake Campground. Her mission apparently wasn't as urgent as mine so often is. Perhaps her kidneys aren't routinely pounded by copious cups of coffee and other sundry beverages. Still, it was a no-nonsense decision; she made the turn-off smoothly, sped to the same toilet facility she'd used the week before, jumped sprightly from the car—and was apprehended by a stout, no-nonsense matron wearing the DFW&P brown jacket with a DFW&P shoulder patch. The matron demanded two dollars.

"All I want to do is use the restroom," Jane said. "I'm not planning to stay all night."

"Yes, and that will be two dollars," the matron replied.

"Two dollars just for using the restroom for a few seconds?" There was no change in expression on the warden's face. "I'll hold it," Jane said, clambering back into our car.

Can you imagine what would have happened had Jane been someone with less...umm...*intestinal fortitude?* Me, for instance? I can't imagine my kidneys holding the question open for debate. Mine are more the "go now and pay later" type.

Being both long in the tooth and weak in the bladder, I recollect when pay toilets were standard in bus stations and railroad terminals. Back then, the fee was a nickel—which seemed like extortion to someone who was hardly in a position to be philosophical about it. (Let's see, should I pay a nickel now? Or can I hold it until the bus gets to Peoria?)

I was young and agile in those days and usually solved the dilemma by clambering over the stall. That ploy had its risks, however, particularly if the toilet was already occupied.

Pay toilets in public places are long gone—a relic of extortionistic ancient times. They were condemned by a federal government that deemed them discriminatory against the poor.

Montana, of course, doesn't discriminate. Two dollars to wee-wee is crass to rich and poor alike. But I'll predict the policy will fail to generate the expected revenue. Instead, at two bucks a throw we're likely to price ourselves out of the market. Tourists may hurry through the state in order to avoid extortionate urinal- or bidet-use fees.

And will tourists dollars be the only ones to flee the Treasure State?

No.

I find it ludicrous to expect Treasure State citizens to divvy up usurious rates to piddle in Montana when Canada lies just a few hours north.... ∎

*Really enjoy your articles in the **Tribune**. Please, more often!*   Jim and Helen Shortridge • Great Falls, MT

*This is to thank you many times over for your articles that have appeared often in the **Great Falls Tribune**.*
Mrs. Bill O'Neill • Great Falls, MT

We are avid readers of your various articles in Montana papers.   Stan and Marilyn Gossack • Great Falls, MT

Backcountry Don't List

The following is a backcountry *don't* list based on years of all too close observations:

Don't trust a Coleman stove stand in a windstorm. True, the stand lifts the stove to optimum working height. True, the windscreen allows you to cook in a breeze. But it's also true the windscreen provides enough surface to flutter an anvil and the wobbly stand provides a perfect launch pad. Jane discovered this truth when she tried to catch a falling pot of boiling water. Fortunately, she didn't have to pack horses or row a raft until the next day.

Don't try breaking a renegade horse while on a wilderness packtrip. One of our guides gave this a go when we were thirty miles into the Bob Marshall Wilderness. By dint of good luck and hard riding, the emergency ALERT crew helicoptered him to a hospital the same day of his compound fracture.

Don't leave a double-bit axe sticking in a block of wood. Fortunately, the slice I received when I stumbled into it required no stitches.

Don't try to nail shoes on a nervous pony while wearing only swim trunks. One of our guides volunteered on his day off to nail a shoe on a stranger's horse and the torn thigh he received when the horse jerked his hoof away required several stitches. Fortunately, we had a doctor along who had needle and thread. Unfortunately, the doctor had no anesthetic. Fortunately, my guides were tough.

Don't wear new boots on your once-in-a-lifetime packtrip. Over the years, two or three of our hunters tried this tactic. Inevitably they became bored from sitting around camp with crippled feet.

Don't tie your saddlehorse to a hollow tree that houses a yellowjacket nest. The horse will be hard to free from his tether amid the resulting violence.

Don't forget your insulin, allergy pills, nitro glycerin tablets, or whatever medication is vital to your disposition on wilderness excursions. As a result of such forgetfulness, your being cranky can work hardships on others in your group.

Don't expect others to come looking for you if you don't show up at camp for supper. After three days they might divide up your stuff and swear to God they never heard of you.

Don't try riding a horse up a hill so steep he might power out before scrambling to the top. Mine made it, but Jane's stopped to rest. Unfortunately, when he did, he toppled over backwards. Fortunately, she wasn't hurt. (Oh, a little blood here and there—but not *really* hurt.)

Don't let your saddlehorse crowd the horse ahead. The lead pony might not like being crowded, and he's got twin persuaders aimed at your kneecap. The ALERT team stands by for this kind of thing, also.

Don't gawk too much at the scenery when treading a perilous mountain trail. It naturally distresses an outfitter to watch his guest flip-flopping down a mountainside.

Don't take shelter under a tree during a lightning storm. No, we've had no direct association with this don't, but it's been close. The difference between "close" and "don't," in this case, is "don't" ain't there no more. ■

Women in History—What Happened?

I have trouble picturing Northern Plains life before the advent of the horse. Examine domestic animals, for instance:

We tend to take our present-day pets for granted. Today's farms can include coops for chickens, ponds for ducks, yards for geese or guineas or goats, pens for hogs, pastures for sheep or cows, barns for horses or mules, corrals for llamas. They also usually include a porch for a dog to snooze under and a parlor couch for a cat to snooze upon.

It wasn't always that way. Before the sudden appearance of the horse to spice the life of the Northern Plains Indian, dogs were the sole domestic animals. Did early Native Americans treasure dogs as the hard-riding Indians of recent history treasured horses?

I've read that Indian dogs were capable of carrying up to fifty pounds on their backs or pulling seventy-five pounds on a travois. Man's best friend as primary beast of burden—imagine!

Think about an entire Indian village on the move: hundreds, perhaps thousands of snarling, barking, whining mongrels strung out among villagers for miles. No fireplugs. Dog fights common. Slippery moccasins. A female in heat.

What a din!

The pre-horse era is designated in scientific circles as the Pedestrian Culture. Pedestrian Culture—think of it! Modern folks are apt to refer to a drive from Idaho to North Dakota in an air-conditioned automobile as a hard day. Think about having to *walk* the distance! And doing so with a noisy dogpack howling for a can of Alpo.

Come to think of it, how *did* they feed that canine multitude?

After all, dogs competed directly with their masters for available meat and bone. We assume hunting was more difficult before the advent of the horse, so how did a tribe provide fresh meat for themselves *and* a slew of transport animals?

How valuable were those animals? Did enemy tribesmen conduct dog-stealing raids, as happened with horses in a later era? What clamor might have ensued in an encampment of hundreds of dogs had even one pup discovered a skulking enemy amongst the tipis?

The horse apparently nibbled its way to the Northern Plains around the mid-1700s. What a godsend. Horses carried warriors to battle, ran down buffalo during the hunt, packed huge loads for long distances. More importantly, horses never competed with humans for the same food. Kill a buffalo during the pre-horse era and feed a large percentage to your canine beasts of burden. Kill more buffalo using horses, then turn the ponies out to graze and keep all the hump steaks for yourself.

Horses, on the other hand, couldn't be kept in the lodge overnight and they seldom gave advance warning that strangers neared. Did protecting grazing herds from enemies turn into an endless chore?

With the advent of the horse, luxuries—impractical during Pedestrian Culture days—suddenly blossomed among the tipis: roomier skin lodges, ceremonial clothing and decorations, superfluous pots for cooking, bundles of trade gear. Avarice developed a certain social acceptance, and with it the unforeseen necessity of protecting thy wealth from thy neighbor's greed.

But, then, I'm only recounting history everywhere, am I not? The industrial revolution was to bring us more leisure time, a more relaxed lifestyle. So where are we? Working longer hours in order to buy more Tinker Toys; commuting extra hours every day in order to live a more relaxed life that we hardly ever glimpse because we're seldom home.

To get back to the Indian's Pedestrian Culture days, I returned to the book I was reading (Ewers: *The Horse In Blackfeet Indian Culture*, 1955). It was there I stumbled across an interesting passage and went to find Jane.

My wife is ordinarily a swell gal. She's tough and adventuresome and curious about what makes people and things tick. But I soon found out she has little interest in history.

"Do you realize," I said, holding out Ewers, "that this book says Indians used women and dogs as primary beasts of burden before they acquired horses?"

"Hmph," she replied.

"It says here that a good pack dog could carry fifty pounds on its back or pull seventy-five on a travois." I frowned while scanning the next couple of pages. "But there doesn't seem to be any breakdown on what a woman could carry or drag."

Jane said nothing. A more observant husband would have recognized her unaccustomed silence as a first hint she was more interested in home economics than history. She began banging pots and pans. Her Brittany spaniel, Tess, crawled under the table.

Meanwhile, I returned to my recliner and mused about how difficult life must have been. A camp with laden women and dogs on the move could apparently travel only five to six miles per day—if there was to be enough time for those same women to set up the hide shelters, fetch wood and water, and prepare a suitable evening meal for their hard-working spouses.

How primitive and scant must have been their possessions, limited of course by their available transport. No roomy tipi, no heavy cooking pots, no luxuries such as beaded finery or other womanly foofaraw.

Acquisition of the horse changed all that. Plains Indians became far more mobile and enjoyed luxuries unknown during earlier days. Indian horses, according to Ewers, regularly carried two hundred pounds and could easily drag three hundred by travois for ten to twelve miles each day.

Four times more weight for double the distance—horses, then, are capable of performing eight times more work than dogs.

Women's status improved immensely because of the horse. Lodges were roomier and enjoyed elaborate furnishings. Horses for transport meant the luxuries of clothing changes, extensive supplies of fresh or dried meat, wild fruits and vegetables. All would have been considered excess baggage when dogs and women were the only dependable transport.

By contrast, life today is so simple: flip a switch for light; twist a knob for heat; all sorts of fingertip kitchen appliances; telephones instead of smoke signals; trucks and trains and airplanes for easy transport to distant places.

I thought of our wilderness adventures, Jane's and mine, where we load up our horses with down-filled sleeping bags and lightweight nylon tents and enough food to dine like royalty for a week. To some folks, rinsing their hands in ice-cold creeks and sleeping amid nights of intense silence would be unthinkable. But me? I *thirst* for adventure. How unlike those primitive Indians. What experiences they must have had with only women and dogs to carry their plunder!

I ambled into the kitchen where pots and pans continued to bang. "Jane …"

"Don't even think it!" she snapped. The dog growled and bared her teeth.

Like I said, no interest in historical perspectives.

<hr>

I learned, much later, that social ramifications exist to preclude in-depth research into modern applications of the Indian's Pedestrian Culture days. This was all gleaned accidentally, rather than through applied science.

It was in the fall of 1990—our last year of outfitting and guiding others to adventure. It was late enough in hunting season that most folks had already pulled out of our part of the Bob Marshall Wilderness and begun planning their safaris after Garfield County antelope or Hill County mule deer.

Because of a vehicle failure, we were late getting away from road's end and had to make an adjustment in where we planned to spend our first night. Because of the unforeseen emergency, we needed a few extra supplies, so I threw a light pack on my saddlehorse, planning to walk the thirteen miles to our emergency camp while leading him. Which I did—most of the way.

Jane, bless her heart, took pity on me and let me ride her horse after ten miles, or so. As luck would have it, that short reprieve was when we met other hunters on their way out of the wilderness. There my hunters and I were, perched like King Tut in our saddles while poor Jane trudged behind leading our laden packhorses. I knew the folks we met. They eyed our line-up. First their eyes revealed amazement, then disgust. Caustic comments were made about an outfit where all the men were mounted while the lone woman struggled behind.

Yes, I found it embarrassing.

Jane found it amusing.

What's wrong, for heaven's sake, with our social system that we men tolerate such behavior? I doubt Tutankhamen himself, that splendid Egyptian pharaoh, would have considered walking while his many queens rode. Can you imagine a Cossack afoot while his woman perched in his saddle? Hey, I saw the movie *Taras Bulbas* and the Cossack Yul Bryner rode everywhere he went.

Right here in Montana, for God's sake! Did Sitting Bull and Crazy Horse trudge afoot into battle with Custer and his 7th Cavalry while their women went berry picking by horseback? On the contrary. The American Indians had their priorities right: men rode and women walked.

Women also packed the horses—after first breaking camp. Upon arrival at the next campsite, women unpacked the horses, set up camp, gathered wood and fetched water. They cooked meals for the men and served them. And woe to the woman who shirked her duties.

It is only we Anglo-Saxons who've become so mixed up that we're embarrassed by social behavior the rest of the world finds normal.

How did we come to such a pass? Where did we go wrong? Some of the depicters of the great American West portrayed wagon trains crawling across the Great Plains with men driving and women trudging dutifully behind, through the dust. So our loss became woman's gain sometime after 1860.

How much more are we to lose? Must we soon set up our own tents, butcher our own game, cook our own meals, pack our own horses, fetch our own water, cut our own wood?

Unite, men! have we lost all historical perspective? We must immediately return to the good old days or lose everything in the end.

"Huh? What's that? Oh, you want me to carry out the garbage? Yess'm, dear. And should I bring in firewood and draw your bath after that?" ∎

Fire In the Cooktent!

F ire!" I leaped the corral gate shouting, "Fire! Fire!"

Flames danced into the night sky and sparks shot up to blend with stars. "Fire in the cooktent!"

Hunters and their guide boiled from the connected sleeping tent; from the warm comfort of their down-filled sleeping bags. The guide collided with me as I darted through the cooktent flap.

Blackened tent fabric fell on a cherry-red cookstove and into the bubbling coffee pot and the dishpan full of steaming wash water. I grabbed both, ignoring searing heat, and flung them at the licking flames. The guide snatched the five-gallon pail of drinking water and sprayed it overhead.

"Don't waste—" I moaned, but he was already gone in a mad dash for the creek. When he returned, the hunters and I busily beat at the last pockets of flames with empty burlap grain sacks. This time we threw pans of water at the fire's last remnants. Then dampened the stove I'd stuffed earlier with too much pine pitch, and an eerie silence fell over the camp.

One hunter gazed up into the night sky and remarked that this was his first time to stare at the Big Dipper from *inside* a tent.

I fingered the asbestos and metal stovepipe liner that had failed us, my knees shaking from the near tragedy. "John," I said to the guide, "you want to pull the feed bags from our horses while I'll see if I can clean up this place and start breakfast?"

He looked down at the skivvies he wore, and at the felt-lined Sorel boots on his feet, grinned, nodded, and left abruptly.

Later that day, as I temporarily repaired the gaping roof hole with canvas pack covers, I thought how lucky we'd been that I'd turned from brushing and graining our saddlehorses when I did; how fortunate that we'd had so much water on hand; that we'd all been so quick to react to the emergency. A couple of minutes later and....

Then I thought about how I'd stuffed the stove with too much tinder in order to hurry things along that morning; how I'd left the cooktent unattended; how I'd obviously not been vigilant enough to note a sag in the tent canvas that must have hung dangerously close to the stovepipe.

Reflections—that's how we learn, I'd reckon. But the experience became even more painful when later I forked out several hundred dollars for a new tent.

Additional pain was there that same day of the fire when it began to rain softly and there was simply no way we could fend off every drip, no matter how carefully we covered the charcoaled edges of the burned-out tent hole with the canvas manties.

Rufus (one of the hunters) later told me that the morning was his most exciting during the seven years he hunted with us. And both hunters and guide accepted with considerable grace the fact that their soup was diluted with rain drops and their bacon more boiled than fried.

Me?

I learned something, too, for we've not had a tent fire since. Of course, after that terrifying day our tents were equipped with a better grade of stovejack and there was someone on hand when a blaze roared in any tent.

By the way, that's good advice to you, too. ■

MESG [answering service]: 934 IN:EVE 7/20 10:57
Which book did you wish to order: *TALK BEAR, PHANTOM GHOST, BOB MARSHALL*
Community/State   Name: *FRANK MORGAN*
Address: City: *WILLAMINA*   State: *OR*   Zip:
How did you hear about the book: *HE JUST FINISHED "DANCE ON THE WILD SIDE." IT IS A WONDER-FULL!!! BOOK. HE WAS UNABLE TO PUT IT DOWN. DID NOT DO ANY OF HIS CHORES UNTIL HE FIN-ISHED BOOK. WANTS HARDCOVER OF BOB MARSHALL.*

Comparing Household Hints to Outdoors Tips

Did you know that old linen dinner napkins make good dust rags because linen is usually lint-free?

Or how about old newspapers? They can be used to wipe window glass after washing. They, too, leave no lint.

Or listen to this: a quarter cup of vinegar per gallon of water used for washing windows reduces spotting (apparently the acid in vinegar cuts lime in the water. (At least it cuts *our* lime.)

These are everyday things my wife knows about house cleaning. Her simple household hints started me thinking….

There are, you see, a plethora of simple hints that make most endeavors easier. People familiar with those hints tend to take them for granted and apply them as a matter of course, never thinking about their doing. Like me with outdoor stuff.

Layering, for instance. I've read for years about how advisable layering is when dressing for foul weather. Yet I never understood the technical aspects for some time. Layering sounds complicated—as if you need to understand garment weaves or the merits of polyester versus wool, or windbreaker nylon versus down-filled canvas. But it might be nothing more complicated than wearing three sweaters during a blizzard while your buddy is shrouded in a heavy, down-filled, satin-lined, Gore-Tex outer-shelled parka that is impossible for him to shed a portion of as the temperature and body sweat rises.

Or did you know that gaiters—leg coverings lapping boot and trousers—are effective for more activities than the cross-country skiing for which they were designed? Fall hunting, for instance, or tramping through tall grass after a soaking June rain.

A bottle of drinking water can be very important in winter when dehydration can accompany lowered body temperatures to make you more vulnerable to hypothermia.

Have you ever had a boot eat your sock? That is, have you ever worn a pair of socks that seemed determined to work down to your toes while hiking? Of course you have. If not, you've done little hiking. But did you know that stocking-creep can be prevented by tying a knot in your bootstring right at the peak of the arch? Try it. You'll be surprised.

How do you apply waterproofing to your boot? The way we did it in our fall hunting camps and prior to our spring hiking trips was to heat a can of boot grease until it was liquid, then apply it to the boots with a one-inch paintbrush. No muss, no fuss. Yet all nooks and crannies received a good coating.

If you insist on using spray for waterproofing, then use it outdoors. The odor lingers longer than the protection such kid-stuff gives your boots.

For your day hikes or hunts, think about using a small pack to carry the things you'll inevitably need during the day, such as lunch, camera, field glasses, etc. Some people use a fanny pack that belts around their midsection, but I prefer a small packsack called a daypack. You can stuff more things into a daypack than a fanny pack: items like a windbreaker, plastic square to sit upon snow or damp ground, small first-aid kit.

And I have no backaches from carrying a daypack, as opposed to a fanny pack.

Simple things. So simple I sometimes forget to tell others about them…. ■

Discovering Day-Hiking

For the better part of my life I've roamed the most remote regions of the mountain West. During my youth, anything within a day's walk from road's end was too civilized for my attention. And in middle age I guided others to the same places I'd visited earlier. It's only now, during my dotage, that I've discovered the advantages of day hiking.

There are still horses in the back pasture and all the right saddle and pack equipment in the barn to throw on 'em. And there's a four-horse trailer squatting in the yard alongside a three-quarter-ton pickup that can pull it. But right now I'm too busy discovering how much snazzy country I passed by on my way to the farthest reaches of America's outback.

So far this year I've hiked to Scalplock, climbed to Tranquil Basin, visited Marion Lake. I've seen the South Fork of the Two Medicine, Picnic Lakes, and Mt. Aeneas. I've skied to Grinnell Lake and Elk Calf Mountain during the winter, and hiked the Ole Creek Trail in the spring. And each night I slept in my own bed.

No camp to pitch, no ponies to pack. No staggering up-trail under an overloaded backpack. No firewood to cut, no horses to hobble, no water to carry. In the mornings there've been no wet socks or stiff boots or cold stove. And the view from Mt.

Aeneas or Scalplock Mountain is every bit as spectacular as any I've seen in the Bob Marshall Wilderness.

Day hiking has opened up an entirely new world for me. It's easy. It's affordable. Compared to a week-long packtrip, it takes little planning. It's even something you can decide to do on a moment's notice. Very little equipment is needed for day hiking, and only minimum preparation. Provisions amount to nothing more than lunch, water bottle, and a soda or a beer in your cooler for the return to road's end.

In addition to those provisions, I carry a camera and extra film, binoculars, matches, a raincoat, a down vest, and a small first-aid kit. I also have a few rubber bands and a chunk of light rope, a couple of plastic bags, and a small foam pad to cushion the camera. The entire pack weighs less than fifteen pounds.

Even a single overnight horseback junket into the back-country requires hobbles and bells, nosebags, picketlines, oats or pellets—all for the horses. For your own comfort, you'll need a camp kit when cooking and eating, a small tent, sleeping bag and sleeping pad, and an axe, shovel, and water bucket.

If the weather sours, chances are the tent will leak and your firewood will get soaked. The ground is a whole bunch harder and colder and lumpier than your waterbed back home. The campfire will either be too hot or not hot enough for quality cooking, and it's hard to tell how much black pepper to sprinkle when your scrambled eggs are full of ashes.

Just about dark is always when your ponies decide to head for home, and that's also when you'll discover a hole burned in the socks you were drying and your boot toes have wrinkled to look like dried prunes because you also had them too close to the fire.

How in the world did I put up with it so long? ∎

*Can you please tell me what station your program is pre-
sented on in the Tri-Cities area of Washington? I listen to
you every day on the way to work each morning on KSEI at
Pocatello.*   **Len Corey • Pocatello, ID**

*I enjoy your program as it gives me something else to
think about as I head for work.*
                       Gary Lofing • Billings, MT

God's Big Picture—No Small Thing

Book reviews are rare in the kinds of stuff I write. Even
more so are reviews of books that have been in print for
a while. But when I finished *Cataclysms on the Columbia* by
John Eliot Allen and Marjorie Burns, I figured it's a book
worth telling about.

Cataclysms on the Columbia is about the greatest scientifically documented floods on earth: the emptying of Glacial
Lake Missoula some twelve thousand years ago. Written
engagingly, the book takes the reader on tour as the great continental ice sheet creeps down the Idaho Panhandle's Purcell
Trench to finally butt against the north end of the Bitterroot
Mountain Range near the head of Lake Pend Oreille. The ice
effectively plugged the valley of the Clark Fork of the Columbia River like a giant cork.

The damming of the Clark Fork behind the massive Purcell ice lobe gradually inundated valleys, turning much of
western Montana into a huge impoundment. It is estimated
that, at its highest level, Lake Missoula contained half as
much water as present Lake Michigan and covered an area of
three thousand square miles.

The lake's surface was 4,150 feet above sea level, which
translates to a depth of almost 2,500 feet at the ice dam. Lake

Missoula backed up until it was within just a few miles of the Continental Spine, near Butte, Montana. It was almost a thousand feet deep at present-day Missoula, and over two hundred feet deep at Darby. It is estimated the lake was eleven hundred feet above the level of today's Flathead Lake.

> *At the Clark Fork River's present flow rate, it would take one hundred and thirty-five years to fill Lake Missoula until water began overflowing the ice dam. But it is thought that twelve thousand years ago the river was augmented by glacial melt and a wetter climate and would overflow in about sixty years.*

However long it took, when the river breached its ice dam, all hell broke loose. Water roared through the ice, cutting rapidly down from the top and ripping apart the ice walls by undercutting until the dam collapsed. In fact, research suggests the dam may have collapsed in the passage of a mere day—or two!

Here are a few lines from *Cataclysms on the Columbia* revealing what actually happened when, after several decades, the river breached its plug:

> *When the waters in Lake Missoula broke through the 2,500-foot high ice dam ... they poured south for 20 miles, and then southwest along the Purcell Trench across the Rathdrum Prairie ... to Spokane. The maximum flow was more than 9.5 cubic miles of water per hour, which could have drained the lake in two days....*

In real terms, the draining of Lake Missoula—and it happened more than once—produced the greatest scientifically documented floods known. "Swollen by the flood waters, the Columbia grew to contain ten times the flow of all the rivers in the world today and 60 times the flow of the Amazon."

Perhaps of special interest to visitors to the region, terraces—developed as a consequence of Lake Missoula wave action—can be seen nine hundred feet up Mount Sentinel, above the University of Montana complex. And across the south side of Markel Pass (Highway 382 south of Camas Hot Springs) are giant ripple marks (20 to 30 feet high and 200 to 500 feet apart) caused by water rushing from the lake. From the book:

... They could only have been formed by floods at least 800 feet deep plunging across the pass at velocities of up to 55 miles per hour!

As should be patently clear by now, ice is a powerful geologic force. But as powerful as is the solid (ice), it cannot resist the liquid, (water).

The wall of water that went through Spokane was several *hundred* feet high. The wall of water was *still* several hundred feet high when it went through the current Tri-Cities area of Pasco, Kennewick, and Richland. And it was nearly four hundred feet high when it hit the area that is now Portland, Oregon.

In fact, water flowed *up* the Willamette Valley from Portland, almost to Eugene. The reverse flow carried an iceberg from the collapsed Purcell Lobe ice dam *up* the Willamette River for almost fifty miles to near McMinnville, Oregon. That iceberg was of sufficient size that it, in turn, carried a boulder weighing as much as eighty tons. The boulder, which is a Canadian import via the Purcell ice sheet, still perches where the iceberg brought it to rest.

So ice, and ice and water, are gigantic forces indeed. Leave a soda can behind the seat of your pickup and find out how powerful ice can be when temperatures plummet.

River ice buckling and heaving against bridges and abutments can ravage the most careful engineering. Frozen water pipes, shattered water pumps, and burst engine blocks are all part of the testing process one endures while learning to live in the mountain West.

Ice in its most gargantuan form—glaciers—is mind-boggling. Icebergs are but tiny fragments of glaciers, but they're capable of sinking ocean liners, punching holes in great oil tankers, and threatening every form of seaborne commerce. Manifestations of glacial ice at its most powerful are yet evident over much of the northern hemisphere.

Great sheets of ice built up on the Arctic cap sixteen thousand years ago, and moved south. Moraines—ridges, mounds, or irregular masses of boulders, sands, gravels, and clays left by glaciers—are clear to the perceptive traveler all along the southernmost advance of the great ice sheets: in New York and North Dakota, as well as Washington and Wisconsin.

The Great Lakes, of course, are nothing more (or less) than God's wash basins—manifestations of His sculpting with ice. Montana's best example of what is known as the "terminal moraine" of the great northern ice cap can be found in the Blackfoot Valley around Ovando, east of Missoula. Gravel-shot hillocks and knobs known as kames and drumlins, along with tiny potholes known as kettles, were shoved and gouged. The moraines mark the southern face of an ice sheet towering thousands of feet and covering most mountaintops in Glacier National Park and the Bob Marshall Wilderness.

Farther east, that same great ice cap shoved the Missouri River from its former route through what is now the Milk River Valley, pushing the angry river southward for scores of miles to its present bed.

Great ice sheets crept out from other ramparts—the mountains of Yellowstone Park and isolated mountain ranges like the Little and Big Belts, Elkhorns, Crazies, and Bitterroots—to scrape the sides of river valleys and leave gathered detritus at their farthest advance.

A tremendous volume of water was released when those glaciers began their retreat. Added to seasonal precipitations, they left evidence of general flooding greater than can be imagined today.

Well, let's try....

Imagine one huge sheet of ice covering most of Canada, down to, say, the northern twenty percent of the continental United States. That ice may have been upwards of two thousand feet high on its leading edges. In addition, ice sheets crept out from most high mountain ranges.

Now, imagine most of that ice melting in a mere thousand years. Add that massive annual melt to the usual spring floods we get today and figure how high the Mississippi would've been at New Orleans when the Gros Ventres were trying to use woolly mammoths for stone-spear pin cushions.

❧

Water and ice. Ice and water. Given all that evidence of the enormous power of ice, it's no wonder we credit glaciers with more geologic force than they deserve. You see, though great periods of glaciation shaved the land, nobody said glaciers *shaped* it. Glaciers scraped, scoured, scored, and skewed bits and pieces of Montana and Northern America, but as an agent of real change, they were minuscule. Glaciers followed river valleys that were already in place.

But neither did the rivers really *shape* the land. Rivers flow from mountain peaks that were already in place. Those rivers have cut valleys that glaciers may just soften around the edges. And a few mountain peaks might have had their summits shaved.

God used glaciers to sculpt a few heavenly wash basins or take rough edges from His new construction. And He may have used rivers to put character to the land, just as He uses laugh wrinkles and squint lines to add character to faces. But what we must wonder about is where the figure behind that character came from.

So glaciers can soften mountains and rivers can carve them, but where'd the mountains come from in the first place? Mountains are the *shape* of the American landscape. Rivers are the result of that shape. Valleys are the result of that shape. And prairies? Prairies are the raw material waiting to be shaped.

The science of geology tells us the Pacific Ocean once lapped the shores of North Dakota. Since then, God made the Rocky Mountains, the Cascade Mountains, the Pacific Coast Range. Before that, He made the Appalachians. He also made a passel of smaller ranges like the Little Belts in Montana and the Wasatch Range in Utah. There are the Wallowa Mountains in Oregon and the Toiyabe Range in Nevada. Colorado has the San Juans, and California has the Sierras. There are the Black Hills in South Dakota and the Mogollons in Arizona.

Where'd all these mountains come from? Tectonic plate collision and vulcanization. The Rockies and the Appalachians, geologists tell us, were the result of tectonic plates colliding: The North American Plate colliding with the East Pacific Plate to push up the Rocky Mountains. Something had to give. That something was a buckling at a weak spot in the North American Plate. Wrinkling took place. Some of those wrinkles ran a little oversize—like, say, twenty thousand feet into rarified air.

The collision of these two giant crusts floating on the earth's magma took upwards of fifty million years, ending twenty-five million years ago. That's when the plate we're riding on won this battle of the titans and began riding up and over the East Pacific Plate. As a consequence, the East Pacific Plate is currently bumping along the edge of our North American vehicle, heading for Alaska. The present contact point between the two plates is a series of fragile fault lines where the land shifts sometimes inches at a whack. The best known of these earthquake contact lines is the San Andreas Fault that some wags claim will eventually deposit Los Angeles somewhere in the middle of the Aleutian Islands.

A consequence of all this continental grunt work is that the body supporting these heavyweights gets a belly ache. All the gases created by the belly ache and all the molten magma get churned up, and the only way for the body earth to get relief is to let a little out from time to time. The last time she did this was at Mount St. Helens.

In short, the Cascade and Sierra mountains were created largely by volcanic eruptions along lines that were weakened while the titans struggled. The island ranges spreading across most of the mountain West and sometimes out onto the plains are products of that same vulcanization; though they busted loose not so much along fault lines as sort of pustules on the earth's skin.

Some of those volcanic pustules, of course, make gorgeous scenery today, as anyone who's ever oohed and ahhed over the Grand Tetons in Wyoming, or the Olympics in Washington, or the San Juans in Colorado, or the Wallowas in Oregon can attest.

It's difficult to grasp, I know. But after one understands what *really* shapes the land, it's easy enough to see that both glaciers and rivers, as monumental geologic agents, are largely overrated in God's big-picture scheme of things. ■

Just thought I'd take a moment to let you know how much
*we enjoy your program, **Trails to Outdoor Adventure**.*
When I heard the demo tape you sent I knew we were on to
something, and I haven't been disappointed. You bring a
quality to the program that doesn't exist with other similar
programs, which often give great information on fishing or
hunting. But your show weaves the outdoors into everyday
lives. I love it.

Jerry "G" Miller, Program Dir, KSEI • Pocatello, ID

Crow Chief's Legacy

In his autobiographical account, *Blankets and Moccasins*, Crow Chief Plenty Coups reputedly said this about mountains:

Of all things created, the mountains only have escaped
domination of the white man. The valleys are scarred
by the plow man, ridged by the trail maker and gut-
tered by the taker of water, but the mountains are still
as God made them, and to be near them is to be on the
pathway to peace.

There's a modicum of truth in the chief's observation, although I wonder what the sage Indian leader would say about today's heap-leach mining in the Little Rockies, or clearcut logging amid forested ranges over west. Valleys "guttered by the taker of water"? What would the wise old man say if he sat cross-legged on a hilltop and stared down at mud flats behind Hungry Horse or Libby Dam?

The litany goes on and on: skunk-smell air permeating a university town—legacy of a paper mill and frequent air inversions. There are pine trees killed by fluoride releases, mine tailings and settling ponds polluting river valleys, subdivisions in key wildlife winter ranges, surface value of farms and ranches destroyed by strip mining....

Drill into Yellowstone's thermal system, anyone? Oil and gas exploration in the Bob Marshall Wilderness, anyone? Back water into Glacier Park with a hydro dam, anyone?

No, I'm not suggesting we give it all up and go back to the land of our ancestors. But, like Plenty Coups, I am suggesting we take a second—or perhaps a third—look at those things we're doing. For frightening examples of what can happen to our land, I need look no farther than my own state. Five will get you ten, you can come up with an equal number of outrageous cuckoo-land examples from your own home country.

Where do we get off even *thinking* of mortgaging our children's heritage in order to buy a few more baubles for ourselves. Can we really believe we can have no-holds-barred development and still have the land God gave us? Do we think we can compound the upper Clark Fork Superfund debacle of epic-proportion smelter tailings into the state's other rivers and still have sparkling water? Can we extend the dubious benefits of what's happening in the Little Rockies to the Treasure State's other Island Ranges and still have those mountains for contemplation, water storage, scenic grandeur, and physical challenge?

Let's get real. If the Canadian mining conglomerate continues to crush tons of rock from the top of the range in order to heap-leach an ounce of gold from it, the Little Rockies may have the dubious distinction of being the first Montana mountain range to disappear from the face of the earth.

Drilling to tap Yellowstone's geyser system for power generation was *a real proposal. So were dams to back water into Glacier Park. Oil and gas exploration into the Bob Marshall really was proposed.* It's a sad joke that mill tailings between Anaconda and Deer Lodge became America's largest Superfund site. But will it eventually be overshadowed by careless development in places as yet unknown?

Plenty Coups died in 1932. His legacy lives on among his people, and let us hope his wisdom is accepted among all people. That Montana's mountains have escaped domination by the white man is less a testament to our wisdom than to our frailty—we've not yet become efficient at destruction, but we're working at it. The great Crow chief said:

"… the mountains are as God made them, and to be near them is to be on the pathway to peace."

I'm looking at a mountain while writing this. It dominates my valley. Columbia Mountain is still the way God made it, upthrusted by plate collision, sculpted by glacier, scarred by avalanche and wildfire. Considering God's awesome alterations, could man change this mountain even if he tried?

Perhaps. But it would not be the pathway to peace. ■

Showers of Gold

I've never quite figured out why folks leave this country to see fall colors. With entire east-side hills burnished with sunshine-colored quaking aspen, and west-side forests a-glitter with golden tamarack from valley bottom to mountain summit, what's all this fuss about seeing New England in the fall?

The east side of Glacier Park is particularly lovely with turning aspen in early September. So are most of the Island Ranges sprouting from the prairies: the Highwoods, Little Belts, Snowies, Crazies. And Lord, Lord—have you noticed the trees along the Yellowstone or the upper Missouri rivers, or framing the free-flowing Bitterroot when cottonwoods are turning?

One of my wife's (and my) favorite mid-September hikes is into the Lubec Hills, just out of East Glacier. A place of picturesque views into the Park mountains, it's a land of beaver ponds and elk trails. And it's a place where—when we hit it right—there is a magnitude of absolutely stunning fall colors. It's paradise for camera toters.

September is like that. It's a month where there are not so many vari-colored license plates parked in front of the plethora of P.T. Barnum-type milking parlors for cash-cow tourists. Nor are visitors fighting over park trails or camp-ground sites. In addition, September is before serious hunting season gets under way, so the entire landscape belongs to the ones with the gumption and curiosity and elan to get out and find it.

Though one should keep a wary weather eye out during September, skies are usually blue, bugs nonexistent, and temperatures in the tolerable range.

September is when Jane and I do our serious hiking in Glacier. And I'd imagine folks dwelling around Yellowstone or Grand Canyon or the North Cascades or Boundary Waters or the Great Smoky Mountains might employ similar tactics. It's a time when trails are lonesome and regimentation relaxed. It's also when National Park wildlife move back to areas they abandoned earlier as a result of summertime's press of biped humans. September is a time for, well, natives.

October is great to hike in Glacier, too—even more lonesome than in September. But October storms can close the high country. And those storms can be inconvenient to anyone improperly equipped. After hunting season opens (if we choose not to hunt on a particular day) Jane and I will usually hike in the park so we can stroll the shores of Bowman or Kintla or McDonald lakes and be confident we're not interrupting someone else's hunt.

Look for the vast western larch forests to begin turning to gold around mid-October. At the highest altitudes, alpine larch will turn by early September and their needles will loosen soon after. But alpine larch is so rare it's difficult to spot the tree from roadways. I know of only three or four places—all within the wildest country—where the tree exists in large enough enclaves to present a significantly colorful show. The more common western larch, however, provides performances that run throughout October. Gradually, the deciduous conifer's needles begin to fade from bright green to light green to orange to gold.

By the end of the third week, the needles begin to fall. Riding or hiking beneath a tamarack forest as needles drift down is like experiencing a soft, golden rain. Better than that, it's sort of like God is showering gold dust on His favorites. ■

Dumbing Down or Preparing Up?

Any veteran wilderness hunter knows that proper preparation contributes to success. Most often it's little things, like sighting in your rifle before you slide it into your saddle scabbard, pick up the packhorse leadrope, and swing into the saddle for the first day's ride.

A veteran hunter doesn't wind up in the middle of the Bob Marshall Wilderness with a stove generator that won't work—as happened to me. He'll fire up that stove and maybe his gas lantern and check them out before departure time. And if he's really smart, he'll stock an extra generator for each. He'll also carry a little more fuel than needed and lay in a spare lantern mantle or two.

Flashlight batteries will be new and so will backup batteries. And if he's extra sharp, he'll carry a spare flashlight bulb.

A veteran hunter should know better than to do as I recently did when I rolled out my duster-type raincoat and found it mildewed because I'd not properly dried it after my last bad-weather trip, some months before.

His tent will have a carefully placed stove jack to protect fabric from the stove pipe. My tent is equipped with more than merely a metal jack. It sports heavy-duty fireproof material replacing fabric around the pipe hole. This is because my cooktent once caught fire after I'd stoked it with pitch-wood during a cold snap, then went outside to grain horses. That stove turned white-hot in my absence, igniting the tent's canvas around the stovepipe.

We put out the fire with copious gallons of creek water, but there's something disquieting about facing a blizzard thirty miles from the nearest road with only half a tent!

A veteran hunter will break in his boots before his adventure. And he'll adequately care for them during the hunt. Caring for feet and boots means clean socks and it means cleaning and properly drying boots and applying manufacturer's recommended waterproofing to them. He'll *not* do as I once did and place boots so close to a fire that they shrink and wrinkle to resemble a dried prune.

A veteran hunter will don layers of clothing, rather than one all-purpose garment that commits you to one type of action. Coveralls and a down-filled raincoat might be okay for sitting on a whitetail stand in tough weather, but it's poor attire for chasing elk through a lodgepole blowdown, or mule deer up a mesa slope.

A veteran hunter will take care to pack necessary maps, matches, compass, and a first aid kit. He'll lay in necessary horse tack, such as bells and hobbles and nosebags. He'll itemize and inventory his kitchen gear, making sure each utensil, pot, and pan is serviceable and included in the kit.

A menu will be carefully checked off and food stowed to avoid breakage or spillage. Horse feed will be packed. Last of all, just in case fortune smiles, a smart hunter will check and pack his tools to care for his meat: sharpened knives for skinning and boning, game bags for hanging.

How do I know all this? Because at some time or other during my hunting and horseback packing, I've erred on one or another of each of the above items. I've broken eggs, spilled grain, tried to cook in a cracked frying pan, sat outside during downpours without a raincoat, had flashlights grow dim, used dull knives.

I'm not proud. But by now, I am experienced. ∎

Where Culture and Chaos Collide

I've always admired culture. Got a nice ring to it. Goes beyond obvious phonic similarities like vulture, rupture, suture, and troglodyte. Makes a body think uplifting thoughts:

"Janie, did you sew a new button on the back flap of my union suit?"

Cultural sites are supposed to be tourism's new wave. Distinct possibilities arise for previously undisclosed centers of Treasure State enlightenment, such as Havre's underground town (prohibition era), Butte's Mercury Street (there were no prohibitions), or Helena's Capitol Dome (neither prohibitions or inhibitions there).

We Montanans have distinct cultural advantages over folks elsewhere—unfortunates who have to make more ado about much less. Take transport, for instance: While Californians can only trace reliable conveyances to post-World War II and the advent of BMWs and Toyota Land Cruisers, Montana's mobile record can proudly be tracked to the American Indian's embrace of the horse; and before that, their dog-culture days.

Montana waterways floated canoes and pirogues and steamboats while Kentucky was settled via ox-drawn wagons lumbering through mountain gaps.

Tennessee travelers wearied of slogging the mud of the Natchez Trace, while up in Montana nail-driving men laid steel that eventually crossed a Continent so fiord-loving Norsemen and women could search for dryland wheat farms along the railroad Jim Hill built and promoted.

Early Santa Fe traders went mad for want of vistas and water while crossing New Mexico's Llano Estacado—the Staked Plains. But up north, Canadian-bound whiskey haulers plying Montana's Whoop-Up Trail enjoyed scenery galore and used water sparingly, only to be added to the rotgut pilfered from barrels amid their freight.

Montana's first inhabitants were much less mean and conniving than those of eastern persuasion, engaging in spirited fun-filled competition with newcomers in places like Little Bighorn, Big Hole, and Bears Paw. Eastern natives, on the other hand, bilked the pale-skinned newcomers of $24 worth of valuable trinkets in trade for Manhattan Island—at least twice what the place was worth then and now, even after more than three centuries of inflation.

The Treasure State has a leg up on art, too, as a quick comparison between Charlie Russell and anybody else will prove.

And ours is not called the Treasure State for nothing—even though a few other places make idle claims concerning Mesabi iron, Comstock silver, or Homestake gold. Only in Montana can folks point with pride to the "richest hill on earth" (now the deepest lake in town).

In Montana, citizens hung their sheriff, and not the other way around. Meanwhile, corporate empires like the old Anaconda Company distributed suitcases full of long-green largesse to legislators, and bought office for their very own U.S. Senators—until the companies went belly-up in their own swill.

We've got grizzly bears snoozing in suburbs, mountain lions eyeing schoolyards with interest, and wolves inoculated against canine diseases. We have horse sales where dumb— but rich—folks bid real money for horses that buck. We snag prehistoric fish that wear built-in paddles. And we still shoot buffalo and hunt sandhill cranes.

You want culture? In Montana, we got all anybody needs. ■

I met a grizzly one fall while leading three horses loaded with meat and riding a crazy thing. I had read that in Alaska they talk to bears they don't want to shoot. I talked but was afraid he might be hard of hearing.
Russ Kinney • Missoula, MT

Admirable Conclusion to an Admirable Program

The beast paused in a shaft of moonlight, lifting her nose to test the air's gentle downhill drift. It was an odor so delicate, and from such a distance, that only the olfactory nerves of one so wild could sense it. She turned to stalk the breeze.

Minutes later, the animal stood motionless behind a screen of spruce saplings. Only her eyes moved, first around the tiny forest glade, then to the pile of debris on its far side. Again she tested the wind; her tiny ears flicked rearward, momentarily flattened, then pricked ahead. The odor here was pungent. She took a step nearer. Another. And another.

Despite the enticing odor luring her, the approach to the jumble of logs took a half-hour. Finally she could see the juicy venison hindquarter tucked far back within the rubble. She took another step, bent her head and reached inside. The snap was sudden! She smashed the top logs from the pile with an instinctive leap, then crashed to her side, roaring and bawling hideously, held fast by a steel cable around her right forefoot.

"Looks like we may have 183 down," the biologist said to his partner as a rising sun peeked above the eastern horizon.

The man snapped the off switch on his receiver and carefully folded and stored his antenna. "Let's go."

A half-hour later the men approached the forest glade where they had set the baited trap, every sense alert. One carried an autoloading 12-gauge shotgun, the other a plain-looking broomstick in one hand and a canister of capsaicin pepper spray in the other. Faced with an ominous silence, they parted the last spruce branches. The animal lunged for them!

Neither man leaped aside, but both blinked as the giant grizzly crashed to the ground, brought down once again by the ensnaring cable.

"Easy, girl," one of them said.

The two biologists shrugged from their daypacks, and moments later a hypodermic syringe gleamed from the end of the broomstick. The team leader warily approached the recumbent sow. She made one more lunge, again was jerked back, then squirmed to face her stalker until the second man approached from her other side. At last, the first man maneuvered into position and with a lightning thrust, jammed the needle into the fat animal's thigh.

She roared and lunged and again crashed to the ground. Minutes passed. Her eyelids drooped. The first man poked her with his broomstick. She didn't stir. He moved in and removed the bear's radio collar.

That's right, the man *removed* the bear's collar while his partner pulled the cable snare from her leg and dabbed the worn spot with disinfectant. Then they packed up their gear and hurried from the mountain.

The South Fork Grizzly Study, conducted largely amid the northern Swan Mountains, was designed to achieve clear objectives over a ten-year span. This single study provided the public with more and better understanding of bear behavior than any previous research—ever! The study should serve as a model: completed a year ahead of schedule, objectives accomplished.

Now the unheard-of: actually removing research equipment from wild animals that unwittingly and against their will contributed so much to our—and their own—futures.

It is an admirable conclusion to an admirable program. ∎

I couldn't resist writing a few lines since I have come to feel that I know you. I listen to your radio program almost daily and relate to your experiences very often. I'm a retired Idaho State Trooper and currently drive a courier route and listen to you while going over a small mountain pass between Montpelier and Preston, Idaho. The scenery goes well with your stories.   Ed Appleton • Pocatello, ID

Booger-Eating Poop Stains

How could someone do this?" my friend asked.

I shook my head. I've always struggled when confronted with conclusive evidence that there are jerks among us. My friend's wife exhibited far more eloquence—she called the unknown creeps "booger-eating poop stains." Her passion surfaced when we discovered someone had ripped a log from a deteriorating Missouri Breaks homestead cabin to use for campfire wood.

The cabin was about ten by twenty, with a low ceiling and a shallow-pitch sod roof. There were no remaining doors or windows. The remnants of a barn thrust against a flat sky a hundred yards to the east. Two fallen-in dugouts, or root cellars, beckoned from across a tiny grass-filled draw to the west.

More precisely, according to my excellent BLM-produced map of the Upper Missouri National Wild & Scenic River, the abandoned homestead perched on a bench some hundred yards back from the broad and muddy Missouri at a place called Greasewood Bottom. The bench is a hundred miles from our launch site at Fort Benton and fifty from our take-out boat ramp at Kipp's Park.

The night before, we'd camped just upstream. Our friends

spotted the ramshackle homestead while on an evening hike. Thus, shortly after morning launch and with their direction, we put into shore to explore what was certainly a site with some historical significance.

Then we found the half-burned log. I walked a short distance in the deep grass and, with the toe of my boot, rolled over the fat-bodied remains of two fish. Their heads had been removed, but the entrails were still in place. What was left appeared to be at least sixteen inches in length. I'm hardly an expert on Missouri River fish, but big encircling red and black side dots said char to me: brook trout or dolly varden. I muttered a curse.

No doubt about it, Colleen was right: Somewhere ahead of us floated one—maybe two—"booger-eating poop stains."

Even after seeing the evidence, I choose to believe that the anglers' destruction was the result of ignorance rather than malice. I simply can't believe they paused to consider the hours, days, weeks, months, and years those hard-working, lonely settlers had put into that homestead.

Those pioneers harbored end-of-the-rainbow dreams, too, just like you and me. They smiled with a good planting and laughed with plentiful harvests, slapped mosquitoes while rolling an evening smoke, cursed the riverbottom mud, and shed tears during floods and fires and hail and drought. They worked hard and played but little. And their legacy of dreams and work and disappointments lives on in the crumbling remains of that isolated homestead.

A time will come when its last evidence will melt away, returning to the soil from which it came. But until then, our own lives can be enriched by contemplating their passage.

It is that opportunity for contemplation that thoughtless booger-eating poop stains steal. If each passing individual burned cabin logs from the dilapidated homestead, and left rotting fish for others to bury, soon nothing would be left. Then we could all show our kids faded photographs and brag about how good it was back in "the old days" and there'd be nothing tangible left to show any different. ■

For several months I have enjoyed listening to your radio broadcasts on KXLE, a local station. Especially enjoyable was your story this morning about your "big pony" (Buck, I think). Letting you know there is another Cheek who appreciates your work gives me a good feeling.
Immojean Cheek • Ellensburg, WA

Your show is on WIGL at 6:30 a.m. I try never to miss it. It is a great way to start a work day with a little outdoor perspective (you help me keep my priorities in line).
Bill Cheek • St. Matthews, SC

Straight Talk About Horse Magic

The best horse handlers I know get inside the animals' heads to work their magic. They know the powerful beasts are capable of only one thought at a time—sometimes on an intelligence level somewhere between a box of rocks and a hop toad. They know, however, that even dunces in the herd have excellent memories. But memory needs constant reinforcement if a pony is asked to do something not of his own choosing.

For instance, on foot I can drive my four horses from a sixty-acre field into a corral located at one end, provided they haven't just come in for water and are feeding their way back into the pasture. In that case, their minds are set to graze out, not drift in. I must then take additional time to turn them from drifting for the pasture to drifting toward the corral. In other words, patience is needed to change their mindset. Try to drive them against their will and they'll break around and dash for freedom.

They *can* be driven against their will, yes—if I get enough people shouting and throwing stones and waving their arms. Or a couple of well-mounted cowboys can do it, whooping and hollering and pounding pell-mell behind. But the corralled cayuses will then be wild-eyed and snorting and blowing and hard to catch. You might have to shake out a lariat and rope 'em and snub 'em down until you can get a halter over their heads and tied off in a corner. Even then, they might take to fighting the halter rope until they throw themselves in a frenzy. And who wants to ride an animal that's crazy?

So why not do it the easy way and get them used to your idea until they think it's theirs. Then you can trail along behind, kicking at an occasional clod in boredom. Into the corral. Close the gate. And the relaxed steeds are standing there as if to say, "What's next, boss?"

When a horse sets back on a halter rope, it's because he's momentarily alarmed. But when he comes up short, he might fight the rope until he's crazed, then exhausted.

If I have a halter-puller, I won't tie him hard and fast. Instead I'll take a couple of wraps around the hitchrack and leave it loose. Then if the animal becomes monetarily alarmed and sets back, the rope slips with him, to his surprise. Usually it's enough to change his attitude, giving him something else to think about. Instead of snorting and fighting something that's offering no fight, he looks around, sees the other ponies standing placidly, and decides to stand placidly himself.

The best horse handling is a bit like judo, where you never pit your strength directly against your opponent. Instead, you go with the flow, using the opponent's own strength and movement against him. A prime example is a pony that tries to break away from you; a good horseman won't fight him directly, but holding to the halter rope, get him going in a circle until he tires of fighting something that's not fighting back.

There's another way to train a horse: the carrot and stick approach. It works. Sort of. Sometimes.

It's true you can change a pony's mind through force, but you'll only have him working *for* you instead of *with* you. And bribery? Yes, ponies will come for a sugar cube or a nosebag full of oats. But again, you'll have them working for you instead of with you. And what happens when you have no bribe?

Get into your ponies' heads and wriggle into their minds often enough and you'll reach their hearts. Along the way, you'll learn how they think. Pretty quick they'll take pride of ownership in you—that you have joined them as a team.

They'll begin to trust you, eager to do whatever it takes to make the team work.

And if you're unusually lucky, you'll someday be owned by a really great horse. That's what happened to me.

⁘⁘⁘⁘

Just north of the Flathead Lake town of Bigfork there's a pasture full of what I'm told are Norwegian Fjord horses. All are of the same near-palomino hue. Each is stocky, like a draft horse in miniature—sort of Welsh types, or bigger Shetlands. I can't imagine 'em hiking up a mountain trail.

"I don't care what you say," my wife mused, gazing out the auto's side window at the animals scattered across the rolling, green-carpeted hills, "I think they're picturesque."

"Why?"

"I don't know. Perhaps because they're all the same color."

I thought back to the times I've gone "color-blind" while shopping for a horse: invariably I paid inflated prices for an inferior pony when I let color grab control over conformation and spirit and obedience and training.

Let's see, there was Jackpot, one of the most beautifully blanketed appaloosas I've seen. Jackpot was still a stud at seven years old. I paid twice the going rate, only to discover the colorful horse rated high in vitamin Z. Like in la-z-y.

Then there was April, a beautiful smooth-riding palomino. She was a bunchquitter who caused more after-dark, long-riding grief while searching for her than any ten common-colored ponies.

Of all the reasons to buy a horse, basing a do-or-don't decision on color is the poorest. That's not to say a pony shouldn't have a pleasing color. It's nice, too, if it's distinctively marked. But let me say it again, you should never judge the quality of performance by the color of a coat.

My taste runs to buckskins. Make it a gelding the color of a faded manilla envelope and add an inky-black mane and tail and pasterns and you'll have me slobbering all over him. Throw in a dark line down its back and a few tiger stripes to hock and knee and I'll go and sin some more for that pony.

Know why? Because the best horse ever to own me was colored in just that manner.

But did I buy a look-alike when Buck passed over the Great Divide? I did not. By then I was broke of sucking colored eggs. By then I knew the things that made Buck the epitome of Roland's equine pleasure lay with his temperament and wisdom, strength and agility, willingness and audacity. That and the fact that the big buckskin loved me as much as I loved him.

The horse I ride now—my second best pony—is a big, white, poorly marked appaloosa with the stub of a worn-out broom as a tail and a mane that wouldn't make a rat proud. Rocky, my newest saddlehorse, is a mare instead of a gelding. She has red-rimmed eyes and a head that wouldn't fit inside a thirty-gallon barrel. She's a tad clumsy at a trot and gallops like a sick Holstein. But ever since I bought her as a four-year-old, her only concern has been to discover what I wish her to do, then to do it to the best of her ability.

And what is her ability? To walk. Tirelessly. Incredibly. Squatting astride that big, ugly appaloosa while she treads a mountain trail is like sitting in a porch swing, watching all the world's best scenery march by for your private perusal.

There were thirty head of horses in my outfit when I retired. I chose the ugliest for my very own saddlehorse. Some were of better conformation, *all* were more colorful. But color be damned—I picked the best. Like with people, the best in ponies lies between the ears. ∎

My father and I really enjoy listening to your program on WCKR and WLEA in Hornell.
Sharon L. Willis • Greenwood, NY

Just a note to let you know that I very much enjoy your program. Dugan Coffee • Lakeview, OR

I listen to your program nearly every morning over KERR radio station and read your articles in the local newspaper. Don Smith • Hot Springs, MT

The All-Important Question

There is no delicate way to approach this subject. Of all problems associated with middle-aged outdoors adventure, the single biggest concern among my guests during the two decades I guided people through the northern Rockies was, "How does one go to the bathroom in the woods?"

Funny. I'd trained for leadership by manhandling ten-horse packstrings over distant mountaintops; by learning that a certain flash of silver in the middle of a whitewater cascade reflected from a thirty-inch bull trout with a girth of seventeen inches; by knowing snow brushed from the limb of an Englemann spruce was caused by a six-point bull passing through at a trot at 6:38 in the morning.

And all my clients really wanted to know was how to go to the bathroom.

I didn't know it was optional. Nothing I'd trained for told me internal waste movement was subject to debate.

Now, however, it's different. Now that I, too, have reached middle age, I'm beginning to understand the question. In other words, I feel their pain.

The approved U.S. Forest Service way is to use the "cat method." But that's not always intelligible to first-timers, as demonstrated by the land-clearing contractor from North

Carolina who muttered, "I've got two D-8 Cats and a dragline at home that I'd like to have here to help me out right now.

I have a friend who once turned over a rock in lieu of digging a hole, only to discover that someone had previously turned over the same rock for the same purpose.

Official Forest Service interpretation of the cat method is to dig a hole to mineral soil, do your duty, then fill the hole with dirt. Careful research, I assume, has disclosed rapid breakdown of excrement.

The method I've found most effective at my advanced age is to find a sapling lying horizontally about two feet off the ground. Saplings, of course, are easy enough to find in a lodgepole thicket, but tough to locate in an ancient Douglas fir forest. Ideally, the sapling should be situated above soil you can easily excavate. Another criterion you should insist on in selecting your sapling is that it be sturdy enough to support your weight for the entire period it's employed—surely you can conjure images of sapling failure at an inopportune moment!

Naturally, if you're staying for several nights at the same location, you can invest more energy to secure more comfort. Our hunting camps were regularly occupied for six weeks by as many as eight people. There, we went first-cabin with a superb open-air throne complete with a magnificent view of surrounding mountains and a commercial seat rescued from broken porcelain.

Even such creature comforts aren't sufficient for everybody, however. One gentleman told me, "It took ten thousand years for civilization to perfect flush toilets. I owe it to those who went before never to get far from one." ∎

We live in a small, quiet town that has a local radio station. Each morning early they have your program. My husband, about six months ago, was given an AM/FM clock that he promptly put in the bathroom to listen as he gets ready for work at our locally owned body shop. He's listened each day since and during our cold spell while starting the cars, missed a couple of days and was disappointed.

Shortly after he became involved with your program, I, too, began to listen and find myself rushing to turn the stereo up when it's time for your program to air. I like the logical and funny sides, as well as the good advice you have.

Pam & Carey Rose • Colville, WA

Attitude Is Everything

My friend stopped to adjust the bindings on his cross-country skis. My friend doesn't often swear. Good thing, too, or the air would have been blue. His face turned the color of raw pot roast. "I'm getting too old to bend over like this," he said.

I snorted. "You're not much older than me. And I'm not too old."

"I am, too. I'm a lot older than you."

So he's six or seven years older—what's that when both of us count decades like we once counted fence posts along the back forty? We struck out along the twin ski ruts left by our wives.

Our friends retired a few years ago. The couple built a beautiful home on a spit of land between two lakes. With the building project behind him, the guy now builds model airplanes and flies them. Only his model airplanes run thirty feet long with forty-foot wingspans, and will transport him and the missus across America. In addition, this retired workaholic cuts trees and builds roads on a tree farm he owns. He and his wife also hike amid Utah Anasazi ruins and canoe down Arctic rivers. It wears me out just trying to keep up with these friends.

"You are not growing old," I said over my shoulder. There was no reply, so I added, "'old' is a matter of attitude. You might grow older, but don't you dare grow 'old.'"

"I'm just grateful that I have my health," he said.

The women waited for us at the top of a rise. I pointed. "Look at that. That's where we're both maybe the luckiest guys alive. We not only have our health, but so do our ladies. On top of that, each loves doing outdoors things. Our wives are our best friends, and we all prefer to lead active, simple lives. So we're not as supple as we were at sixteen. Big deal!"

"We've always been active, Roland—all of us."

"Which might help explain why no one sees our names on the obituary page."

Jane and I have other friends we admire a great deal. They recently left their beautiful country home for a more centrally located retirement spa. "Our new quarters is ideally located," the husband recently told me. "The hospital is right next door and the cemetery is just across the street."

One of my guides, the late Ken Averill, was diagnosed with inoperable cancer at age seventy. What did he do? Went out and bought a brand-spanking new Western leisure suit, a Stetson hat, and a pair of Justin boots. Then he went dancing. With only a couple of months to live, the grand old man confounded his doctors for almost a year. Of his last eleven months, he *lived* for nine.

There may be several reasons why people enjoy longevity. But chief among those reasons you'll find attitude. A healthy attitude prompts one to be active physically and mentally. An unhealthy attitude leads to physical torpor and mental stagnation.

Our skiing friends spent much of the past summer learning to handle a river canoe while preparing for their Yukon journey. They not only enjoyed the physical adventure, but benefitted by learning techniques and maneuvers previously beyond their ken.

It's an attitude that allows one to grow older without growing old. ∎

Deuces, Nines, and One-Eyed Jacks

I have a neighbor who owns a farm. His animals are diverse: a few sheep, a few goats, a small herd of cows and one bull, half a dozen horses, and even a llama. The crops are varied, too: alfalfa in the bottoms and spring wheat on the bench above, plus experimental patches of mint, lentils, and canola.

In an upland draw is a stand of fine yellow pines. Patches of firs, lodgepole, and aspen are also spotted about the place. The entire spread is watered by an artesian spring of the sweetest water imaginable. By some trick of atmospheric dynamics, the skies over the farm are usually cloudless blue.

A few days ago, a couple of gents drove up to my friend's home in a big black automobile sporting out-of-state license plates. One of 'em carried a briefcase. "John," the briefcase-toter said, "we are going to make you an offer you can't refuse."

John, being typical of the nice kinds of people found in rural parts, invited the gents in to squat around his kitchen table and slurp down a cup of sugared coffee. "Okay, fellows," John says, "what's the pitch?"

"We are going to make you rich beyond your wildest dreams," the big one says, opening the briefcase and lifting out a sheet of paper. "Keep you and the missus in a style to which you'd like to become accustomed, send the kids to college, maybe even have enough left over to hire a man to help out around the place. All you got to do is sign this paper allowing us to dig around under your ground some, looking to strike a little black gold. We'll take the risk, all you have to do is sit around and watch."

John chuckled. "Me and Lucy presently live in a style we prefer, one kid has already graduated from college and she's a medical doctor in St. Louis, and the other is a senior in ag school and will take over the farm when me and momma retire. And for your information, I already have not one but two hired men."

"Well, if you won't think of yourself, think of others. If the rainbow we think we spotted on the way in is the one with a pot of gold, it'd benefit this entire godforsaken country by bringing newcomers to your schools and on your roads and over your bridges. Man, you can't think of just yourself on anything this big!"

John picked up the paper and studied it. "This doesn't say a thing about my artesian well. There's no guarantee it won't be affected."

The big guy grunted as if my neighbor had punched him in the belly. "Some things you got to take on faith."

"And this road right up my yellow pine coulee …"

"All the better to log them old, overmature trees with."

"And how about my fields of lentils and mint?"

"Read the fine print. It says we'll put the gravel back when we finish … maybe." The big guy squints and pulls out a deck of cards. "Tell you what we'll do. We'll play you one hand of five-card draw. Deuces, nines, and one-eyed jacks wild. You win, we'll stay off your farm. We win, you sign. What do you say?"

John studied the cards as the gent shuffled. He couldn't put his finger on it, but something didn't sound … quite … right.

Maybe it's just me, but the foregoing neighbor-parable sounds eerily reminiscent of what some folks want us to do with our Rocky Mountain Front—the richest unaltered native wildlife habitat in America. ■

Since I work two jobs I rarely have a quiet moment, but that seems to be when the kids are getting ready for school and I am enjoying the morning's first cup of coffee. I hear your voice come on and it catches my attention and I love hearing your hunting and Western life stories.

Jan Davis • Gunnison, CO

Abusing Your Feet Doubles Your Troubles

It felt as though ten thousand needles were jammed at all angles into my feet. Just seconds before, I'd been unceremoniously shoved from exhausted sleep by an insistent bladder. Still sleep-drugged, I was nearly upright before excruciating pain swept all other considerations aside. A scream of mortal anguish and the subsequent thump as I hit the floor jolted my wife from bed.

"My feet," I moaned through gritted teeth. "It's my feet. They're burning."

She switched on the light. Each toe was bright red. So were the heels and the edges of both feet. She asked, "Can you stand?"

"Stand? I can't even stand to touch them."

I crawled to the bathroom, then crawled back to bed. After daylight, I crawled to the kitchen. Later, Jane drove me to town and I crawled into the doctor's office.

"Hmm," the doctor murmured, callous to my suffering as he twisted first one foot, then the other. "Looks like frostbite." When I only growled, he added, "But since it's the dog days of summer, that can't be."

He dropped my feet to his examination stool and as I winced, he leaned back in his chair, lacing his fingers behind his neck. "Have you had those feet in water for any prolonged period?"

I nodded. "Yeah. I was fishing at a mountain lake over the weekend. Packed in a rubber raft. It leaked. Sat with my feet in water for three days. But the water was pure. Why?"

"Immersion foot," the ex-Navy pilot said. "Fairly common with shipwrecked sailors and downed aviators who spent time in a raft before they were rescued. Works like frostbite by restricting the blood vessels to the extremities."

It was an interesting clinical analysis, but what I really wanted to know was, "How long will I be down?"

"Oh, I'll prescribe some medicine to open the vessels. It's just a matter of time, say three days."

That was more than forty years ago. But, as with frostbite victims, my feet still remain susceptible to any prolonged exposure to water. When hunting, it's routine for me to carry an extra pair of socks in my daypack. And if my feet become wet from either outside moisture or inside perspiration, I stop to change socks. Over the years, I learned that I could place the damp ones next to my skin at the waist and they would dry in a couple of hours. Then I could change again.

Just a couple of years ago, my valley experienced an unprecedented rise in ground water due to an unusually wet winter and spring. Water crept into the pit housing our well pump, drowning it. I donned rubber boots and stood in ice water for nearly eight hours while working on the pump. Inevitably, water sloshed over the tops of my boots, and my feet were soaked. When the job was at last finished, I pulled off my boots and socks. After just eight hours of exposure to chilled water, each toe and heel and the edges of both feet were shiny red and itched fiercely.

The moral of this story is that we're all too inclined to take our feet for granted; careless treatment is common. We undertake long backpacking or hunting excursions without first breaking in new boots; we tolerate worn or broken arches because the boots feel comfortable; we dry our boots too close to a fire; we buy shoes too large or too small or too narrow or too wide; we choose soft cushion insoles and disregard proper heel lasts, arch supports, or outer and inner fabrics.

No wonder our feet play out before the head that abused them. ■

From the lovely way Roland refers to his life's partner, I addressed this card to both of you: You have explored and enjoyed [the northern Rockies]—when I hear your program it's almost as tho I've smelled the pine, I've seen the sunrise and I've heard the elk bugle. I'm glad you've been able to do so and thank you for sharing your joy with me and countless others.   M. J. Jackson • Bozeman, MT

Walkie-Talkie Time

My wife calls it "walkie-talkie time." I like the term. She uses it to describe the quality time we spend together simply walking for our health.

Jane began walking years ago, while I still guided in the Bob Marshall Wilderness. She, too, wished to maintain her health, and walking through the woods behind our home was the perfect way to exercise while staying close to nature. After I retired from outfitting, she pestered me to join her. Now we both enjoy the hours spent walking together, talking of private things.

Our daughter, a successful businesswoman in California, marveled at our dedication and perseverance until she, too, discovered her forty-year-old body wasn't built to last forever. And she also began walking for her health. Her husband joined her. They walk an hour each morning and evening. She tells me the most surprising benefit is the quality time it gives them together.

Cheri says their twice-daily walkie-talkie sessions are better for them physically and provide more psychological therapy than they could ever get through counseling. Less money, too.

Besides the physical and psychological benefits, our walks through the woods have been educational for Jane and me.

We've spotted great horned owls, foxes, pileated woodpeckers, a moose, a bear, a few elk, loads of deer, coyotes, turkeys, skunks, squirrels, ruffed grouse, and a whole bunch of LGBs—little gray birds.

We thrill to spring's first buttercups, then follow the advance of other flowers until, always around Mother's Day, I pick Jane a single fairy slipper for her very own orchid.

The woods are warm when the winds blow cold across the fields, yet cool during the dog days of summer. They are soothing for Jane during periods of financial stress and help me to creativity during mental blocks. They offer shade from the sun and air sweetened by juniper and firs and carpeted with the needles of spruce and pine.

During the long winter of 1996-97 and its record-breaking snows, we did not walk in the woods. Jane tried her skis twice, only to discover the snow too soft or blizzards too biting. With the advance of spring, we were like frisky colts let out of the barn.

We're into our sixties now and we're fortunate to be in reasonably good health for a couple of old duffers. We attribute 90 percent of our good fortune to regular exercise and 10 percent to heredity. We know many older folks who are in remarkably good condition for their age, too. Almost without exception, they keep active and exercise regularly.

Jane and I believe firmly in a regular outdoors regimen. We think its benefits are so apparent we wonder why there's anyone at all who cannot recognize that truth. It's not just longer life we want, but to continue the same excellent quality of life we're living now.

If you have a partner during your exercise, so much the better. But partner or no, you must do it. Begin slowly. Do only as much as you enjoy. Today around the block. Months from now through your neighborhood. Next year across town. But only as much as you wish; that way you'll find plenty of gain with no pain.

There is no better quality time than that spent maintaining your health.

No one reaches advanced age without making accommodations with reality. For instance, I've learned not to spit into the wind, go one on one with Michael Jordon, take over a foreign embassy in Peru, or sword fight with the Three Musketeers. And as for braving flood-stage streams to experience whitewater thrills, huh-uh. The catch in achieving advanced age is: Where do you draw the risk-reduction line if you still want adventure?

Perhaps the line lies within the individual. Or maybe not. After all, one can hardly live a life of adventure after one is dead.

But one cannot avoid all risk. Drive down a highway, punch a time clock, ride an elevator, climb on a tractor—there's risk there somewhere. The truth is, we who've survived to our dotage owe something to Providence as well as to prudence and proficiency. We have, in some part, been lucky. Pick up any newspaper on any given day and see how lucky.

Recently, two men drowned after overturning a canoe. I've canoed and so have many thousands of others. Was our survival a result of our dexterity with the craft, or simply luck because we weren't hit by the same freak storm that capsized the canoe of the victims? Or might their ultimate misfortune have occurred because neither man was wearing a life preserver?

Yes, mishaps befall even the most cautious. But it's likewise true that mishaps occur more often to the unwary than to the vigilant. My own rule of thumb is that I listen to an inner voice.

Self, says I, "I don't like the way this trail is sloughing off over yonder cliff."

"Then don't cross it," self says. "Turn around and go back the way you came."

"Self" tells me he doesn't like to raft rampaging rivers. He says it frightens him to shoot over dishonest standing waves that one moment might leave you feeling cheated with your ease of passage and the next moment flip your raft end over end like the deuce of diamonds in a whirlwind.

I don't like rivers where undertows whisper to me—when the whispering water cuts short my passage through a pool of surface eddies and the rear of the raft is sucked down before release. It's times like these when self murmurs, "Boy, life-jacket or no, if you'd been in the water just then you would be at the bottom of this river."

Self also whispers that there's danger in crossing a late-summer snowfield on a 65-degree slope; that carrying insufficient water in desert country is patently stupid; that leaving home to face a November storm without proper clothing is idiotic.

What has happened with us old geezers, of course, is that we've learned through experience. What may be even more pertinent is that to learn, we must first live through a few bad experiences. To do so requires luck, skill, and/or caution.

At sixteen I depended on 90 percent luck and 10 percent skill. At twenty-five, it was 90 percent skill and 10 percent luck.

Nowadays I'm not sure of the percentages, but both are seasoned with prudence. ■

Clown Prince of Fools

The man waved frantically. Others ran to his side, then wheeled to wave at me and point toward a clump of hawthorn bushes. I ran to them. The men crowded around, pointing and whispering as I approached. "What is it, Roland?" a breathless guest asked.

A bright red bird perched on a thorny limb. I'd never seen one like it. Certainly no grosbeak; or even a tanager. Much too red. "I don't know." Curiosity overwhelmed me and I took an involuntary step beyond the others. The bird remained motionless.

I heard the whirring of Dick's expensive Bolex movie camera, but my attention was on the bird. Then one of the Saginaw, Michigan, fishermen whispered, "Isn't that a cardinal?"

"Yeah," another said. "It sure is. I didn't know they had cardinals this far west. Do they, Roland?"

I shook my head, took another involuntary step forward, and whispered to the crowd behind, "I've never seen anything like it. I guess it really is a cardinal."

There was really no question—the bird was about the size of our steller jay, with a similar topknot. But he was bright red with maybe a couple of darker red feathers in a wing clasped tight to his body. Dick, the cameraman, said, "Is it true they'll jump on your finger if you don't rush them?"

"You know," one of his buddies said, "I've heard that."

"Go on, Roland," Dick murmured. "I'll get it on film. Go on and see if he'll hop on your finger." There was a buzz of approval.

I glanced back at my guides, Hazen and Carl. Both stood just beyond the ring of Saginaw fishermen, every bit as intrigued as I. "Go on," Dick urged.

I took another step toward the bird. Did he cock his head and peer more directly my way? Another step. No more than twenty feet now. Fifteen. Ten.

"Hold out your finger, Roland." Dick's whisper was insistent. Others took up the chant. I pointed a forefinger.

"There!" one guy said excitedly from behind. "He moved. Careful, now."

"Oh he didn't move either," another said. I didn't see the bird move.

"Closer," Dick urged. "This film might make history."

They were a rollicking group, calling themselves the "Saginaw Fin & Bottle Club." It was an apt title for a collection of friends who, each year, fished a different place, with good fun had by all. This year—1975—they'd chosen Big Salmon Lake and the South Fork of the Flathead, in the Bob Marshall Wilderness.

"Closer, Roland," Dick muttered, camera whirring.

"Yeah, mon," another said aloud.

I moved up, held out my forefinger at arm's length. I couldn't believe the bird still perched there. Four feet. Three. So close I could see thread stitches along his belly. The forefinger joined its mates in a clenched fist and my arm dropped. A slow flush crept from my collar as I turned. Both guides were rolling on the ground and my guests were all pointing their fingers and guffawing at the clown prince of fools.

And it was all on 16mm movie film! ∎

Shivers of Impermanence

It's tough for us mortals to come to grips with time in terms we can understand. For instance, I'm told the Fort Union coal layers below the topsoils of eastern Montana were decaying vegetation laid down in shallow seas and swamps fifty to sixty million years ago. That lush forests once sprouted in the arid country around the isolated hamlet of Jordan cannot be doubted, for Jane and I have picked up fossilized cones from giant Sequoia trees that grew there.

But the mind is boggled by the concept of elapsed time so enormous as to account for tropical jungles flourishing amid what is now barren prairie verging on desert. It's difficult enough for us to think in terms of the life of one tree, let alone an entire forest regime. Then consider cyclic changes so immense as to include desert, then jungle, then desert again and ... and....

Oceans once lapped the western margins of North Dakota. Most of Montana—if not all—was under the sea. Those sea margins retreated to the west, then returned east again. Water trapped in polar caps during periodic ice ages could be one reason for fluctuating ocean margins, but hardly the only reasons.

The equator, we're told, differed from its location today,

and a Montana risen from the sea was tropical. Giant beasts stalked the land and floated in marsh. Their fossilized bones are found as far west as the East Front of the Rockies.

The Continental Spine began pushing up, so we're told, fifty million years ago, and quieted after twenty-five million years. The terrible lizards disappeared in but a short time, vanquished by some traumatic cataclysm of the earth, the source of which is still being debated by scholars who study that sort of thing.

The Rockies are several thousand feet above today's sea, rising as giant wrinkles in the surface, pushed up by tectonic plate collision. Erosion began at once: wind and water wearing away at the mountains almost as swiftly as plate collision pushed them up. But not quite, leaving the spectacular mountains we see today.

And we're only talking about events that occurred "last week" in comparison with the age of our planet. It is estimated that the earth is four billion years old. And these days, the science of astronomy is discovering that elsewhere in the cosmos, four billion years seems a tad youthful.

How do we mere mortals grasp those kinds of time lapses when the age of human life is, comparatively, a mere blink of the eye. I've seen sixty-four years of that blink and, truth tell, I've forgotten most of that.

That's why it's ludicrous for us to think we're preserving Glacier or Yellowstone or the Bob Marshall Wilderness or the Selway-Bitterroot forever. Those lands are changing even as I write. The great northern ice cap will once again grind and carve and sculpt in Glacier—probably before our species goes extinct.

That's just as well, because if it continues to move in its same direction and at the same rate of march, the Yellowstone Caldera is certain to be in downtown Billings in a mere five million years.

Given enough time, the Rocky Mountains might once again be mud flats and the seas may lap the margins of North Dakota.

I don't know about you, but all the foregoing causes me to have shivers of impermanence, despite my sixty-four years. ∎

Enjoy your program at 7:10 a.m. on KBBS. I'm in a wheelchair and my wife is on oxygen so we'll never see the Bob Marshall Wilderness through our own eyes first hand. But we can see it through your book. Please autograph it to "Mary Lou Hudson, Christmas, 1994: Enjoy God's handi-work." **Rodney Hudson • Buffalo, WY**

God's Better Gardens

Giving up her flowers was one of the more difficult things about Jane's involvement in our outfitting and guiding business. There simply was no time to garden—to till, plant, weed, or prune—during our hectic spring, summer, and fall wilderness adventure periods.

Gradually, her once well-tended flowers withered and died, taken over by yard grass that seldom was mowed to maintain a carpet-like appearance. Yet, as one of our guides was quick to point out, she really didn't give up her flowers. Instead she discovered new ones. "And," as Larry Gleason said, "they're of a kind that never needs tending by mortal hands."

In May it was buttercups and glacier lilies, wild crocus and sugar bowls and shooting stars. The month of June brought orchids: ladyslippers and fairyslippers and coralroot. There were valerians and mariposa lilies and beargrass, too.

July brought harebells and penstemon and entire fields of lupine. August owned the late-bloomers: pearly everlasting and goldenrod and groundsel, and an abundance of asters in the high country.

And there were more. Many more. Through the years, Jane learned to identify well over one hundred and twenty different species of Bob Marshall wildflowers. There were hedgerows of serviceberry, red osier dogwood, mock orange, and chokecherry. Because flowering plants were so important to her, I learned a great deal about forage plants critical to winter survival for ungulates—elk, deer, and moose—as well as when they matured to be palatable to wildlife. Along with them came an understanding of the palatable sequence of other shrubs, grasses, legumes, and broadleaf perennials.

Because wildlife held my particular attention, I learned by osmosis quite a lot about how, why, and where different creatures dwell at particular times of the year—a not unimportant element of the outfitting occupation.

My earlier years spent in the woods and in the mills of the wood-products industry helped me to learn about the fifteen or so tree species native to the wilderness I roamed. Nor did we neglect the exotic introduced plant species, such as leafy spurge and knapweed.

All in all, during the course of three decades spent trekking forest trails, game trails, and no trails in the Bob Marshall, Jane and I learned to identify upwards of two hundred different types of plants.

The kinds of observation demanded for amateur botany led eventually to wondering about other wonders of nature: sedimentary layering, mountain upthrusting, glaciation. We can now recognize faulting—both thrust and tension—when we see it. At least sometimes. We know about the "kames" and "eskers" and "kettles" common to glaciation.

And it all came about because Jane gave up her flowers.

Now that we've forsaken outfitting for a more sedentary life of fireside chats and backyard cookouts, my lady tells me she still doesn't plan to jumpstart her home flower beds.

No. Instead she figures to satisfy whatever horticultural urge strikes her fancy by checking into God's own better plantings whenever we hike or ride into the wilderness.

And she says she knows right where a bunch of His flowers will soon be in bloom. ■

Becoming Partial to Equine Transport

Although there are good ones in the thousand-pound
range that pack heavy loads over long distances, mountain horses, as a rule, weigh in excess of eleven hundred
pounds. Jane's saddlehorse is but a nine-hundred-pounder.
But then, Jane weighs only one-twenty soaking wet and she's
apt, by choice, to walk half of any distance, so her pony fares
well.

All the same, it takes a big horse to carry a big load. That's
why most outfitters you encounter along mountain trails will
be leading a string of big horses.

Big horses aren't cuddly. In fact, to most people—especially to folks unfamiliar with the oversized creatures—they're
frightening. Actually, even small horses are big enough to
intimidate most inexperienced riders.

As daunting as horses are to many people, I sometimes
wondered why, year after year, the timid continued to line up
for a demanding week-long horseback packtrip into the middle of one of the largest wilderness areas in America.

Answers to that question are as varied as one might imagine. Some folks seek escape from their normally hectic world.
Others want to view natural beauty. Still others reach for
peace of mind, physical restoration, the challenge of polishing

wilderness skills, ad infinitum.

Most surprising are those who become partial to equine transport as a result of those wildlands adventures. Kay Rahlf, an athletic, fortyish, emergency-room nurse from Rhinelander, Wisconsin, wrote:

"I have become addicted to horses and am presently leasing a horse and plan on buying one in the spring. I've learned quite a bit. Our goal is to do trail riding and camping. I manage to ride a couple of hours about every other day or so (in the woods, trails, etc.). Also have taken lessons.

"… Anyway, I am quite excited about all this. It's fun to go look at a horse for sale that sounds good.…"

Along with her husband Roger, Kay does a great deal of hiking and backpacking. For Kay Rahlf, horses became an immediate love after joining us for a Bob Marshall adventure.

In fact, after Jane and I retired, Kay and Roger came back to the Bob a couple of times with other outfitters. One of those times, Jane and I happened to be camped near a trail in Big River Meadows as a string of riders chanced by. Jane was outside our tent with her faithful Brittany spaniel companion, Tess.

One of the riders said, "That looks like Tess." Then she said, "That looks like Jane!"

Jane said, "Kay!"

Kay said, "Jane!"

It was like old home week that evening around our campfire.

Horses never came quite as easily for Tink Mendel. This diminutive wife of a University of California professor was terrified of horses. However, her husband Verne, a one-time Montanan raised near Winifred, wished desperately to join two other couples on an adventure into the Bob, and he persuaded her to do it, too.

Before their trip began, Verne confided Tink's fear to me. He said she'd once been astride a runaway horse and had suffered for it. With that memory on her mind, Tink, quaking with fear, mounted our most reliable and gentle horse. And either Jane or I rode nearby at all times. Afterward, Tink had this to say:

"Now I am your real convert. My 'call-of-the-wild' experiences have been almost nil, and horses suited me best on the other side of the fence. And also, my blood is happy in Palm Springs. However, I would not have traded any of our week in the Bob for anything. It was wonderful—after that first day."

After the first day it gets to 'em every time. I know it did with Tink, because after Jane and I retired, Tink and Verne also returned to the Bob with other outfitters.

<hr/>

There is no sound as pleasing to a wilderness horseback traveler as the dinging of horse bells. Nothing is as comforting as awakening in the dark of night and listening to the muted "ting-ting" of far off bells, or searching for lost horses and hearing a sudden jangling from behind a screen of trees as an unseen horse fights flies.

To be out of sight and sound of loose horses is as frightening for the experienced horseman as a swamped dory is for a landlubber. And the longer the horseman goes without the soothing sound of nearby horses munching pasture grass, the greater the terror.

Aside from an obvious outlaw horse, having a bunchquitter mixed into your string is the worst possible scenario. Either an outlaw or a bunchquitter is tantamount to disaster. One will leave you dead. The other will leave you and you'll wish you were dead.

How can you know a bunchquitter before the fact? You can't, always. But I'm automatically suspicious of a horse who isn't buddied up to another in the band. If you've got a pony that doesn't seem to mind when the others are out of sight, that's the one to which you should pay special attention when he's grazing.

If you're mixing horses—that is, if you've got a couple of head of stock and your buddy has a couple, and you're taking those on a mountain holiday—turn one of yours and one of his loose to graze while the others are tied. Then swap the tied ones with the loose ones every couple of hours.

If the ones that are tied become agitated as their buddies graze away, and if they begin to stamp and paw the ground, slap a pair of hobbles on the troublemakers. I've never known one to paw dirt from around a tree's roots while his front legs are snared.

If the worst happens and you suddenly come awake to find your pony is gone, check your back trail first. Odds are ten to one he'll head back the way he came. That's why most experienced horsemen will stop on the near side of the meadow where they wish to camp. If you set up camp on the side nearest your backtrail, the loose horses will graze farther into the meadow. Then, when their bellies are full and their eyes load with wanderlust, they'll head back the way they came—and run smack into your camp. But if you set up camp on the far side, there's nothing between the ponies and downtown Denver except miles and miles of freedom.

Should you find tracks of a wandering horse in trail dust or mud, kick the pony you're riding into a lope. Carefully scan every glade you pass; your lost horse might be standing in a nearby patch of brush fighting flies. Keep watching for his tracks. Pray.

I've talked a lot about "him," but a bunchquitter will most often be a her. Mares, you see, are more prone than geldings to wander away from other horses.

If you've got a bunchquitter that flees your society and heads up-trail instead of back the way she came, get rid of her as soon as you hit civilization. Sell her for whatever you can get and be happy you didn't lose a hundred cents on the dollar!

Now, ain't the sound of those bells beautiful? ∎

Woolly Mammoths and Saber-Tooth Tigers and ... and ...

We'd been climbing steadily for three hours when at last we topped out at the Summit House. The building was locked, its windows boarded. The huge lift stood motionless, its chairs appearing poised for a leap from mountaintop to empty parking lot shrouded in clouds far below.

We detached our skinny skis and walked around the porch and catwalk, pointing out distant peaks thrusting above the cloud layer. A raw breeze bit inside our jackets and parkas, so we gathered on the lee side of the shuttered alpine restaurant and elected to eat lunch. A mid-November sun slanting in from the south reflected from building walls with surprising warmth. Conversation ebbed and flowed. I tuned out.

The top of the cloud layer was a good thousand feet below and I recall being disappointed that our valley's big lake wasn't visible. Nor the Bad Rock area where our home is located. Let's see, it'd be over there, near Columbia Mountain. Columbia and the entire Swan Range thrust far above the cloud layer. So did the distant Mission Mountain Range. I thought the towering pinnacles of Glacier Park absolutely gorgeous. And there was Teakettle Mountain surrounded by clouds that appeared to be flowing down from the north. I pondered the phenomenon, then the discovery hit me!

"Is this what it looked like when glaciers lay across this land?" I blurted.

"Huh?"

"What did you say, Roland?"

"Look out there," I said, throwing an arm out like a revival preacher at a tent meeting. "Clouds have filled the valley. Only the mountaintops are visible. Is that what this land looked like when the great northern ice sheet moved in? Geologists tell us only the highest mountain peaks stood visible above the ice."

Silence fell over our little group as the vision was confronted or embraced—I couldn't tell. But how could they not capture the image? The cloud layer's top was white, with tiny hillocks and crevasses breaking the monotony—just like present-day glaciers of Alaska and Greenland. Though the layer was motionless, it appeared to follow visible creek valleys into river valleys. From the Stillwater and Swan and Whitefish river valleys, from the North, Middle and South Forks of the Flathead, the cloud layer flowed forward and onward until it merged into one massive sheet stretching south toward Polson and Missoula and Salt Lake and Mexico City—as far as the eye could see.

It *must* have looked like this during the glacial age: jagged peaks standing as islands above the ice; isolated pockets of spruce, whitebark pine, and alpine fir surviving on these islands to re-seed the barren land as the ice began its slow retreat; lower-elevation species such as cottonwood, larch, and Douglas fir no doubt crept up from the south and over from the west to reclaim land belonging to them prior to glaciation.

I began to pant, so caught up with the image was I! I tried to imagine what other vegetative successions took place during glacial retreat. Grassland first, no doubt, then brush and trees. Grazing animals must have followed the grass, with carnivores in hot pursuit: woolly mammoth and saber-toothed tiger. No doubt the huge cave bear was in there someplace, and small three-toed horses, and camels, and great stags, and packs of huge wolves. And man! Where was man?

"And so, what did Doris say when you told her that?" Jane asked.

Phyllis shrugged. "What could she say?"

POP!

I sighed. We were, after all, looking down at clouds, not ice. ∎

Just Another Overgrown Coyote

Roland!" Jane's voice, though subdued, held a note of urgency. "There are two wolves on that mountain."

I made a wry face and stared at the inside of the outhouse door. I've always dreamed of seeing a wolf. I *beg* to see a wolf. I'd like to hear one howl. But after two decades guiding people into some of the wildest country in the northern Rockies, the only evidence of wolves I'd ever seen was an occasional large canine track that had no vibram boot prints beside it.

We were in a little roadside picnic ground at Many Glacier. It was mid-April and snow still covered the tables. Snow was spotty up on Mount Altyn, but there was still too much for hiking. We'd already spent much of the day glassing several bands of bighorns and smaller bunches of mountain goats. Then, just before we headed home, I had this urge to more closely examine the campground's little outbuilding....

"Where?" I asked, hurrying to her side.

She still held my Zeiss binoculars to her eyes. "I ... I don't know. I lost them."

"You *what?*"

"They were right up there. Trotting across the hillside. They were dark. I know how badly you want to see a wolf. I just took my eyes off for a second to call you. I'm sorry."

I lifted the hatch on our car, took out the spotting scope, and began adjusting its legs. "You didn't mark them?"

When she failed to answer, I said, "You know, ma'am, probably the first thing I ever taught you about wildlife viewing is when you see something, pick out a nearby feature you can easily find again and *mark* that spot so you can go back to it."

She lowered the glasses. There were tears in her eyes. "I know. I thought I did have them marked. And I can't see how they could have disappeared."

"Okay, now where were they exactly?"

"See the band of sheep lying just above the big angled snowbank?"

I focused on the bighorns—a couple of dozen rams and ewes, all lounging calmly and comfortably, chewing their cuds. They were scattered across a hundred feet of grassy slope, all at ease. Not at all like one would expect wild sheep to be if wolves had just trotted past. Still, I've come to trust Jane's wildlife spotting abilities and if she says she saw wolves there, I wouldn't want to bet against her. "How far from the sheep were they?"

She raised the glasses. "Up the hill and to the left. I'd guess a hundred yards. Ten o'clock. Above the rock ledge. They were headed left, up the canyon."

I began systematically sweeping the mountainside, pattern scoping; starting low and working left to right in zig-zag increments, ratcheting the 20-power scope's objective lens up the hill to insure covering everything. As the lounging sheep again came into view, I muttered, "Those bighorns hardly look like a couple of wolves just trotted through their camp."

She became testy. "I don't care what you say. I know what I saw."

"How do you know they weren't coyotes?"

"Roland, I saw wolves. I know I saw wolves. They were dark. It's not as if I've never seen a coyote before."

The scope's lens swept over a ledge. I paused and swung back. Something strange was there. "Are those ears?" I muttered.

"What did you say?" Jane asked, still sweeping the hillside for her lost carnivores. When I didn't reply, she turned to see me focused on one spot. "Find something?"

"Mmm." The ledge had to be at least six hundred yards away. Yet, what looked to be ears poked up. I studied them for a few more moments before deciding my imagination was running away. Jane again lifted her binoculars as I resumed methodical sweeps with the spotting scope. A few moments later, however, I came back to the ledge and the ears. The ears were gone. I scratched my head and gazed over the top of the spotting scope. Yes, that was where I saw it, or them, or whatever. Again I peered through the scope. The ears were back.

Intent now, I watched until the wolf—and wolf it was—swung his head to peer up Swiftcurrent Canyon, then back to gaze down at the Bighorns lounging below. "Jane," I said, stepping gallantly from the scope.

"Ooh, do you see something?" She stretched to look. "Yes, you do. It's just his head peeking over that ledge. But this one is white. Mine were dark."

Again the wolf turned his head toward Swiftcurrent Canyon. "Maybe he's looking after his buddies."

We watched the wolf for nearly an hour. During that time, he laid his head on his paws several times, presumably to doze. Then he would lift it to look first down at the sheep, then up the canyon after his pack mates.

Still, I'd been unable to see anything but the animal's head as he lifted it to peer about. Apparently he was sprawled upon a ledge, with his head to the front, and because he was several hundred feet higher in elevation, we couldn't see the body. I tried howling—other wolf spotters tell me howling sometimes evokes replies.

"That got his attention!" Jane said, eyeing the animal through the scope. Sure enough, the wolf gazed straight down the hill at us. I howled again. Again he studied us. Then he popped to his feet and trotted off up-canyon, after his pack mates. The sheep watched him leave—just as some of them had all along been watching him lounge.

Meanwhile he'd studied them, watched after his buddies, looked our way, napped when it pleased him, trotted away when he wished. There was, as Jane said, no doubt this was a wolf.

There could easily have been a question, however, had he been slumbering in, or trotting through, or watching over a rancher's meadow—a question of whether he was wolf or an Alaskan malamute.

The wolf was cream-colored, with black ear tips. His legs were long and sturdy, his tail bushy and carried at half-mast. He exuded power; there was no slink to him. He was a wolf, pure and simple. Until then, the wolf was the one animal that had eluded me during all my wilderness adventures.

What surprised me most, though, was how the bighorns seemed to view him as just another overgrown coyote. ■

A Matter of Age and Degeneration

I knew I was in a world of hurt when cute young girls started smiling. These days when they see me waddling down the street or leaning against a lamp pole to catch my breath, every lady I meet will look me squarely in the eye and smile sweetly; perhaps they'll even pass along a few encouraging words. Back when I was younger and full of vinegar, members of the opposite sex wouldn't even stay in the same public auditorium I chanced into, let alone allow me to catch their eye. And speak? May the saints preserve them!

We're talking here of age and physical degeneration. Mine, not theirs. It's embarrassing that when I was twenty the Monicas and Celestes of the world helped me across the street with a spike heel planted firmly into my hind-side, while today they do it by taking my elbow and murmuring reassuringly.

I even tried leering at one in an attempt to recapture some of my lost youth. But all she said was, "You poor man—and Medicaid doesn't pay for good dentition, does it?"

Earlier this summer, a fashion model in sleeveless blouse and short-shorts picked me up in her red roadster. It could've been my dream come true, but she took me to my house instead of hers. Turned out she was on vacation; she's a home health-care giver in Connecticut. And she and my wife Jane spent an hour with their heads together on how to get more mileage out of Jane's old beater—which, I gathered, meant me.

It's strange, though, that I don't even know when the transition from "cease-and-desist" to "hold-harmless" began. Up to a certain age I was a pariah to half the humans on earth. Then I blinked and of a sudden gray-haired ladies spring from their seats in subway cars to offer me a place to collapse and rein in my racing heart. Perhaps fumbling for the nitro pills had something to do with it.

The truth is those tiny crimson nitros are really cinnamon Red Hots I pulled from the supermarket candy counter and transferred to a plastic pill bottle with the image of a lightning slash through the skull and crossbones.

Another truth is that I'm comfortable with my cover. Learning the doddering limp twenty years before I eased into it naturally took intense study and superb physical acumen. Instead of perfecting the artistic style of an Alan Alda, I spent all my time developing into a shuffling Alfred Hitchcock. At least this way, pretty young things smile at me and older, more mature things cluck with pity and feed me slices of apple cobbler with cups of warm milk.

There are definite advantages to maintaining my ancient, debilitated facade. This way I get to stand in the same storefront alcove with the opposite sex and wait for a bus. If I do it right, the cute one will assist me on board and help me to a comfortable seat. If I really do it right, she may even sit beside me and hand me a kleenex for my runny nose.

It's something she wouldn't do if she saw me striding over mountaintops in my normal Jim Bridger gait. If she knew how virile I yet am beneath the turned-down brim of my slouch hat, she'd probably have taken another bus.

What's that? No, no. The lady has nothing to fear. After all, I *am* on Social Security. ∎

Solicitors of Solitude

We hiked to scenic Rock Lake in the Cabinet Mountains Wilderness. The trail—actually an old, brush-filled mining road—climbed along the East Fork of Rock Creek, passing through a series of tumbledown corrugated-iron shanties and old prospect holes. The buildings and diggings provided mute testimony that the region once crawled with secretive men whose single object in life was to keep their nearest neighbors oblivious to discovery of an offbeat streak of color snaking through a chunk of quartz.

As our trail switchbacked up the mountainside, we passed the dark hole of a horizontal mine shaft that seemed to leave an entire mountain exclaiming "Oh!" in surprise. And there were rusted remains from an old stamp mill: an eight-foot-diameter flywheel and a disintegrating metal boiler.

Mining men, so I'm told, are still interested in this hillside, this drainage, this mountain range. It was gold that attracted them before, and it's gold now. And silver. And perhaps copper. Before, they scratched with pick and shovel. Today, such mining is done by boring mammoth holes to accommodate giant motorized ore trucks carrying millions of tons of precious metal-bearing ore from the mountain bowel to canyon mouth.

Rock Creek is a beautiful, clear, cold stream that has sufficiently healed itself from the effects of yesteryear's mining for westslope cutthroat trout and bull trout to call these canyon waters home. A broad, basin-bottom beaver marsh spreads along the creek's upper reaches. Telltale tracks in its mud show that the marsh is home to moose and whitetail deer. Wood ducks float its ponds. Harlequins, I'm told, fly the cataract mists where Rock Creek tumbles down-canyon.

I paused and marveled where men had labored. Just to penetrate this boulder-strewn mountain canyon was testament to stubborn will. Each square nail, each sheet of rusted corrugated iron roofing, each bridge timber and fallen-in outhouse and pile of mine tailings represented a dream, a prayer, loads of sweat, and buckets of tears. Especially the tears.

The day I climbed to Rock Lake was the first time I realized that prospectors of yore had to be at least the equals of my mountain-man heroes when it came to backwoods savvy and survival. True, trappers from David Thompson's Northwest Company brigades probably penetrated to these beaver ponds shortly after Lewis and Clark passed through to the south, but the beaver men were only here a brief time and left. And they limited themselves to poking up stream bottoms, leaving the brooding mountains to themselves.

Miners, on the other hand, stayed until they starved, hope died, or they struck it rich. They clambered up the highest peaks, dug holes into the most dangerous mountainsides. (The mine shaft and remains of the old stamp mill on the way to Rock Lake was athwart an avalanche path!)

Mountain men were, by the nature of their work, given to gregariousness during their summer rendezvous. Miners, conversely, were solicitors of solitude, secretive, suspicious. According to tradition, even on the rare occasions when they were driven by weather or hunger to the outside, they slipped surreptitiously about towns, ferreting out saloon corners so dark and dreary even sheepherders shunned them.

Those miners are gone from anything but history. Today's variety occupy boardrooms and employ engineers, geologists, and chemists to do their exploration.

I found it difficult to reconcile the differences between the two on my way to Rock Lake. ■

Cats in Question

I've tried. But I simply cannot regard mountain lions in the same detached way I view grizzly bears. With the big ursids, I'll trust a modicum of understanding on my part and prudence on theirs to lead to mutual survival. But with mountain lions?

Is there something sinister about the big cats? Grizzlies can certainly kill you; even eat you. But seldom does a bear pine after sunburned rib steaks wearing sunglasses. Cougars, on the other hand, rarely eat huckleberries, and usually think of any creature, four-legged or two-, as nothing more than potential pot roast.

I'll take my chances with either. But at least I can expect *Ursus arctos horribilis* to be up front about it if I displease— say, by rounding a trail bend and bumping unexpectedly into a grizzly sow with suckling cubs at her side. In that case, I'll expect things to grow sticky in a hurry.

But there's little up front about the sneaky felines, and God made them that way. They stalk their unwitting prey, attacking by surprise from the rear. A cougar attack on humans is never—as it is with bears—preemptive to quell a threat. With cats, their attacks are predatory. You're their breakfast porridge. *Finis.*

Do I fear mountain lions? No, not especially. I'm a six-foot, two-hundred-pound, adult male human. I'm a predator myself—I don't fit their prey mold. But my grandson does. And maybe that's what makes the big cats seem especially sinister.

In widely separate Montana incidents, six-year-old boys were recently attacked by young male lions that were beaten off by bystanders. In an Associated Press report of one attack (at the Birch Creek Trailhead), Joey Wing spotted the cougar watching him and shouted, "No! No!" Then the boy turned and ran. The boy's flight actually might have triggered the cat's predatory instinct.

There have been hundreds of mountain-lion attacks on humans across Western America. It's disconcerting, however, that cougar/human encounters seem to be accelerating. Most attacks are on children—the humans better fitting the cats' prey image. Sometimes the attacks have been on a lone child; sometimes an individual has been selected from a group. Surprisingly, given the big cat's efficiency as a killing machine, not all attacks are fatal, probably because most cougars preying on humans seem to be young and inexperienced.

That lack of feline perfection in the killing art is one reason many experts on *Felis concolor* believe the big cats have expanded in numbers to fill their available habitat, requiring immature animals to establish their territories in less desirable places—where humans congregate.

Contributing to the alarm are the youth and inexperience among us humans who may be viewed as survival food by hungry cougars. How can parents prepare a six-year-old in proper response when staring through a hedge row into the yellow slits of a mountain lion's eyes?

How, in fact, do we adults respond to a cougar sitting on the edge of an elementary schoolyard watching kids at play? Folks at Longmont, Colorado, constructed an eight-foot chain-link fence around their playground.

Montanans, it seems, are more inclined to select cat-elimination as their preventive medicine. ∎

Bears and Men
Different Strokes for Different Folks

I picked up the phone on its second ring.

"Roland, the reason I'm calling is to let you know the bear that you wrote about was at my place last night."

"What bear that I wrote about? Which one?"

"You know, the Dairy Queen Bear. He was at my place last night."

Uh-oh, is this early morning caller a bear lover or bear hater? Is he mad at me for writing the truth about an animal he hates or is he fascinated by the animals? To buy time, I said, "How do you know it was that particular bear?"

"Big. Real big. A grizzly. Big hump. Hell of an animal."

Still no hint about how he feels toward the bruins. "Did you actually see him?"

"Oh, yes, in the yard light. We had it on. He nosed around our garbage can. Ate some bird seed. He tore up a bird feeder."

I sighed—probably a bear hater.

"I don't mind," the man continued. "It was wonderful just to see him. He's been here before, you know. In years past. That's what makes him so special."

So he's on the bears' side. I asked, "And you live along the Swan River, near Ferndale?"

"Yeah. Right on the bear's travel route. That's why we've seen him before. He's a beautiful animal." When I said nothing, the man added, "He's really shy around people, though. One time I flipped the light off and on and he really took off."

"Listen," I said, "I think it's great you'd call, but why me?"

He hesitated only a moment: "Because I know you care. I've read everything you've written about the bears. I learned a lot from your stories. I had no idea they were out there in this valley. Because of your stories, we started paying attention. Everybody who lives around me feels the same way. They all have copies of your story lying around the house and they're all rooting for the bears, too."

Well, maybe not all of them....

I knew Digger, the big male bruin that is officially registered as No. 22 in the Swan Mountains Grizzly Study, the so called Dairy Queen Bear, had recently lost his radio transmitter collar. So I asked, "Did the bear you saw last night have a collar on him?"

"No, not that I could see. But I've seen him when he did and this is the same bear."

"Any ear tags?"

"Not that I noticed."

I thanked the man for the phone call and asked him to keep me posted. Then I slammed the phone down, calling, "Jane! Jane! I've got news of Digger!"

That the giant grizzly is still out there, still okay, still moving as a wraith through the populated Swan Valley, should rate as a wildlife miracle. It was in 1992 that I wrote my first newspaper column about a radio-collared grizzly inhabiting the environs of Bigfork. It was then that I passed along the animal's latest nickname: the Dairy Queen Bear. Magazine articles followed, and eventually a chapter in a book about the great grizzled beasts.

Digger—or the Dairy Queen Bear—was first trapped in 1989 as a three-year-old by biologists working Montana's long-running Swan Range Grizzly Study. That means the animal is now into his teens.

That a male grizzly has lived so long in the wild is unusual.

That he has lived so long while spending much of the last six years amid the fleshpots of mankind is phenomenal.

If you have news of this great beast, let me know—I do indeed care.

⸻

Jane's and my closest encounter with a grizzly bear came the morning after a Spokane book-signing tour. We'd arrived home late, slept in later than usual, then decided, what the heck, let's go hiking.

Jane was perhaps ten feet behind me, hurrying to catch up after pausing to tie her shoe.

"I'm not sure how interested in bears Spokane people are," she said, picking up our conversation's thread. Just then she screamed as dense willows and tag alders to our right erupted!

I whirled, shouting, "What is it?"

"Bear!" And as if she'd waved a magic broom, the woman was in my arms, with me between her and the bear.

"Get your bear spray!" she ordered, as if I wasn't already fumbling for it when I spied the brownish streak bursting up the hill.

"Get your own," I snarled, shaking free from her, freeing my canister and flipping off its lock.

The encounter was close. And it was sudden. Too sudden, too close. We were hiking the trail to Glacier Park's Huckleberry Lookout. Berries were ripening along the path, as expected in late summer. Since Huckleberry Mountain is prime grizzly habitat, and since we'd spied evidence of bear activity along the trail, we were both on high alert, carefully scanning hillsides around each trail bend, talking, making noise.

The bear, after crashing away, paused a mere thirty feet from us and lifted his snout to the wind—I clearly saw his nose wrinkling. Then he wheeled again and crashed away. "I can't believe this," I said. "He's acting as if he didn't know we were here."

"Do you suppose he was asleep in his day bed?" Jane asked.

There could be no better explanation of why I had missed spotting him in the brush. Obviously I would've been looking for a standing bear, not one sprawled on his belly fast asleep. The bruin must have slept hard, too, or he would have heard us coming. But, my gosh! when he rocketed from the brush, he was only six feet from either of us—almost within handshake range.

After our palpitations slowed, I noticed Jane staring oddly at me. "Something bothering you?" I said.

"Just wondering ... do you *really* know how to talk to bears?"

I grinned. "He went the other way, didn't he?" Then I sobered. Had it been otherwise, an attack would have been instantaneous, and nothing we could have done would've prevented it. No time to jerk out a canister of pepper spray. No time even to throw ourselves to the ground and cover up.

But the bruin took care of us. He did what ninety-nine percent of his cousins do day after day, year after year. And more often than not, we don't even know it happens.

Still, it's sobering. We were hardly unsuspecting novices. After we'd spotted the first telltale digging and fresh bear scat, we'd adopted every known precaution short of turning back. And not once did we dream we could get so close to a fully grown animal without his taking fright or otherwise letting his presence be known.

"Perhaps someday I'll write a book about bears," I joked.

My wife gave a nervous laugh. "It's hard to believe that less than fifteen hours ago you were in Spokane talking to hundreds of people *about* bears. And here we are the next day, absolutely alone in the mountains, talking *to* bears."

<hr>

It was our first November grizzly. I believed it to be a male. He wandered lackadaisically across a riverbottom gravel bar, almost under our feet. The animal was as big as a small pony, his color a dusky silvertip, perhaps muted by the river water still dripping from his fur. When he turned to amble away, his hind end was as broad as that of a Wild Kingdom hippopotamus. And when he swung his head to stare our way through a few leafless cottonwoods, he looked as though his tiny-eyed face could hide an oncoming Peterbilt.

We whispered too loudly, nor could he have missed the oohing and ahhing coming from seven throats. But the awesome bruin simply didn't give a damn. He wandered idly for a few yards, then began tearing at what must have been the remains of a long-dead animal. Then the bear plopped down and was hidden from us by waist-high dead grass. So we moved to a better vantage point—still on the high bluff—and in the doing, stupidly lost his location altogether.

Minutes went by while we whispered back and forth, discussing whether the bear would move again. I told the others, "We have maybe an hour until dark. If he doesn't move soon, we'll have to give up."

Then Marilyn gasped. The bear was sitting up, staring directly our way through the dry grass. He was approximately two hundred yards distant. When I focused my ten-power binoculars on that massive head, the shock of our eyes locking made me involuntarily step backward. Again the animal plopped down.

But he was up and moving within five minutes, shuffling like a hospital patient staggering from bed to toilet and back again. "He's lethargic!" I said. "He's so close to hibernation that he doesn't want to move."

As if to punctuate my observation, the bruin sat abruptly and stared about, tiny eyes only half open. Then he was up and turning our way.

We eyed nearby trees, selecting suitable ones to climb, just in case.

Again the bear plopped his hind-end down and stared about. Something about a nearby twig caught his eye and he bit it from the branch and chewed methodically. Then he collapsed into a heap, laying his head on outstretched forepaws. The animal appeared to snooze for upwards of ten minutes before sitting up again to gaze about. He focused for a couple of minutes on his human observers, then lay back down to snooze once more.

The next time he roused from his slumber, it was to amble nearer our high post. Apparently he was only interested in drinking at a spring flowing from beneath our feet. Again the bear lay down. Again he rose to a sitting position; again he sprawled.

A hundred yards was his nearest approach to our position before he wandered in the other direction. Then darkness settled along the grass-filled slough that swallowed the giant. I shouted, "Thanks, bear!" And we turned for our car.

What was such an animal doing out and about the North Fork river bottom so late in the year? Was he one of the big males that have learned to stay out all winter by taking kills from wolves and mountain lions?

Tell the truth, we didn't care. We cared only that he was there.

I was at a press conference on a controversial proposal to reintroduce grizzly bears to the Selway-Bitterroot Wilderness. My role was to report my findings (researched for my book on bears) concerning the changing attitudes of folks living around grizzlies. Instead, I fielded a couple of questions not previously considered. I did poorly. The lesson was that it's hard to come up with answers until you know the questions.

The questions I found especially troublesome were from Idaho reporters: (1) What do you say to Idaho people who tell you they simply do not want the grizzly? (2) How do you respond when people tell you they have an unreasoning fear of bears?

Now that I've had time to think, I could probably take another shot at those questions.

For the first: Whether it's appropriate to reintroduce grizzly bears to Idaho may not be a decision of Idaho residents alone. The question strikes at the heart of the Endangered Species Act. The Act, it seems to me, is a manifestation of the will of all the people of America to retain certain species of wild animals—manatees in Florida, condors in the Canyonlands, and grizzly bears in the mountain West.

In every part of the United States there are wildlife species in short supply. Some of them require habitat peculiar only to certain regions, and it's within those regions that recovery must take place. Idahoans, if they had their druthers, might druther recover manatees instead of grizzly bears. But Idaho hasn't the proper habitat; Florida is where manatees must live. Remote Idaho mountains, on the other hand, must be grizzly country if grizzlies are to be. Grizzlies once roamed Idaho's central mountain country. God put the creatures there; we wiped them out.

For the second press-conference question, I should have said something like this:

If it is the will of America that grizzlies are to be returned to Idaho's remote wilderness, the question of the Gem Staters' fears of the great bears must be addressed. Will those fears cause Idahoans to shun recreation in their own wildlands?

Not if we judge by the experience of people living where bears roam in Wyoming and Montana. Not even if we judge by the experience of folks living in North Idaho's Panhandle, where as many as fifty grizzlies roam the Selkirk Mountains.

It's true that some Idaho residents may not choose to venture into backcountry inhabited by grizzly bears, just as there are some Montana and Wyoming folks who fear to venture outdoors for fear of bears, cougars, snakes, wasps, and unknown boogeymen. There are also Idahoans and Montanans who've never taken up downhill skiing, flying in airplanes, or even swimming. But does that mean no one should have the opportunity to ski, fly, or swim?

Each of us must confront fears throughout life. In fact, overcoming unwarranted fears—fear of height, darkness, snakes, bugs, mice, or mumps—might well be the essence of life itself. If your fear is greater than your love of the wilderness, you'll stay home and more's the pity. If not, you take sensible precautions and venture forth.

Boy Scout troops and church youth groups tread Bob Marshall Wilderness trails. So do grizzly bears. How many kids have been injured by bears?

None.

As one man said when I was researching my book:

"To me, it's a gift to live in a country so rich in life's quality [that would allow an occasional grizzly bear to pass through]. You can have a million dollars, but no one can buy such a gift." ■

Dostoevsky vs the Compleat Angler

It's a giant paradox, this obsession we each have for trying to please our mate; a terrible nightmare almost as bad as stumbling through a blizzard after a wasted evening arguing politics and religion at the Dog & Duck.

Am I really as bad as she thinks? Yes, it's true I can't pass a fingernail test, but my leprosy cleared up last week and the ebola virus hasn't reached my bathroom yet, so I ought to tell myself I'm a happy man. But how can I when my wife takes stock of the man in her life and is disappointed? After all, I wear underwear without sleeves and shun garters to hold up my stockings. So I don't sleep in pajamas—so what? There are precious few tattletale smears on the collars of my boiled shirts and she won't discover any catty women whispering behind their hands about me.

While it's true my suits sag, they only do so because they were cut for a man thirty pounds heavier. It's her fault. She's the one who suggested I lose forty, then starved off fifty—the real reason I woke up in the Dog & Duck in the first place.

So I'm no mechanical genius, and electrical squigglies leave me squirming, so what? Truth to tell, there are just too many complications. Take battery-powered electric socks and dual-control electric blankets—I'm just not the type. I'm not even the type who sleeps or smooches with one who is. My taste, you see, runs to snuggling with descendants of pioneer women who baked buffalo, shot grizzlies, and had babies, simultaneously, while reading Thackeray and Dostoevsky before breakfast.

Our problems, Jane's and mine, are more cosmetic than substantial: she wants a sporty roadster, I want a four-wheel-drive pickup. We buy a lemon-yellow sedan. Its color is blue. The lemon denotes the fact the speedometer was rolled over twice. And the yellow means I'm afraid to drive such a piece of junk.

If she wanted a younger man, she should have married me earlier instead of waiting clear up 'til I reached nineteen. I will admit, however, there's no way she could've known about my uneven teeth since I smiled but little and laughed not at all during our courting years. Too, nice folks didn't chew or smooch with mouths open in those days. And she's got to agree the bald spot shining through my curly locks caught us both by surprise.

The lady might have a valid complaint about all my fishing and hunting. But her complaint would carry more weight if she didn't occasionally whip out her six-shooter (actually my six-shooter, but she never lets me carry it) and pop the heads from grouse at forty feet. And danged if the little woman can't float a grey hackle through a ripple as neat as any man alive.

Bake a buffalo? Naah, the last one came out on the tough side. Shoot a grizzly? I hope not, her six-shooter is loaded with .22 Shorts. Have babies? Yep, they were grand. Then they turned into teenagers.

Her real problem is Dostoevsky. Thackeray she digs. Even Chaucer. But when it comes to Dostoevsky, my woman still struggles at suppertime. She plugs for Tolstoy instead.

Now you can readily see why we have such monumental marital problems, Jane and I. But we'll work 'em out. How do I know? I just gave her a copy of Plutarch for Christmas and she handed me *The Compleat Angler*. ■

Writing About It Brings Tears

Whatever do you people do with all the horses?"

We'd lived in Montana only a few years when my favorite aunt visited. Her home was in the hill country of Texas, where she and her late husband had farmed and run a small dairy. She was apparently surprised at the number of horses she saw scattered on ranches and farmsteads during her drive through Montana.

"Do with horses?" I said. "Maybe I don't understand the question. What're folks supposed to do with horses? We ride them."

"Why? Why ride a horse when you have a perfectly good pickup truck in the driveway? And a car in the garage."

I chuckled at this lady who'd proven so kind to a hell-raising kid during a particularly unmemorable period of my youth. "There are lots of places in Montana where we can't take vehicles. We ride horses into those wild places."

Just then a couple of neighbor kids passed our place astride their ponies. "Lots of folks ride for pleasure, too," I added.

Aunt Lemma clucked disapprovingly—I suppose at the thought of wasting perfectly good grass and hay on something as uncommercial as the useless nags in our pasture.

"I thought Texas had lots of horses," I murmured.

"We do. But nothing like I'm seeing here. We have breeding farms and ranches—some run to thousands of acres. But it seems like every home in Montana has a horse behind it. Sometimes, like yours, more than one."

I've thought of Aunt Lemma over the years—how she was appalled at the unsensible way we Montanans keep horses for pleasure instead of profit. Times change, of course, and in the last thirty years even Texans may have discovered methods to waste money over and above bare necessities.

Today's Montana has a generous share of breeding farms and ranches specializing in blooded stock of all breeds. There are show horses and performance horses, racing horses and rodeo horses. There are draft horses big enough to shade a freight truck. But still, by far, most equine types in the Treasure State are just plain "usin'" horses.

We're so serious about it that often our blooded stock are also usin' stock. They labor up mountainsides laden with heavy packs just like grade nags from down the road. They all scramble over rock outcrops and windthrown trees, plough through bogs and snowdrifts and swollen rivers because we cherish our legacy of mountain men and mounted warriors, gold-seekers and cowboys. We recollect how hunting parties once trekked for weeks by horseback through forbidding wilderness. And we wish to be part of that legacy, carrying it into the future for our kids.

Economics be hanged. No matter how mean the farm, ponies graze. Behind most Montana homes and cabins, horses take shelter from keening winds. In a corner of tumbled-down sheds, well-worn saddles and bridles and halters and nosebags collect dust. And occasionally that dust is blown off and those ponies are saddled. It might be when cutthroats are biting up the South Fork, or when elk are bugling in the high basins.

But the when isn't important. What's important is that it's done. And we and our horses are the better for its doing.

One of the paradoxes of horseback packtrips into mountain country is that the more proficient you become in the art of packing horses, the less memorable such adventures become.

My first attempt at horsepacking the vitals for an overnight trip into mountain country took place almost fifty years ago. It was such a fiasco that for a decade I shuddered every time I got close to equine troublemakers. Then I took another trial run. This time my nerves quit banjoing after only a year as a consequence of that drubbing. So I tried an extended packtrip into the middle of the Bob Marshall Wilderness. That took another year to get over. In time, though, the peaks got lower and the valleys shallower until I hardly remember the later, easier excursions. But every single one of those earlier "adventures" is subject to total and vivid recall, even after decades and with the burden of an aging memory.

There's a funny metabolic process that takes place if a fellow is a slow learner, though. By going back and going back, my horses got better and I got better. Our gear got repaired and refined. I trained a wife, grew my own helpers, and gained the confidence of most people who don't know me. My horses became resigned to their fate and even began to enjoy working their way into the freedom of the wilderness. Nowadays Jane and I can unload the ponies at the trailhead, hang nosebags on their heads, brush 'em, saddle 'em, sling packs, and be on the trail before they come fully awake.

Eight hours later, we'll pull the packs, hang another nosebag, unsaddle and brush the creatures, turn 'em out to roll. Jane will go for water, I'll gather a little campfire wood, and we'll both set up our tent and be relaxing with an evening cocktail before the sun moves toward the western horizon.

But once, it wasn't so.

In the early stages of my horsepacking fetchin' up, we'd blow two trailer tires on the way to a trailhead and get there long after lunch. One pony would ropeburn while backing out of the trailer and another would be halter galled while fighting the pine tree to which he was tied.

None of the saddles fit, no two packs weighed the same, we forgot one packpad, and the lady picked up the dry heaves on the crooked road from civilization. The trail was muddy, I lost my sleeping bag somewhere between Black Bear and Independence Park, the heaviest packs rolled three times, and one of the ponies learned how to shed his load, having watched how it was done so many times before.

The trail we followed was full of windthrown trees, and somebody was already camped where we'd planned to take up residence. It was okay, though, because full dark came when we were halfway to our destination and we had to pitch our tent in the middle of the trail five minutes before two Forest Service mule trains happened along.

We were up at first light because nobody could sleep with all the strange noises coming from the brush that closed in around our tent when the moon went down. Joe forgot the whiskey, and the extra I brought for medicinal purposes got broke the second time the damnfool mule rolled coming down Switchback Pass.

No wonder it took ten years to get over the first time.

※

Shoeing horses, pouring concrete, and cutting wood all rate as the toughest kind of grunt work for me. Especially shoeing horses.

I just get no peace of mind from climbing under a 1,200-pound animal, picking up the leg upon which he's determined to lean, using a set of rusty nippers from the bottom of my tool bag to pare a hoof he keeps jerking away; then pounding with a sledge on a piece of stiff iron to shape it to look like a shoe to fit a hoof that no longer looks like an equine footpad. Where's the fun?

Back in the days when I ran thirty head of stock in my outfitting service, I'd bring in a professional farrier to do the job. Don Stafford could do in a day what it would take me a week to accomplish. Owen Klapperich can shoe a steady two horses per hour.

Me? My back is sprung, pants torn, and hair disheveled just thinking about it. I'm grimy of face and palms and under every fingernail that's not ripped off from the effort. In addition, my boots are trampled from the top and soiled with road apples from the bottom. My face has been tail-switched for flies, and the last pony took a nip out of my hinder when I quicked him with a nail.

No, thanks. Having found out how easy it was to bring in an

expert to shoe an entire herd, I adopted the same policy for the four ponies Jane and I kept after selling our guide service. Perhaps there's irony in asking a professional to tack footware on what may be the four most gentle steeds God ever made. But collectively, those four horses weigh well over two tons and I have only a one-ton back.

Horseshoes and I have an exaggerated history of histrionics. The only thing that kept one from breaking my back was the fact that the horse planted it in my belly and there was sufficient padding between.

Another horseshoe once caught me in the thigh. It had a horse tacked on the other side of the shoe. What happened was I tried to cut him off as he darted for an open gate. He won the race. I lost the ability to walk without a crutch for a week or two.

But the most nimble piece of footwork I ever saw was with a horse named Jughead—the one who never learned to gracefully accept folks fiddling with his feet. On the day in question, I'd hefted Jughead's left front to reset a shoe.

The pony didn't like it, of course, but what could he do? After all, I'd lashed him to a stout corner post that was actually an old railroad crosstie planted three feet into the ground. I was whistling Yankee Doodle when that horse kicked the watch from my wrist with the hind foot from the same side—without falling on his buns. Jughead was back standing on all fours before I figured out what had happened.

I had another horse named Lobo that might have more properly been named Loco. No, he wasn't crazy—he never had enough brains. In fact, standing alongside a chunk of busted asphalt, Lobo appeared severely retarded.

Lobo especially impressed me the day he stepped on my foot while I adjusted a pack. Naturally, I howled. The horse turned clear around to see what was bringing me to a screech—without once lifting the foot that pinned me to a rock outcrop.

Just writing about it brings tears to my eyes. ∎

Are Yellowstone Bears
More Aggressive?

Grizzly bears following the sound of gunshots to an elk
carcass—and charging the hunters who were butchering their winter's meat? Sounds far-fetched, doesn't it?

That's what I thought, too, when I started research on an
article for the Rocky Mountain Elk Foundation's *Bugle* magazine. My assignment was to find out whether the grizzlies
around the Yellowstone Plateau might be honing in on gunshots. I went into the assignment somewhat—uh—skeptical.
Imagine my surprise when biologists for both Wyoming's
Game & Fish Department and the Fed's Interagency Grizzly
Bear Study Team told me they believe it's happening.

When I told them I outfitted for over twenty years in the
area south of Glacier Park, the biologists rocked my beliefs
about grizzlies even more by telling me I may have dealt with
bears less dependent on meat for their diets than are Yellowstone bears.

"Down around this park, we don't have the lush plant
growth—the berries, rootstocks, nuts—like you do up there,"
I was told. "But what we do have is a lot of protein hitting the
ground in the form of gut piles from elk at the precise time
when our bears need to put on weight for hibernation."

"What kind of verification do you have for that hypothesis?" I asked.

I was sent to Dr. Charles Robbins, Professor of Wildlife Biology at Washington State University. For a number of years, Robbins and his students have studied hair and bone samples from bears all over the world. Robbins' research has disclosed that meat makes up roughly eighty percent of male bears' diet in the Greater Yellowstone ecosystem, forty to fifty percent of females' diet.

By comparison, according to Robbins' research, meat (protein) makes up just two percent of the diet of Glacier Park grizzlies.

Here in simplified terms is how Professor Robbins and his students research grizzly eating habits. Living matter is made up of a combination of elements. The elements present in the hair of an animal are a reflection of what he or she has been eating. Hence, the atomic signature of the bear's hair tissue reflects the animal's diet.

Nitrogen atoms are the key to the bears-eating-meat-in-volume conundrum. Most nitrogen atoms have a mass of 14, but roughly six of each thousand atoms in living things have one extra neutron, giving six of each thousand a mass of 15. Nitrogen-15 accumulates as it moves through a food chain: plants may have two atoms of naturally occurring nitrogen-15, but deer feeding on plants will contain six, and wolves feeding on deer will have ten. Thus scientists, analyzing the nitrogen-15 composition of a bear's hair tissue can accurately assess his diet.

So grizzly bears around Yellowstone really do appear to be more dependent on meat than the bruins of Glacier. But does that make them more aggressive in pursuit or defense of protein? Are Yellowstone bears more protective in defending a gut pile left by a hunter butchering an elk than a Glacier bear in protecting a rich huckleberry patch?

And are Yellowstone bruins honing in on gunshots? If so, what does this learned trait portend for elk hunters?

Nate Vance guided hunters in the Thorofare area, south of Yellowstone National Park, in northwestern Wyoming. Before daylight one morning in the autumn of 1994, the unsuspecting outfitter and a hungry grizzly wound up trying to get into the same bear-proof camp grocery box at the same time.

The food cache was a pit in the ground. Heavy-duty metal packboxes containing perishables were stashed in the pit, then covered with a frame-reinforced plywood lid. Two 24-inch logs pegged with horsebells for burglar alarms lay across the heavy cover. It wasn't the handiest set-up from which to retrieve a slice of bacon, but thus far the camp's food supply had not been hit by marauding bears.

Breakfast comes early in Wyoming hunting camps. A few days before, in order to expedite its preparation, the slender mid-forties cook had rolled the 250-pound logs off the cache alone. Her reward was a sore back. As a consequence, outfitter Vance tried to be on hand to help the lady access her larder.

It was long before daylight on the third day of the Cowboy State's archery season when Nate struck a cooktent fire, lit a couple of lanterns, and sat back with a cup of coffee for a moment's respite. He'd just taken a sip when he heard the cache bells ring. Thinking the cook had awakened early and was again moving the logs without assistance, the outfitter hurried to help.

"I knew I'd made a mistake when the cooktent door slammed behind and there was no light at the cache."

Coming from the illuminated tent into close darkness, Nate could see nothing. He said he'd just taken a step back, fumbling behind him for the door, when he was struck a mighty blow on his forehead. Mercifully, the blow knocked him unconscious.

A half-hour crept by before Nate Vance's eyes fluttered open. Blood soaked his shirt and pants and trickled into his boots. He ached as though he'd been struck by an eighteen-wheeler.

He pushed to his feet and staggered into the cooktent; the effort started his wounds seeping anew. Grabbing a lantern, Vance stumbled to the guides' tent. It was a hell of a way to begin the day with the boss bursting into their sleeping quarters, weaving in the flickering lantern light, bathed in blood. "I need help!" the injured man croaked.

It was Nate Vance's good fortune that a doctor hunted from his camp on that fateful day. Surgeon Byron Brown of Dallas,

Texas, had become something of an annual archery-hunt fixture in Teton Wilderness Outfitting's camp.

Pepper, salt, and napkins were swept from the cooktent table and the injured man laid upon it. Buckets of water boiled as Dr. Brown assembled the instruments of his trade. Some eighty stitches later, the outfitter was helped to his feet so he could limp outside amid bright sunshine and survey the attack scene.

There was a pool of blood where Vance had lain unconscious. "But," he said, "the end of the cooktent was sprayed with streaks of blood, like I was flung around like a rag doll." The man paused while reflecting on the little he remembered of his mauling. "There was a big center post that holds the ridgepole for the fly [a large plastic sheet covering the cooktent]. There was a big splash of blood on that center post, too, like he'd thrown me against it—but I don't remember."

"So you don't know how long he worked you over?" I asked, looking up from my notes.

"No." He paused, then added, "I surprised him. It was my own fault. I just didn't think. I thought I heard the cook out there; by rushing outside without giving the bear a warning, I got inside his space and he acted on instinct to remove what he thought was a threat. He probably threw me around like a puppy wagging a dirty sock. Then when I didn't move, he quit me."

"You don't even know for sure that it was a grizzly?" I said.

It wasn't the most brilliant question I'd ever asked, and Vance looked down his nose in disgust. "The tracks told us what kind of bear it was."

"You refer to it as a 'he'—how can you know?"

"I just know it," the man replied. "I'd spotted a big male only a half-mile from camp the day before. He didn't scare. He was—well—he was arrogant. Then, too, the tracks around the tents were all *big*. It's sort of marshy behind camp and the mud was all tracked up. There weren't any small ones there. It was that big boar. I know it."

Nineteen ninety-four was a bad year for Teton Wilderness Outfitting, with hunters or guides stumbling into repeated field confrontations with grizzly bears on the prowl for nourishment to sustain them during hibernation. It's called

hyperphagia—the autumn process of bears laying on sufficient fat for winter—and bears are implacable and can be
ferocious during their search for the food that will sustain
them.

"Why do you feel 1994 was such a severe year for bear
encounters?" I asked.

Nate shrugged. "I guess their natural food failed—I don't
know. Maybe the pine nuts just weren't there. Or strawberries
in the summer. Maybe the fish runs were down. All I know is
we could hardly turn around without running into a grizzly."

<hr />

After five years of leading hunters from Vance's camp, Todd
Sanner was one of Teton Wilderness Outfitters' most experienced guides. Just a day after his boss tangled with the
food-cache bear, Sanner called in a bull elk to his hunter's
bow. It was just at dusk when Jimmy Wages put two arrows
into the bull. Mortally wounded, the elk fled down the mountainside.

The men tracked the bull in fast-fading light until they
spotted the animal standing against a tree, apparently dying
on its feet. Night fell. Fearing the animal might yet bolt and
they'd lose him in the darkness, the hunter and his guide
headed for camp, intending to return the following morning.

With frequent bear encounters weighing on the guide's
mind, Sanner asked his boss for advice on how to approach
the bull. Vance, who had deigned to return to civilization with
his injuries "because I already had the best doctor in the country," suggested that Sanner take Wages and the man's hunting
buddy to help bring in the elk. The outfitter said the men
should take a position above their quarry, watching the area
carefully for a while to make sure no bear was in the vicinity.
Then—and only then—should they go down and begin
butchering the bull.

Sanner, equipped with a .44 Magnum sidearm, led the way
from camp, followed by Wages and Jim Privia. Neither man
carried a bow, but Privia packed a .357 Smith & Wesson
revolver—grizzly bears weighed heavily on his mind, too. The
party found the bull where they'd left him the previous

evening. The animal lay on its side, lifeless. Taking their outfitter's advice, the three men watched the elk for nearly an hour before approaching. No bears had visited the carcass. Sanner started to work.

Two hours later the quarters were skinned and bagged, and the guide had the cape nearly removed, with only the critical nose left to peel. Suddenly, Privia yelled: "There's a bear!"

Sanner leaped to his feet. Seventy-five yards down a steep hillside meadow, a sow grizzly led two half-grown cubs along a game trail. The sow stopped and lifted her nose into the air. In an instant, she broke into a gallop up the hill, directly for the men.

Sanner got off two rounds from his magnum, both into the dirt ahead of the charging bear. Then the sow was upon the guide, leaping a log and smashing him down while airborne.

As bear and man went down in a heap, the sow had Sanner's head in her mouth. She left canine-tooth punctures on the underside of his jaw and atop the head. In desperation, the man jammed the muzzle of his .44 against the bear's head and pulled the trigger. At the same time, Privia rushed forward and fired two rounds point-blank into the bear's torso.

Dust and twigs and grass and leaves flew. So did the bear, dropping Sanner and rushing back the way she'd come, spurting blood all the way.

"We never did find her," Nate Vance said. "When Game Warden Tim Fagan came to investigate, he and I tried to track her down. But it just wasn't any use."

⚬

Nate Vance's hunting area lies hard against the southeast corner of Yellowstone National Park. The camp itself is sited in the Teton Wilderness, close to the headwaters of the Yellowstone River, thirty miles over Deer Creek Pass from road's end. Few places in America are so remote. Perhaps no other place in all the lower 48 is home to so many grizzly bears. Vance says grizzlies are increasing, alarmingly so:

"When I first started outfitting twenty-six years ago, my hunters would often ask if they might see a grizzly bear. I'd tell 'em that if they're lucky, they might spot a *track*. Now we're bumping into them all the time."

"How often?"

"Between me and my guides, we'll see one pretty near every day."

"Every day!"

"Sometimes more."

A broad grin spread across Vance's face, then faded. "When I first started outfitting, we considered it a treat to just see a grizzly bear, even at a distance. Now, it's getting to the point where you see so many it's scary. It ain't fun any more."

He dropped his eyes to stare into his glass. "Now—and it's a hell of a thing to say—but I just hate the thought of being around grizzly bears."

The man pleaded for understanding: "My hunters and my guides—they're counting on me to take care of them. And I try. But after a while, with bears so close and so frequent, a man starts to get complacent. Maybe you'll let 'em get too close one too many times—you know what I mean, don't you?"

I don't really know what Nate means because I've never, during all my years guiding near Montana's Glacier Park, encountered grizzly bears with the same frequency as this veteran Wyoming outfitter. I do know enough about the massive animals to respect their strength, agility, and intelligence. And they're still thrilling for me to watch. But could there be too much of a good thing?

"This past season," Nate continued, "I was in the backcountry for sixty straight days ..."

I leaned back in my chair, tapping a pencil against my notebook.

"... and there was only two days that I didn't have either myself or my guides within a hundred yards of an adult grizzly bear."

I thought of the adrenaline rush that comes with finding yourself within a few yards of a grizzly. Then I thought of having that happen day after day, for eight to ten straight weeks.

"They're close to camp. They're out in the woods. It's no joke that they follow gunshots to downed elk."

The outfitter has had grizzlies attempt to take meat away from him before he's through butchering it. "I've had maybe eight to ten assault charges over the last fifteen years. Some were bluffs, but some were not."

Nate is a great believer in a relatively new innovation for dissuading grizzly bears. "I've stopped two of them with pepper spray within ten feet. I know each of 'em would've been all she wrote if I hadn't blasted them with the spray. Nowadays I work on butchering an elk with a can of spray in one hand, my knife in the other."

Nate's wife Julie had listened quietly. Now she murmured, "What about that moose this last year?" Her husband grinned. "Nate went back to get horses while we skinned and quartered the moose. Then one of our hunters walked down the trail a little way and came running back to tell us grizzly tracks overlaid the tracks of Nate's horse." She shook her head. "He was out there someplace, watching. So when Nate came back, we stood around in a circle while he caped the animal—two men armed with high-powered rifles and me with a can of pepper spray. It was like Wells Fargo agents standing guard over a gold transfer."

I asked the outfitter if he had trouble with bears while guiding for summer trips. He shook his head. "Maybe they're all up in the high country turning over rocks for moths or feeding on pine nuts. Then, too, there's so much daylight in the summer. We're never out at dawn and dusk on those trips—not like hunting season. Morning and evening is when grizzlies are most active—you know that—and hunters are poking into every tiny forest meadow or wet spot or thick patch of timber…."

Julie said, "During hunting season we even run into them on the trails at night."

Vance nodded. "Nobody believed me when I first told them grizzly bears were following horse trails, cleaning up bits of grain that pass through our stock. But when they started looking and found no horse poop around any more, they began believing."

Nate Vance retired from outfitting five years earlier than he'd originally planned, selling his business at the end of the 1998 hunting season. "I just couldn't take it any more. Too much responsibility. Too much weight. Too much danger."

Still, the man doesn't hold a grudge against the bears. He

considers the grizzly to be one of the most magnificent creatures God ever made. "But we've got to do something to control problem bears. There's just getting to be too many of them. And some of 'em no longer have any fear or respect for us."

"Some people propose limited hunting of problem bears," I prompted. He nodded. "But, Nate, I know how hunters might sit up over gut piles from previous elk kills, and I know how random are the bears that might be attracted to one. I also know we hunted black bears by spotting them from a distance and stalking. How can you be sure limited hunting will take out the problem bears?"

He nodded again. "Maybe we have to give the job to a warden."

"Like a government hunter?"

"Roland, I feel there are only eight or ten bears in all the Thorofare country that no longer respect humans. They're the ones causing all the trouble. There must be *some* provision for eliminating those animals or *all* grizzlies will suffer."

Nate must have mistaken my thoughtful silence for hesitation because he added, "The grizzly recovery program is a great success. They're back in a big way. It's time the Endangered Species Act was modified to permit some way to exert a little more local control."

I *was* thinking of the Endangered Species Act, and how it has unquestionably contributed to the bears' return. But a second thought stole in while Nate talked: Exit the Colt and the Winchester and what does a grizzly bear have to fear? Absent the Colt and the Winchester, will *Ursus arctos horribilis* once again occupy the throne that was his during the stone age? Will the playing field then be level? If so, will I, like Nate Vance, no longer wish to play on that field?

As I closed my notebook, Vance said, "Our hunters and guides were all gone and it was just Julie and me alone at the end of the season. We broke camp for the last time and headed out. You can't possibly know what relief we felt when we loaded the last eight head of stock and started for home, knowing we didn't have to come back."

"You will, though," I said. "You'll go back because it's in your blood."

He shook his head. "No I won't. I'll never go back to any place that has grizzly bears. From now on, I only want to visit places where we *won't* ever see another one."

Julie Vance shook her finger at her husband. "Even on that last trip out, we ran into a grizzly standing in the trail in the dark. Remember?"

Nate Vance nodded. How could he forget?

On December 10, 1998, Nate and Julie Vance sold their Teton Wilderness Outfitting business to Clanton Lindsay.

Other Yellowstone area outfitters besides Nate Vance have had encounters with grizzly bears over elk carcasses. Dean Johnson, an outfitter in the region for more than thirty years, said he never even saw a grizzly bear during his first seven years, but now he and his guides average one a day between them. Johnson's hunters lost two elk to grizzly bears just last year.

Lee Livingston is another Cody area outfitter with considerable experience. I asked Lee what his policy is if a grizzly bear tries to claim an elk carcass. "I give it up. What else can I do? I'm not going to shoot the bear. Same with the guides. I've instructed all of 'em to give up an elk if a grizzly wants it."

I'll confess that I began researching this story about conflicts between grizzlies and elk hunters with several preconceived notions. Grizzlies defending a carcass or a gut pile they found unattended? Yes, that was easy to visualize. But grizzlies trying to take a carcass away from hunters while the humans are butchering it? That seemed far-fetched to me. During the course of my research, however, there came some shocks.

The fact that some bears can be essentially carnivorous contradicts my experience.

It's also remarkable that success rates for elk hunters are so high around the borders of Yellowstone that grizzly bears are changing their feeding habits to hone in on a seasonal bounty of gut piles.

But I'm still dubious about bears cuing on rifle shots for two reasons:

1. Lots of rifle shots occurred during my outfitting and guiding years that did not result in kills—target practice and clear misses, for instance. In fact, there were so many rifle shots echoing around the mountains we hunted that if a grizzly had honed in on them he would've starved from spending more energy in chases than he recovered in calories.

2. Bears are also coming to bowhunter kills.

My wife is not so sure. She reminded me that a Brittany spaniel who once owned us learned to distinguish the sound of the cookie-cabinet door opening from the sound of the other cabinet doors. She also points out that our horses obviously recognize the sound of my truck engine revving up at feeding time. She's right, of course. Animals do associate sounds with food, and bears are highly intelligent. On the other hand, the squeak of cookie doors and roar of truck engines have a higher degree of reward probability than does a rifle shot echoing amid the peaks.

Are Yellowstone bears really more aggressive than those in the Glacier area? How could they not be more possessive and thus more aggressive if they are dependent upon meat and find that meat in concentrated but widely scattered gut piles? We're not talking about huckleberries scattered over an entire mountainside. We're talking seventy or eighty pounds of the richest kind of foodstuff that would fit in a number three washtub. And we're talking about some puny human trying to contest it with a huge, hungry grizzly who desperately needs it if he's to survive a tough winter.

It's not a game I'd care to take a hand in. ■

Man's Humanity Toward Man

The man staggered down the switchbacks to the creek crossing. He'd been three days on the trail, and it had been one nasty creek crossing after another. Thank God for the bridges at Little and Big Salmon creeks, and the one up ahead, across the South Fork at Big Prairie. Now, however, he must negotiate Bartlett Creek. And like all the others it was in spring flood.

After shrugging from his heavy backpack, he spent considerable time finding and cutting a just-right staff to help him keep his balance in the torrent. Then he pulled off his boots and stockings, tied the bootstrings together and hung them around his neck, slipped into his sixty-three-pound backpack, and stepped gingerly—barefoot—into the frigid, chocolate stream.

Bartlett Creek in flood is about thirty feet across at this particular trail ford. The swift water rose to the man's knees, but he braced with his staff and picked his way to only ten feet from the far shore. Then he slipped! Fighting to regain his balance, he had only one thought: The boots! Keep the boots dry! So he snatched them from around his neck and gave them a mighty fling.

Unfortunately, they fell short. Somehow the man regained

241

his balance, only to lean helplessly against the torrent and his staff, and watch his well-oiled boots—a pair of hand-made White Loggers—bob down Bartlett Creek, on their way to the Pacific Ocean.

An hour later, men and women of the U.S. Forest Service trail crew from the Big Prairie Ranger Station spotted a lone backpacker crossing the station's abandoned airstrip. One of the lads remarked that the newcomer walked peculiarly. When the backpacker staggered up, they saw he was barefoot. At that point, he was thirty-two miles into the Bob Marshall Wilderness.

"Don't you have at least a pair of sandals?" someone asked.

The man shook his head. What made his plight worse was that he wore size 14s.

Gene Brash, the Forest Service packer, rode in later that day. Gene is a big man, and he wears size 14 shoes.

"All's I got extra is my airport boots," the mule packer said when told of the backpacker's plight. Gene's "airport boots" were a pair of worn Red Wings that he only donned to catch mules in the mornings' dew-wet grass of the old airstrip. "They ain't much, but you can use 'em. But, by God, I gotta have my airport boots back."

The desperate backpacker swore he would return the worn footwear.

Gene forgot about the incident. Three weeks later, a package for him arrived unexpectedly at the Big Prairie Ranger Station, brought in by another packer. Gene opened the package to find a new pair of boots. But wait! These boots weren't new—they just looked new!

They were his old Red Wings, newly half-soled and cleaned and polished to a fair-thee-well. "They looked so purty," Gene later told me, "that I hated to put 'em on to wear out in the wet grass."

There are a bunch of lessons in this tale of the barefoot backpacker—not the least of which is man's humanity toward man. But the most important is the wisdom of taking a second pair of footwear during any wilderness adventure. ∎

When You Should Feel Sorry for Yourself

J ane told me I should've known better.

I said, "What's the big deal? I'm the one who spotted 'em leaving."

The fact that we were camped on a narrow ledge, twenty miles deep into the Bob Marshall Wilderness, and half of our horse herd was headed for neon lights may have had something to do with the lady's consternation. Added to the dilemma were these other deplorable considerations:

1. The trail we followed to this incredibly remote—but hauntingly lovely—place was tortuous and exhausting to both man and beast.

2. The Wind Gods tore savagely at our exposed canvas tent, whipping it mercilessly with rising gales. In my experience, more and bigger storms were certain to follow.

3. Rain squalls screamed over the cliffs towering above, sleet peppered the tent roof, and snow dusted talus slopes down to the ledge where our squalid little hunting camp squatted. The temperature was dropping fast, alarmingly so to Jane.

I peered again toward the two horses: the white mare

grazing placidly as she headed for the distant pass and the docile bay gelding who appeared less certain whether they were doing the right thing.

"I thought you said the grass was so lush here they'd never leave," Jane said, shivering against the chill.

"Umm."

"You said you needn't keep them in hobbles because this is such a great natural pasture."

I grinned and picked up a couple of halters. The departing ponies dipped into a little ravine, then reappeared on the other side, still traveling unhurriedly. I debated saddling one of the two remaining ponies, but simply ambled afoot after the delinquent steeds.

I soon overhauled BJ and made my second mistake by walking directly toward him. After all, I can catch these ponies anywhere, I told myself.

Ha! The gelding bolted just as I neared, triggering the mare to gallop toward the pass, throwing clods as she fled. BJ galloped behind.

It took me another hour to clamber down over a cliff, then follow a second ledge for some distance before climbing back to peek over a rock cleft. As expected, without my pushing them the ponies had settled down to feed.

I slipped farther up-trail, screened by stunted trees and rock clefts until I got between the horses and the narrow pass where they were bound. Now their only escape route was back to camp.

Escape? Who said anything about escape? I walked up to both ponies and slipped on their halters, then led them back to Jane. She breathed a sigh of relief; after all, it was a narrow thing. We returned home the following day. Had the nags succeeded in their daring get-away we would've been more than merely inconvenienced.

I'm a guy with forty years of experience and I still did several things wrong: no hobbles, left them loose after their bellies were full, chased them instead of heading them. Tommy Triplett, a respected former Forest Service packer and outfitter, once passed along this pearl of wisdom:

"Get to feeling sorry for your horses, son, and that's when you should start feeling sorry for yourself. ■

I enjoy your radio program which airs on KMTX at 10:45 a.m. Now that I have caught on to your show, I try to take my coffee break at your airing time, and enjoy your program very much. I find it informative and you are witty and humorous and very knowledgeable about the outdoors. Hopefully this winter while my husband is home tying flies, he too will get hooked on your program.

Rosalie Richards • Helena, MT

Congress Did It, Congress Can Undo It

et's say you have a pond on your place. It has catfish in it. Ducks and geese land on the pond in the spring and fall. And let's say you have a grain field, with scattered, brush-covered foothills snuggling on three sides. You also have car payments to meet, a mortgage on your home, and the little woman's washing machine is on the fritz. Then you must take on some of your mother-in-law's nursing expenses, and the county tells you they're upping your taxes because you have lakeshore frontage. On top of that, you've been downsized to three days a week at the creamery where you work.

The pothole pond is popular with your neighbors, but some folks complain because the trail to it is overgrown with briars and muddy when it rains. You can hardly stretch your declining budget to meet your expenses, let alone their wishes.

That's pretty much the scenario facing the U.S. Forest Service with declining timber sales and a Congress unwilling to dip into the general fund to finance trail and campground maintenance or administrative costs of developed recreation.

But let's assume your neighbors insist on a regularly maintained trail so they can picnic at your lake. What would you do? Charging them a fee might be one solution. And you might tack a surcharge on to pay for cleaning up the garbage some of the slobs leave scattered about. Of course, it costs something to collect the fees, so tack on another surcharge.

From there, the leap isn't long to drain off a little of those picnicking profits to help defray your mother-in-law's medical costs—after all, you must eat, too. Nor will it be long before your wife rebels, demanding a new washing machine, so you decide to up your profits by charging pheasant hunters for entry into your grain fields and partridge hunters for access to nearby foothills.

Naturally, since maximizing profits also maximizes problems, your administration must expand to include fee collection at a variety of entry points. So will enforcement to keep out deadbeats who try to utilize your resources without paying for the privilege. Enforcement and additional fee-collection points will cost money, of course, which must result in ever higher fees.

By now, you're riding high, raking in profits hand over fist. A new expansion prospectus discloses that you'll bring more visitors who'll pay more money if you pave the path to your catfish pond, as well as install attractive welcome gates and dispense hot coffee to hunters visiting your grain field. Welcome gates and paved roads are, of course, expensive. But what the hell, you'll just up the fees!

Incidentally, every farmer along your stretch of road has noticed how you're raking in cash from being neighborly, so they all begin doing the same. If a visitor wishes to hunt your grain field, he'll have to pocket-dip at your place, then do the same at the next farm, and the next. Soon, the hassle is nickel-and-diming visitors to death. The question of whether they'll pay to access your resources may be academic anyway, because word is out that there are no catfish in your pond, pheasants in your field, or Huns in your foothills.

This scenario is, of course, a fictitious metaphor for what may (emphasize the *may*) happen on federal and state lands.

Knowledge of the past is essential for guidance to the future. I'm not the first to say that; Santanyana probably spun his powerful admonition from something said by Peter the

Hermit, who paraphrased Plato, who stole from Socrates, who, ad infinitum....

If you'd like a clear example of how this lesson can affect you in outdoors adventure, let me pass along the results of a recent odyssey Jane and I made to Utah's Canyonlands:

There were no other cars at the trailhead to Moon House ruins. Our friends had, the day before, taken us to the Towers, a mesa-top site of what is thought to be crumbling Anasazi signal towers. There are also ancient Indian pit houses on the mesa.

"You'll love the Moon House," Ruth said as we exited our vehicle. An information sign and registration box stood nearby.

"Let's see, it's going to cost us two dollars each," Ruth's husband drawled, fishing in a metal box at the sign-in spot for a numbered permit envelope.

"I don't have any money," I said. "My wallet is back at camp."

Royce began filling out the form. "It's all right, I'll cover you and Jane." Then he said, "How about a Golden Age Passport—do you have one? You can hike for half-price if you do. All we'll need is the number."

"How the hell do I know what my Golden Age Passport number is? It's in my wallet back at camp."

The next day we visited the Citadel, an ancient Anasazi stronghold. This time I was fortified with both cash and my Golden Age number when we reached the trailhead—$2 for under-age Jane and $1 each for us three senior citizens. This time, however, on our return there was a bright red citation under our windshield wiper because Royce had forgotten to prominently display our payment stub on our vehicle dashboard.

We paid again when, the next day, we visited the Seven Kivas site deep into Roads Canyon.

"Boy," Jane said, "this would get expensive for a family of five, wouldn't it?"

The answer is yes. It's a money-making venture, pure and simple—a public milking machine with your government as sole franchisee.

If there are benefits accruing to the public from fees paid

by visitors, in this case the Bureau of Land Management is doing a lousy job of clarifying them. Regularly marked trails into that stark canyon country are virtually non-existent; instead, trails are defined by wherever people can pick their way below clifftops and down through boulders and along tilted slick rock to reach canyon bottoms.

I can understand recovering the cost of management from folks benefitting from that management. But I saw no management, only collections. There is no rationing of use, no limit to the number of visitors allowed at the Moon House or the Citadel or the Seven Kivas—only limits to how much they can afford to pay for the right to visit their own land.

It's the government's Fee Demo Program come home to roost.

Incidentally, how can struggling young families or the economically disadvantaged cope with these onerous fees? By being shut out, I guess.

When Congress created the Recreation Fee Demonstration Project, permitting government agencies to charge fees for visitors to federal lands and keep the money where it was raised, light bulbs flicked on in agency offices all over America. Hence, four national forests in southern California charge fees for almost all recreational uses of the lands they control; and trailheads on Oregon's Willamette National Forest cost five dollars to enter.

Formerly, there was no charge to park vehicles or to launch a raft or kayak on the Chatahoochee River in South Carolina; now it costs $2 to park and $20 to launch. Formerly, it cost nothing to camp overnight in Glacier National Park's backcountry; now it costs $2 per person per night. And that's a bargain compared to Grand Canyon, where there's a $20 permit plus $4 per person per night.

National forests and the Bureau of Land Management appear to be moving more slowly in my state, but who can doubt that it's a wave of the future? Fee Demo is a sobering trend that has all the appearances of being regressive, coming down particularly hard on the young and the poor. I expect to see a day, shortly, when we'll be nickel-and-dimed to death with fees every time we drive up to a launch site or parking lot, hike a trail, or drop by a lake.

What to do? Search me. All I know is Congress did it. Congress can undo it. ∎

Mountain Lions Grow Desperate, Too

"Can you believe this?" I said to my wife as we slung our daypacks to begin our low-level trail hike from Lake McDonald Lodge to Avalanche Campground in Glacier Park.

"Take it while you can," she said.

You bet—it was almost Christmas. At this time of year this region would ordinarily be socked in snow so deep the only way folks could venture here would be on skis or snowshoes.

We paused at John's Lake long enough for me to wing a flat stone across its surface. "Look at it skip!" I shouted to Jane. "And there's some as would say I can't skip rocks."

"We'll come back after the ice melts," she replied. "Then we'll see."

Perhaps a half-mile past John's Lake, I spotted an unusual elk rub and called it to Jane's attention. She watched as I tramped through brush to a seven-inch-diameter Western red cedar that had been peeled for its first eight feet. Shreds of bark hung down in long strings.

As I examined the rub, Jane pointed to a tree forty feet away. "What about that one?"

I looked, then did a double-take. The tree was sixteen inches in diameter, and it had bark hanging in shreds from a spot fifteen feet in the air.

"That wasn't done by any elk or moose," I said.

"What then?"

"A bear or mountain lion. I'd guess a lion."

She studied both trees, then asked, "Couldn't the first—the one you call a rub—have been done by the same animal?"

"No." I returned to the first tree and showed her how its bark shreds were peeled from the bottom up; how they were only attached at the top. "Can't you picture the sweep of his antlers as he worked on the tree?"

Jane nodded.

"Now look at the other tree. Too high for any animal to reach from the ground, and notice how the bark is stripped from the top down. It's pulled. Like a housecat scratching a bedpost."

Jane returned her attention to the first tree. "And you say that one was made by an elk. How do you know it wasn't a moose?"

"Good question. Considering how marshy some of this land is, it probably was a moose."

"Are there no tracks, so you could tell for sure?"

"Come on, honey. That rub was made two months ago. I'm a pretty good tracker, but I'm not one of Louis L'Amour's heroes."

The amazing thing was that two such fine displays of large animal action were so close to each other. As Jane and I hiked to Avalanche Creek, our senses were sharpened and we discovered dozens, perhaps hundreds, of Western red cedars along that trail had been used as scratching posts by an oversized tabby. The cat had climbed some of them and had stood on hind legs to scratch others. Some of the trees appeared as though she might have sat on the ground while taking a swipe.

But my Lord, the extent of the markings—there are a plethora of red cedars growing along several miles of trail and the cat had marked at least half. It was an impressive display of territorial marking or sexual advertising. I'm a little weak on mountain-lion habits and communiques, so I asked a biologist who is into lion research.

"A mature tom advertising his attributes," the guy said. "Cedars are their tree of choice. From what you've told me about the extent of his marking, I'd say he's desperate." ∎

Tricks in the Outdoors Trade

The campfire blazed merrily, the tent was erected, bedroll laid out. Supper lay behind us. As shadows stole across the quiet land, we had but to slide into the satiny linings of our zipped-together mummy bags. But because we wished to get an early start in the morning, I shaved feathers on a piece of pine pitch for quick ignition.

Jane had seen me do it dozens of times, but she watched nevertheless. "Bud Sayre taught me this," I said.

"So simple. A one-match operation," she replied. "But there are probably a lot of people who don't know the trick."

I closed my clasp knife and reached for the headlamp we would lay alongside our sleeping bags. "There are probably a bunch of great outdoors tips that are routine to us. Automatically, I unsnapped the back of the headlamp case and aligned all four of the tiny double-A batteries.

"Like that one."

"Like what one?"

"What you just did with the flashlight batteries."

I looked down and smiled. She's right, of course. Each night I align the batteries to provide power for the lamp. Each day, especially when we plan to move camp, I reverse two of the batteries so the lamp won't flick on if its switch is accidentally activated.

"What other tips might we know, Jane? They might be worth writing about."

"How about the flashlight itself?" she asked.

"Right," I murmured. We began using headlamps back in the old days, when we operated our guide service into the Bob Marshall Wilderness. Headlamps were so much more sensible than the old hold-'em-in-your-mouth D-cell flashlights, especially for saddling horses before daylight. Even better than hanging a gas lantern from a tree limb because there are no shadowy places a headlamp won't illuminate if you swing your head in that direction.

Jane yawned, stretched, and headed for the tent. A second later I heard her mutter at a reluctant tent zipper. "We need to soap these zippers again," she said.

"Rub bar soap on zippers to make them slide easily," I wrote.

As so often happens when two people have been married for decades, we were on the same wave length: "How about soaping the bottoms of pots and pans before they go on an open fire," she called, just as I was writing the trick down. It was a practice we discovered forty years ago: wipe liquid soap on pan bottoms before blackening them. Cook with them for your entire trip, taking care not to wash the outside of the pot when cleaning the inside. Then at the end of the campout—or sooner if you feel the need—wash the outside. It's messy, but the pot or pan will clean to a shiny fare-thee-well.

"What about getting lost?" she called from the tent.

"Getting lost," I muttered. So I wrote, "Deck of cards."

This one is a tongue-in-cheek trick. If you get lost, all you need do is pull out the cards and begin playing solitaire. Someone is sure to come along to tell you how to play the next card.

The real trick behind this little essay is to trigger your thought processes to recognize some of the little things you already employ to make your adventures easier or safer and thus more enjoyable.

There are more than you think. Share them with others. ∎

Meriwether Wouldn't Recognize It Today

Meriwether Lewis, writing in his journal on June 17, 1805, reported:

"Saw a vast number of buffalo feeding in every direction around us in the plains, others coming down in large herds to water at the river."

The location was at the top of the Great Falls of the Missouri, where the expedition was momentarily stymied. Lewis tells of watching the leaders of the buffalo herd being crowded into the river by others shoving from behind, then plunging to their doom over the precipice.

"I have seen ten or a dozen disappear in a few minutes."

The Captain surmised that buffalo carcasses, washed up below the cataracts, were one reason for the unusual number of grizzly bears inhabiting the region and bedeviling his party.

Farther upriver, Co-Captain William Clark discovered a giant spring. Clark writes: "[It is] the largest fountain or spring I ever saw, and doubt if it is not the largest in America known. This water boils up from under the rocks near the edge of the river and falls immediately into the river eight feet...."

Lewis, on the plain above the cataract and giant spring, wrote on June 30: "Great numbers of buffalo in every direction. I think 10,000 may be seen in a view."

I sat behind the wheel of an automobile at an observation point above the Giant Spring and the Great Falls of the Missouri. The date was August 8, 1997. Much has changed in the 192 years since Lewis and Clark stood here. Such as:

> The Great Falls of the Missouri are a mere shadow of the magnificence chronicled by Captains Lewis and Clark. The reason? Much of today's river flow is diverted through turbines for energy production.

> If Captain Clark wished to view the Giant Spring today, he'd have to pay to see what God wrought since the state of Montana charges visitors to view the spring—as if the governor, legislature, or Fish, Wildlife & Parks had anything to do with its construction.

> Today, the closest approach grizzly bears make to the Great Falls of the Missouri is while traveling through the area on Interstate 15, ensconced in a trailer-borne culvert trap after being removed from some distant campground.

> The vast plain where Lewis watched 10,000 buffalo graze has changed, too. To the southeast, jet fighters rumble from military runways; to the south and west, skylines are dominated by subdivisions and shopping malls. Across the river to the north, where buffalo crowded their own kind into the river and thence over the roaring falls, the scene is still pastoral—but the buffalo are gone, and in their place I counted 182 power poles marching in and out of an electric substation with no more apparent order than an unruly bison mob.

All in all, looking at that landscape and comparing it with the detailed chronicles of our nation's first official Western explorers, I wonder if we've been responsible stewards. Change is inevitable, I know. But a chill washed over me as I wondered aloud what this scene would look like in another 192 years. ∎

You Reckon There's Something Wrong with Me?

Ice fishing has never been a riveting activity for me, mostly because I associate a certain modicum of discomfort with the sport. I get cold.

I'm outdoors a lot during all kinds of weather, at all times of the year, and I've been known to laze away half a day while leaning against a yellow pine, chewing a grass stem and contemplating my navel. But only during mild weather. Wintertime *contemplation* is limited to lounging before a crackling fireplace blaze and scratching an itch. Winter outdoors *activity*, for me, is just that.

Being active—snowshoeing, skiing, sledding—is a highly effective antidote to icy cold seeping into my innards. Squatting for hours on a block of wood with a blanket pulled over my head while staring down a four-inch hole between my feet doesn't exactly raise my pulse rate and warm the cockles of my heart.

The only real rise in body temperature I've experienced during my ice-fishing adventures was while plodding across a frozen lake surface, pulling a sled loaded with necessities: stool, ice spud, fishing equipment, dipper screen for slush removal, tarpaulin or blanket for throwing over my head, thermos bottle, lunch, heavy mackinaw.

All you need in order to learn how unwilling your body is to subject itself to the day's coming activity is to turn around and observe your backtrail. Are your tracks lined out, traveling straight across the lake from point of origin (warm, comfortable pickup) to the frozen, ice-covered weed-bed where the sucker you hope to sucker may or may not be you. Your tracks are not lined out straight and purposeful. Instead, they'll look as though they were laid out by a drunken moonshiner riding a blind mule through a snowstorm.

I have a photograph of a man plodding across an ice-covered lake during a blizzard. The man is wearing snowshoes and, as nearly as I can tell in that near white-out, he's wearing wool trousers and a plaid wool coat. His hands are clad in mittens, his head in a stocking cap. The poor guy looks like he came right out of Sam McGee—you know, "the Night on the Marge at Lake Labarge."

It was an award-winning photograph. It was mine. I wish I had not been there to take it.

The photograph came while my partner and I plodded forlornly up Stanton Lake in what is now the Great Bear Wilderness. We headed for reed beds growing at the upper end. When we reached there, my partner immediately spudded out a hole, lay down on the snow, pulled a blanket over his head, and began jigging with an ice fly. I even have a second photograph to prove the guy actually engaged in this disgusting behavior.

Me? I found a sheltered copse of trees and built a warming fire.

I stayed warm and comfortable. So, by all apparent indications, did my friend. I grew bored. He seemed to enjoy himself. He caught fish. I didn't.

A few years later, I was back on the ice at Stanton Lake, this time skiing with my wife. A winter sun was out. High winds had earlier swept the ice free of snow. Then a trace of powder fell. We've never before or since experienced such conditions—fifteen feet of glide with each stride! Race to the upper end, then race back. Then giggle and laugh and race again.

I caught no fish that time, either. But I enjoyed that second time on Stanton Lake much more than the first.

You reckon there's something wrong with me? ■

I was intrigued by your column on memory nuggets....
There have been several such memories during my lifetime;
but I never thought to give them such an appropriate name ...
[one] nugget which will always be with me happened only
about three years ago. I've always known that monarch but-
terflies pass through Omaha ... I live on the 18th floor of my
apartment building; and it is not uncommon for leaves, maple
seeds, and even hornets to come flitting past my windows,
caught up in the ever-present updraft. But late one afternoon
it was monarch butterflies riding the currents, performing
their exquisite ballet outside my windows.

Gwyneth Hurlburt • Omaha, NE

"Elsewhere" Avoidance - 101

Perhaps it's wise, as we approach the new millennium, to pause and take stock of our changing land, changing people, changing way of life. Most of us, I'm sure, view the coming century with considerable trepidation.

We were comfortable with the way things were. If possible, we no doubt would, as a people, return in a heartbeat to yesteryear. Though we occasionally made snide comments about our relative lack of cultural amenities, we were actually grateful for our location in America's backwater.

Relatively speaking, crime, drugs, gang warfare, and the other social problems of urban centers were alien to us. Our vast natural wonders were still largely intact. Neighbors were still neighborly, government responsive, air clean, water pure, and land spacious to distant horizons.

Only lately have we begun to realize we dwelt in a fool's paradise; that our values—family, culture, opportunity—were subject to the same social laws that govern change elsewhere. Only belatedly do we realize that elsewhere is no longer elsewhere, but rapidly approaching in a wave of discovery by the rest of America and the world.

In some measure, we've begun to defend ourselves, employing all the arguments and tools others have used unsuccessfully to combat changes to their land, their people, their way of life. And common sense tells me we will be no more successful than those who failed in other places.

Change is inevitable, and it does us no credit to rail futilely against it. Not only must we fail at stopping change, but to struggle against the inevitable is to squander energy and resources we can better use to channel change in ways that will benefit the place we love ... and us.

Though in many of our minds all changes are bad, some are worse than others. To see how bad they can be, take a tour through Appalachia or any megalopolis. Check out the slag heaps and decrepit row houses, mile after mile of repetitious subdivision, deteriorating inner cities, polluted air and devastated streams. Look at the beaten peoples; analyze the spread between rich and poor.

There is hope, however. Though our place is changing, the rest of the world is changing more swiftly. I learned that lesson several years ago while attending an outdoor show in Edmonton, Alberta. Several folks there passed our booth and smiled. "Montana," they each said, rolling the word as if they'd not like to let it go. One added, "The last of the Old West."

I stared at him, thinking of voyageurs, the Hudson's Bay Company, the vast reaches of Alberta prairie and northern forest. "Surely," I replied, "you people are part of the Old West, too."

"No," he murmured. "It's all gone."

That's when I realized that although Montana is changing, the rest of the world changes more rapidly. Ours will always be the last of the Old West because no matter how much we change, we'll be nearer to the remembered West than exists elsewhere.

If indeed we fail, it will be because we failed to learn the lessons others have been forced to learn. Simply said, we need to take stock of "elsewhere," and avoid as many as possible of those so called "advanced" elsewhere's pitfalls. ∎

Just thought I'd drop a brief note expressing my appreciation for coming clear over to Noxon for the Saturday night campfire. Really enjoyed your company and stories, and from what I've heard, so did many others. Your talent for captivating an audience is wonderful, Roland, and I'm glad I had an opportunity to stand by the fire with you.
Dennis Nicholls • Noxon, MT

What Really Is Advanced Intelligence?

Ever wonder what makes for advanced intelligence? Is the term an oxymoron? Compare us with the rest of the earth's animals, then tell me who's advanced and who's retarded?

We prefer to describe traits and actions of animals in terms we can understand—by humanizing them. When we train a dog to "shake hands," do we really think Rover does so because he's happy to see us? Given his choice, he'd much rather lick us in the chops. He lifts a paw only because we want him to.

"He's chasing rabbits," we'll say when the mutt jerks in his sleep. But is he? In his canine dreams, he's probably standing on hind legs to purloin a roast from the dining-room table.

Horses are "kid-spoiled," but what really happens is that the pony does the kinds of horse things it prefers, and the kids lack the confidence, heft, or temperament to get his attention.

Our anthropomorphic imagination is wildest when we observe wild animals. The mule deer buck lying on the point of a big ridge might not be "surveying his domain," but sound asleep after gorging himself on red-stem ceanothus just before dawn. The bull elk wallowing in mud might not be "cooling down" after a rutting tryst with a swaggle-hipped young cow. He might not be "fighting flies," either. He might simply like to play in the mud. The point is, *we don't know*.

We do know that the need to obtain food is the primary force controlling wild animals, and tame. Safety from predators is also important for any but those at the top of the food chain. Procreation has its seasonal imperatives, too. And of course there's the need for occasional sleep. But food is the constant biggie, having a bearing on how long animals sleep, what risks to take when hungry, even interrupting the mating process.

That's the way—if we choose to believe fossil records—it was for *us* in the Paleolithic.

In fact, it's the way it still is today, regardless of our false smugness at escaping the laws of nature. Like all animals, we still procreate, still need protection, still sleep. And like all animals, it's in food gathering that even modern humans spend the bulk of their time. Today, of course, we do it differently. Today we call it "work," but in reality it's food gathering. Then we come home to cook, wash dishes, take out the garbage.

Our homes are havens providing security for us creatures who are not so modern after all—so there goes one distinction about which we've been smug for years. And what we refer to as flirting or dating or sex is, in reality, merely a set of procedures leading to procreation. And lastly, what human beings—primitive or modern—get enough sleep during any age?

All the above makes one wonder how we must look through an elk's eyes. Does he think us primitive because we have yet to learn to live near where we gather food?

What must wild creatures think of our insistence on changing bed linens when it would be easier to change beds? How about sewer systems, ground-water depletion, and urban slums?

Just which creatures are advanced and which primitive? Is it possible that "civilization" is really taking us farther and farther from "advanced" living? ∎

Your tales are heartwarming, and I especially enjoy the special relationship you have with your animals.
Jo Ellen Wright • Mineral Wells, TX

I read your column regularly, and I usually find it interesting and informative.
Wendy Whitehorn • Great Falls, MT

God-Awful Horse Wrecks

I didn't see what happened. You seldom do. One minute the packstring is moving well. The next, the tail horse, loaded with an inflatable raft and criss-crossed oars, is straining back for all he's worth while the horse ahead of him is leaning into the strain. I swiveled in the saddle just as the pigging rope parted. It was a kaleidoscopic blur: the tail packhorse slipping from the steep sidehill trail, rolling three times, then somersaulting over a rock outcropping to disappear from sight.

I snapped my head around to look for a tree to which I could tie my string. The high clay cutbank had no saplings growing from it. Silence from below. Dead? I glanced back at the other nervous, stamping packhorses. Poor place to tie a string anyway. Lose another horse over the side if I don't get them out of here. I prodded my saddlehorse and the string shuffled on.

It was but a short distance before the trail crested onto a forested flat. I lashed my pack ponies to trees and ran back to where the rawboned palomino gelding had slipped from the trail.

There! Lying against that big spruce, nearly into the river! I leaped down the mountainside with ten-foot strides to reach the pony. Shattered bits of oars marked the route of the equine avalanche. The horse lay on the inflatable raft, upside down, four feet waving feebly in the air as god-awful moans escaped him.

I jerked the latigo loose from his cinch and unsnapped the breast collar. Then I grabbed his halter rope and tugged. It seemed useless. He was too far gone.

On the other hand, I thought, this horse is an idiot. So I picked up a length of broken oar and thumped him on his hind end. The horse thrashed once, then leaped to his feet to face me. I muttered a curse and examined him. Unbelievably, except for a few scratches, the idiot was unhurt.

Not so his packer, who had a 110-pound raft two hundred feet below the trail and an idiot pony that could no way clamber up where he'd somersaulted down. I began the laborious task of cutting out a winding path over which a clumsy packhorse could scramble back to the trail.

It was an hour later before the out-of-breath, red-faced packer shoved the raft up to the trail. And another hour before the packstring was again underway.

I've seen some awful wrecks during my years packing ponies in the high country. Many are the times I could have sworn there must be busted necks or limbs or hearts in the melee below. But it never happened.

There was even a time when my old saddlehorse Buck stepped into a gopher hole at a full gallop, somersaulted in mid-air and should have broken his leg, but didn't.

That's also the time I should have broken a neck, but didn't.

Once, a pack rolled on a horse, throwing him down a bank into the Spotted Bear River. One of my packers tied his string and hurried to help the first packer save pony and packs. When the second packer returned to his string, they were gone—broken loose and slipped from the trail. They were nearby, however; all of them standing in the river below.

All with packs beneath their bellies. ■

Getting Familiar with a Land

If you don't know how to read it, a map has less value to you than it does to a billy goat. A road map, for instance, is a baffling tangle of lines at first glance. But with practice and use, it's not hard to read.

Most maps have a key printed at the side or bottom. Take time to study it. The key explains that features of the map are in symbols instead of words. A heavy red or blue line is a main highway. Lighter blue lines are less important roads. Thin or broken lines are side roads, usually of dirt that can turn to mudholes during tough weather. Streams, railroads, bridges, roadside parks, and other features have special markings.

The key also shows your map's scale, or how many miles are represented by one inch. This is important to a camper hiking, riding, or pedaling through the countryside.

Geologic maps are usually known as contour or topo (topographic) maps. They're puzzling at first. But when you understand that the curving lines mean different terrain levels, you'll find they soon build pictures in your mind as clear as scale models of the territory. Each line marks layers of terrain that are of equal distance above sea level. The height of each layer is marked on the line in small figures. Circles getting smaller and smaller indicate a hill. Where the lines are close together, the hillside is steep. Where they're far apart, the land is gently sloping. Lines practically on top of each other mean a cliff. A row of V's in contour lines usually show a stream or gully.

The U.S. Geological Survey has most of America contour-mapped down to 7-1/2 minutes of angle (which translates into a rectangular area approximately six-by-nine miles). These maps are sold in many book stores and top sporting-goods outlets. Ask for help in finding maps of the area you wish to visit. Each map is listed by the name of its foremost topographical feature.

USGS maps usually show forest cover, swamps, marshes, depressions, glaciers, and deserts. Some mark buildings, bridges, and campgrounds. Current trails are most often indicated with dashed black lines. The map key is essential in comprehending its features.

After you become familiar with contour maps—I don't believe there's a way to become familiar short of on-the-ground use—you'll discover you can recognize landforms, such as benches, glades, basins, and other intriguing features within the area covered by your map. You'll learn by studying, then by personal application out in the field or forest.

When you're plotting a course to follow, don't choose the longest route you can cover in one day. Choose one that allows you to check out the most intriguing territory indicated by your map. Leave ample time for fun and exploration; for unexpected adventures.

When I'm exploring new country, I usually purchase four contiguous 7-1/2-minute USGS maps, then climb the highest point near where their four corners join. You can learn a lot about the lay of the land if you climb to a high viewpoint, lay a compass on your maps and read the combination, picking out prominent points or features. Then spend a few months—or even years, if necessary—exploring between those places you've identified.

It's the best way I know to *really* get familiar with a land. And when a foggy day comes and you no longer need a compass to find your way around in a country that has the familiar feel of your living room, *then* you'll know you've arrived. ∎

Always enjoy your articles! Especially the one about a guy using his scope to look at other hunters instead of using binoculars. That gets me mad, too!
Greg Muich • Vaughn, MT

I sure do enjoy your radio program, I listen to it while driving to work in the mornings. I have two boys that also enjoy listening to your stories.
Randy Fie • Monticello, UT

To Drag or Not to Drag: That Is the Question

In my opinion, dragging game in from the field ain't what it's cracked up to be. Despite abundant tales of successful hunters who've snaked record-book bucks and bulls from mountaintop to pickup box, I've always found such deeds hard doin's. Maybe it's because some of my successes haven't occurred on mountaintops, but in creek bottoms—and the access road or trail ran along a ridgetop far above.

I know folks who've solved this problem by utilizing a power winch and long cable. I can't address the viability of that method other than to say I'm acquainted with an unfortunate hunter who, while using a chainsaw winch to snake a big wapiti out of a mountain canyon, pulled a two-foot-in-diameter buckskin tamarack over on top of him. It took an ambulance crew most of that day to get my friend to a hospital for treatment of his broken back.

I once tried dragging a small mulie buck down from one of the original "rocky" mountains. Most of his hair and some of the meat disappeared from his carcass; and all of my smiling disposition disappeared with it. I spent several hours more than normal in cleaning and cutting the meat after getting it home. Jane said that buck tasted "wild" and made me vow never to drag again.

I also tried dragging a six-point bull elk through eighteen inches of snow. The mountainside was steep—perhaps sixty degrees—and I could see my vehicle parked far below. I pulled that bull perhaps five rods downhill, then gave up and started skinning and quartering the animal for backpacking.

I have a photograph of that six-point lying at the end of his drag—before I decided that backpacking four hundred pounds of elk meat was infinitely easier than dragging a dozer-blade of snow with an elk in the middle of it. The photo shows a track down that mountain that looks like an avalanche on the Matterhorn.

If you *must* drag your game, there is a *best* way to prepare the animal for dragging. For one thing, there's no reason to drag the animal's entrails. Cut the removal hole as small as you can and still do your job. Remove the entrails. Tuck the liver and heart back inside the cavity and stitch the hole closed with a piece of cord (shoestring will work). Take his legs off at the knees (they'll do you no good), then (if you don't plan on caping the head for mounting) remove and lash the antlers to your backpack—suitably covered with an orange vest or flagging ribbon, of course. If you plan to have the animal mounted, do not—I repeat, do not—drag him anywhere. Instead, cape him on-site and backpack the meat.

For actual dragging, a rope around the neck (a belt will do) with a couple of non-slip loops for hand holds, and you're ready to begin your ordeal. Stay out of the animal's way. Gravity is a strange and powerful phenomenon that can bring a two-hundred pound deer carcass galloping down a mountainside with unbelievable alacrity. If the carcass rushes past, let it go. Even if it plunges over a cliff (*especially* if it plunges over a cliff) and into a boulder-infested river, let it go.

There are, incidentally, better ways to pack out this year's meat than by dragging: backpack, horsepack, pickup pack. But if you insist on believing other folk's wild tales of how they drug a record-book bull across Russian Flats, why, try it.

Then tell me how you liked it. ∎

Our Way May Not Be the Only Way

I stood at the pit's edge and eyed the accumulated debris.
Much of the dump's content was of recent origin, but
some was ancient—if one can consider a teakettle with the
bottom rusted away as ancient. There were worn-out bed-
springs, a broken automobile battery, busted crockery, rusted
steel cans with indistinguishable labels, and an occasional jar
or bottle. Items of recent vintage were a few dented aluminum pans (one with a bullet hole) and copious crushed
aluminum beer cans.

Overall, I was struck by the relative scarcity of bottles and
realized I'd made a mistake....

Jane and I were visiting a friend who owns a huge Garfield
County ranch, some seventy miles from the isolated eastern
Montana community of Jordan. Since my rancher friend is a
noted connoisseur of liquids containing malt and yeast, I took
him a case of bottled finest from a micro-brewery that had
recently opened in my valley.

Our friend greeted us warmly, accepted the case with
gusto, and graciously extended us the run of his ranch for a
few days of wandering, hiking, photography, and—to Jane's
dismay—rattlesnake romping. We discovered the dump on
day two.

It was located in the hole of an abandoned root cellar whose roof had long since rotted away. I was frankly repelled by a sight that once was common to almost every farm family across America—the private dump. Yet … why was I repelled?

My wife and I are into the idea of recycling and think others should be so inclined. But where would these folks take their recyclables? Jordan? How many small communities can support recycling centers? Jordan claims less than a thousand residents. Let's see, Miles City is one hundred and twenty miles away and Glendive is one-thirty. Glasgow? Even farther. So, if not recycling, where was their nearest disposal site? Again, Jordan, the Garfield County seat. But how sophisticated could a disposal site be in a county that is Montana's largest in land but, with just sixteen hundred people, smallest in population.

The beer cans *were* crushed to save disposal space, demonstrating some sensitivity to a problem. There were few bottles because my friend isn't a slob. He's doing what he can in the best possible way, given his circumstances. I was the one who fouled things up by bringing him *bottled* beer.

We Americans are too provincial. We attempt to export our views, thinking our way of doing things is especially virtuous; and we expect everyone else to conform, even if circumstances render that way impossible for them. Worse, if some other world or community or individual fails to measure up to our arrogant standards, we bellyache. Hence the disdain of city dwellers for their culturally deprived country cousins; hence rural dwellers' disdain for city folk of any stripe.

I grew up thinking not so much that I was smart, but that my parents' intellect ranged somewhere between primitive and Neanderthal. Later I discovered Ma and Pa did have a little savvy, and thus began my pursuit of a doctoral degree in human survival. After a while, I even began to think I knew something. Until I stood on the edge of that Garfield County rancher's garbage dump, that is, and discovered how silly I really am when I try to apply my experience across someone else's board.

What is the awkward age? Tell me that. I'm still wondering at sixty-four. ∎

I really enjoy listening to you on KMTX. They air your program at 10.45 a.m., so I try to save that time to answer letters or do something that will keep me in the house then.
Mary Ellen Schnur • Townsend, MT

You're an Outdoor Dude If ...

How do you measure up? You're a candidate for outdoors adventure if:

You'd rather walk in the woods than watch Denver and Atlanta square off in the big game.

You'd rather use an outhouse in a rustic setting than a disinfected flush toilet in a luxury hotel.

You can't stand to camp in a spot where fluorescent yard lights glow from across a distant valley.

You think wild animals and tame pets exhibit more honesty than anything emanating from Washington or Wall Street.

You'd rather sprawl exhausted on a mountaintop than doze on a familiar couch.

You'd rather fish in a secluded stream and catch nothing than limit-out while casting where banks are crawling with other anglers.

You road hunt ... along a trail ... from the back of a good horse.

To you, grouse breasts roasted over an open campfire taste better than the finest cuisine from a posh Manhattan restaurant.

Wind soughing through trees has better resonance than the Beatles' best.

Somehow the dynamic interplay between carnivores and ungulates seem more important than the one between Muslims and Christians.

You'd rather drink unfiltered water fresh from a cascading mountain brook that's surrounded by snowbanks than the finest Perrier ever bottled.

You'd rather rake autumn leaves, shovel January snow, and mow June grass than spend your life searching for parking places.

You want—even if you can't—to do your recreating at elevations where your guides must have oxygen.

You have less fear of things that go "bump" in the night if you're camped in a remote forest glade than if it's outside your metropolitan high-rise apartment door.

You're amused that a beautiful butterfly flutters around the same manure piles as an ugly housefly.

You'd rather squint from a sunrise than from flashbulbs.

You'd rather listen to a rooster crow at dawn than to the wail of nighttime ambulances.

That special "someone" in your life is more attracted to the wonders of nature than Academy Awards glitz.

Ants working from their nest have more fascination than huge earth-moving machines scratching out a new interstate on-ramp.

You're more intrigued with bluebirds migrating along a mountainside than watching a movie of 10,000 orange pickers heading for California during the Dust Bowl.

God's flowers hold more wonder for you than ones growing in your neighbor's garden.

You'd dare think a grizzly bear sprawled asleep in a huckleberry patch demonstrates more raw power than Jesse Ventura flexing his muscles for a television camera.

Silence is peaceful.

Honest sweat isn't a fearful thing.

You find wonder that a bee pollinates as it harvests.

You can accept the certainty you'll not live forever. ■

Family Reunion

I t was but an hour after high noon when we rode your ponies into the delivery room. I should've put a little more thought into our campsite, but the truth was I didn't even see the animals until Bill said, "Shsst! There's a couple of elk!" By then the horses were unsaddled, belled and hobbled, and were hopping out to graze.

We all looked where the guy pointed. Two cow elk stood near the terrace where the meadow fell away to a lower level. Not far beyond, the Sun River's North Fork seethed in spring flood. The elk were perhaps 300 yards away, seemingly curious about us intruders. Eventually they sauntered away, toward the forested hill north of our camp.

The horses took turns grazing, with half waiting patiently at the hitchline while the others were out to pasture. At one point or another, each of the ponies hopped down the terrace to the river for water. Once when we rotated stock, we found all the loose ones grazing amid succulent grasses of the lower level. Bill and Mary strolled hand-in-hand out into the meadow. They moved among their ponies, petting them, then on to the river. Jane walked out behind camp scrounging for firewood and later, I ambled down to where the cows had been, then turned and, also looking for wood, entered the forest. I met the cows coming down the hill. They fled.

"Those elk sure seem reluctant to leave this place," I told the others upon returning to camp.

Eventually, as the sun sank below mountains to the west, shadows stole across the land. Jane had supper simmering in the Dutch ovens as we four lounged about, evening cocktails in hand. "I'll be darned," someone murmured. The two cows were back again, trotting from the forest across the meadow, heads held high, noses in the air. They dropped down the terrace and disappeared. Puzzled though we were, we shrugged their latest appearance off. A half-hour went by. The day was waning and we were all engaged in a race to see who would be first to reach the oven bottoms when Mary said, "The elk are back."

Sure enough, they stood rooted near where we'd first spotted them, staring our way. I still never caught on.

Jane did. She set her plate aside to dig in my saddlebags for binoculars. "They have babies!" she exclaimed moments later.

Indeed they did. By squinting, we could all see the little tykes snuggling hard against their mothers' sides. Now things turned clear for me. The reason those cows never left the area was because their calves were hidden almost under our feet.

The two babies had lain amid the high meadow grass all afternoon. They'd not moved or our sharp-eyed horses would've spotted them and either bolted for camp or been curious enough to approach and sniff.

It was the 29th of May. The calves could not have been but a few days old, perhaps just hours. How frightening the day must have turned for them: abandoned by their mothers, the roaring river, the ground thumping as the monster horses hopped nearby, the terrifying bells dinging multiple dirges. But those two calves never moved even so much as a hair until their mothers returned for them.

Aren't God's goods grand? ∎

Brave Man or Fool?

They were swell people, the couple from Grand Rapids. She taught primary school, he was a retired fireman. They'd come with our little outfit in order to sample some of the fabulous cutthroat trout fishing along the Flathead's South Fork, in the Bob Marshall Wilderness.

Their first day was a long twenty miles by horseback and it was apparent by our noon stop that I hadn't all the facts before we began the journey. So I asked Jack—who obviously suffered from something not readily apparent to me—about his trouble. He said he had a deteriorating hip that pained him while in the saddle. He was quick, however, to assure me he could make it the thirty-two miles to where we'd launch our inflatable rafts on the third day.

Jack gave it his best shot, dismounting to walk often. Despite his every effort, however, the man's pain mounted and eventually the walking took as much toll as riding.

I suggested he try riding sidesaddle—a technique we'd used some years before for another man with deteriorating hips. Jack's problem must have been different because his pain continued to mount. Mile by mile, we journeyed on. But as the day waned, our pace slowed to a crawl that permitted our entire party to stay with the suffering man.

We finally reached our first night's campsite just as the sun sank behind the western horizon. Then it was hurry, hurry to unpack, unsaddle and feed our stock, set up tents and prepare supper before we fell into bed. Jack tried gamely to help, but was finally persuaded to sit on a pack and rest. Even while he was resting beneath a tree, his face mirrored the pain.

Next morning the man insisted on continuing, but we'd traveled only five miles through the magnificent yellow-pine forest at Murphy Flat when I made my decision to abort any attempt to ride the remaining seven miles to Big Prairie.

Jack cried some and cursed some when I told him we'd launch our rafts here the following morning. "I can make it," he said through gritted teeth. "It'll just take me a little while longer, is all."

I shook my head and pointed to a sun that had already passed midday an hour ago. He capitulated when Jane and his wife Jo came down solidly on my side.

The decision was the right one. Jack's pain gradually diminished day by day, as his need to ride or walk was precluded by our easier raft journey.

The man's fishing suffered none at all because he failed to make that last seven miles. Drifting lazily through gorgeous pool after gorgeous pool for five fun-filled days, he caught cutthroat and Dolly Varden trout until his arms wearied.

Jack suffered, yes. The man was still suffering from his trail miles when the float ended days later.

What do you think? Was Jack a fool? Or is he a brave man who'll live longer because he seeks adventure—even at a very real physical price? ■

Listen to Your Lochsa

It has to be one of the scenic wonders of the West. Hoping to find a water route to the western ocean, Lewis and Clark twice hacked their way down to it from the ridgetop high above. Both times they dejectedly beat back up the mountain into snow and bitter cold to follow their Salish guides along the high route to the Nez Perce and safety.

The Lochsa hasn't changed all that much since the intrepid explorers first saw it, at least visibly. Yes, wildfire ripped through the mountains to the south shortly after the turn of the 20th Century, but the land heals itself.

Today an asphalt highway threads through towering river bottom cedars, spruce and firs. But the water still speeds on its way down the valley in one continuous cascade after another, clear and cold and whipped to a froth through much of its fifty-four miles to its junction with the Selway, and finally to the Clearwater, the Snake, and the Columbia.

Everybody should marvel at one of the finest rivers God ever made. My whitewater blood surges each time I do, imagining piloting a raft down its mile-after-mile of never-ending froth. Yet I know it's too much for this wary cowboy.

It's not too much for world-class kayakers, though, answering the river's call like bees to sugar water, from all over

America and beyond. Personally, I can't imagine a greater challenge—the speed and drop of the stream is such that it affords few recovery pools for anyone in trouble.

Jane and I camped along one of the Lochsa's reaches in early June and again in late July. Sitting along its bank, listening to the river talk, first with spring run-off's roar, then with its midsummer rush, one gets a sense of water power at its rawest. Yet we never saw a salmon leap a falls or a steelhead do acrobatics on its way up a cascade. Somehow we felt cheated.

How could we, as our children's stewards, err so grossly in our rush to improve God's creation? It was not intended for us to remake Him into our image, but the other way around.

I don't know all the reasons why the salmon that once fed the starving Corps of Discovery no longer teem in the Lochsa. Over-fishing the oceans and rivers? Downstream dams blocking adult fish from upriver passage? Power turbines grinding smolts as they migrate to the sea? Slackwater reservoirs changing stream regimes and disorienting fish that evolved amid flowing environments? Irrigation pumps moving fry from water to dry land? Overgrazing of spawning streambanks? Poaching?

If one cannot fully know the problems, how can one find answers?

I only know as I sat along the Lochsa and listened to it speak, the river seemed somehow bereft of its virginity.

A Lochsa without salmon is like the mountains around it without grizzly bears—somehow incomplete. The Lochsa is young and shapely and vital, but it's without the light of a maiden's smile. It's like spring without the wild goose song.

I believe everyone should visit the Lochsa, sit along its banks, listen to its pleas, contemplate its dilemma.

Your "Lochsa" might be a different river in a different state. In fact, your "Lochsa" might not even be a river at all, but a mountain, a meadow, a short-grass prairie, a falcon flying overhead.

But whatever it is, wherever it is, we all need to listen to our Lochsa's plaintive cry. ■

Blood-Thirsty Varmints Are a Plight on the Backcountry

I could lie to you and say I'm not into mosquitoes. But you know I'm fibbing 'cause nobody spends time in the backcountry without occasionally coming face to face with the pesky little varmints.

Messrs. Meriwether and William, as well as other diarists of Lewis and Clark Expedition fame, made mention of the annoying bloodsuckers more often than any other wild creature during the epic three years of their journey. And it's a documented fact that, though the men learned to fear the mighty grizzly bear, it was the tiny mosquito who spilled the voyagers' blood—not "Old Ephraim," as later mountain men called the great bear.

Most mountain travelers soon learn to make jokes about the insects under the premise that it's better to laugh than cry. "Mosquito netting doesn't help," I said after spending a fitful night. "The little ones flew right through and the big ones ripped it off."

"There wasn't any little ones," Lyle said. "The ones in my tent were all big enough to stand flat-footed and whip a turkey."

The most savage mosquitoes I ever encountered were at

Timpanagos Lake in the Oregon Cascades. The second-most savage mosquitoes were at that same Timpanagos Lake in a subsequent year. Both encounters left me in shirttail-flapping flight for the vehicle that brought me there. Eighteen-inch rainbows be damned!

But the greatest discomfort I've encountered in riotous take-no-prisoners battle with squadrons of the tiny hellions was on a late-June 1966 family camping trip to a high basin near the Canadian Line. That terror-filled night still clings in my mind.

The Timpanagos adventures were short, swift skirmishes with a stronger enemy. Retreat was the only viable option. The family camping trip began with no more than an occasional swat that escalated as the sun sank below the western horizon.

After dark, the insects called up their reserves. By then it was too late for we besieged humans—who were, by the way, without a tent—to consider pell-mell retreat for the comfort of home and hearth. And thus it was a bloody night-long battle on an evening too sultry for sleeping bags. Therefore, those sheathes turned into sweat bags while insatiably voracious tiny carnivores dive-bombed overhead. It may have been the longest night of my life.

I learned, though. Timpanagos Lake is to be avoided at all cost during June, July, and August. Tents with mosquito netting are much preferable to a plastic rain fly stretched between trees.

I learned even more in subsequent years: During fly time, choose windswept gravel bars as camping spots; long-sleeved shirts and full-legged trousers give added protection; and there are times when an effective repellent is worth its weight in gold.

But what is even more important, I learned that some places are simply worse for mosquitoes. One for instance is the Sun River country. Visit the North Fork after mid-June and before mid-August and one can figure on World War III with the pesky creatures over some of the prettiest camping spots between Biggs Flat and the Klick Ranch. Gates Park is outside the worst of the mosquito belt, however. So is Pretty Prairie on the South Fork of the Sun.

Rain dampens mosquito ardor, and frost puts their aggression into free-fall.

Meanwhile, if I ever perfect my mosquito defense strategy, you'll be the first to know. ∎

Hard-Side or Tent Camp?

The accepted nomenclature is "hard-sided camping"—meaning travel trailers and motor homes. The protection afforded by hard-sided camping makes it permissible where tent campers are considered at risk—for instance, campgrounds frequented by bears.

Travel trailers or motor homes have advantages other than security. Two minutes after arrival, hard-side campers can have "camp" set up and be mixing cocktails. Disassembly is equally easy; simply hook up the trailer or start your motorhome engine, and a happy camper is under way.

Return from a long hike or a hard day's hunt and there's cold beer or pop in the fridge. A twist of a knob and presto! There's flame under the coffee pot and heat from a furnace.

Tent camping, on the other hand, is comparatively Spartan. Some tent camps are more Spartan than others, depending on how elaborate the facilities and how much preparation went into establishing it.

Some hunting camps have separate sleeping tents and a well-lighted and amazingly well-heated cooktent complete with piped-in water and propane cookstove. A backpack camp, on the other hand, might employ a tiny nylon cocoon with barely enough room to roll out a sleeping bag and lay out a clean pair of socks.

The extent of most private-party tent camps used during hunting season range somewhere between a single backpack tent and commercial outfitter's multi-tent camp. They might utilize one large tent for sleeping and loafing, probably heated with an all-purpose woodstove that's also used for cooking. The stove may or may not have an oven for baking biscuits or cakes.

Most hunters, given a choice, would opt for the ease and comfort of hard-sided camping over tent camps established at road's end. But I'm not sure that choice is always wise.

Aside from the obvious price difference—even the cost of a used travel trailer is astronomical compared to setting up for tent camping—hard-sided camp vehicles have a few notable disadvantages.

Enclosed dampness can make it tough to dry clothes in tight camp trailers or motor homes. There's something to be said for wood heat in a tent camp; it's dry and especially comforting to snuggle up to on a cold morning.

Most tents of any consequent size have more cubic space within their walls than even spacious (and expensive) travel trailers and motor homes. This feature is especially apparent in head-room. That overhead space is always employed by experienced campers to dry clothes and boots.

Tent camps are better utilized where roads are bad or where they may become treacherous because of weather. When it comes time to return home, tent camps may be more difficult to strike, but they can be stowed in the box of a four-wheel-drive pickup. This means no snaking an expensive travel trailer down an icy mountain road.

The bottom line, of course, is what you wish to utilize. And what you *should* utilize should be what's best for conditions … of the hunters using it and the terrain in which they choose to establish it. ■

Memories Make the Spirit Soar

The dog may have been an Irish wolfhound, but he zipped by so fast I couldn't be sure. He was covered with rich, reddish-brown hair, except for a big patch of black across one shoulder. He sat upright in a motorcycle sidecar, ears flapping in the breeze. He could've played well in a "Peanuts" comic strip had he been equipped with goggles.

Jane's spirits soared at sight of the dog and she was still giggling miles down the road.

"Whatever possessed the man to put his dog there in the first place?" she wondered.

I laughed at the never-to-be-forgotten sight, too. But instead of wondering what motivated the motorcycle driver, I was curious about the dog. What was he thinking as he sped along in the sidecar only inches above the unfolding ribbon of concrete?

We called him Joey the Bee. He slammed up against our windshield near Lolo Hot Springs and rode the wiper until he got his wits and spirits back. Then Joey crawled out on the glass and rode hunkered down before flying away at Lolo Pass.

I wondered about Joey, too; wondered if he would make it back to his distant hive. Then I wondered about some of the bees in our yard back home. Might some be migrants from distant and exotic locations, arriving via a passing car's radiator grill?

Joey the Bee's technique certainly would take some of the stress out of traveling rush-hour traffic in Salt Lake or Missoula.

———

Fireflies blinked off and on amid lush reeds. The air was humid and damp, as the thunderstorm rolled toward us. Jane and I sprawled atop our sleeping bags, caring not a whit that we would soon be overwhelmed by the approaching storm.

She opened the van's curtains wider to better watch jagged flashes of lightning, then snuggled nearer. "This is absolute luxury," she murmured, "compared to the way we used to do it."

I shrugged. "I liked the way we used to do it, too."

Thunder grumbled and the whites of the lady's eyes were illuminated by bolt after lightning bolt.

"You know what I mean—wind flattening our tents, rain blowing beneath our dining fly. Mud, wet, cold. I don't mind missing that side of our life once in a while."

When I said nothing, she added, "Besides, it's not as if we've completely given up our former life, you know. Now we just don't have to be out there all the time."

I turned my head to glance at her, then returned to the window. "Do you know if you look quickly away, then back, that you can actually see the sky changing. Isn't it beautiful?"

She murmured, then was still and silent.

We slept well that night, swam in a nearby lake the next morning, and drank copious cups of fresh-made coffee before getting under way. The sun was up and burning away the puddles as we motored through a small farming community. Jane wished to mail a letter, so I stopped while she ran into the just-opened U.S. Post Office.

While I waited, a ringnecked rooster crowed from the field at the end of the short street.

Jane spotted my grin upon her return. "What are you on about?"

"Any town where you can hear a pheasant crow from the post office is about the right size, don't you think?" ■

Mother and Child
Only a Mountain Away

We'd been looking for mountain goats for several minutes, scanning the towering hillside above, studying its crevices and ledges, pausing to double-check each patch of remnant snow. Finally we sprawled in the grass to eat lunch, brown-bagging it along the shores of Cliff Lake in the Cabinet Mountains.

"There's a goat," Frank murmured, pointing a couple of hundred yards away, to the far end of the small mountain lake. "We were looking on the mountain for them and they're down here along the lakeshore."

The goat wandered in and out of scattered clumps of trees, heading our way.

"There's another!" Frank whispered. "And a third."

"One has a baby," Jane said.

The goats wandered within a hundred yards, then turned away to circle the lake and come in from our far side. The one we assumed was the mother approached within fifty feet, after first sending her little one up the mountain to perch on a ledge and bleat plaintively.

"They're craving salt," I said. "They've learned to associate us with it. That's why they're coming so close."

"Listen to that poor little one," Jane said. "He sounds as though he's calling, 'Ma-a-a-a, ma-a-a-a'."

The one we thought was the mother bleated only once up toward the kid and again the little guy turned to climb farther up the mountain. Up, up he clambered.

Twice he butted against difficult walls he couldn't scale and had to turn back and circle around until he could continue his climb. Once he came to a sheer precipice and stood bleating down at his wayward mother. "Ma-a-a-a, ma-a-a-a."

I stayed glued to my binoculars, whispering, "We're watching a wildlife drama unfolding—that little kid is going to climb over that mountain and leave his mother."

Jane said, "I should think he'd be vulnerable to a predator—a mountain lion or an eagle—up on that mountain alone."

Still, the baby continued to climb until we could barely see him with our naked eye. The mother seemed unconcerned as she circled the lake.

"More goats over on the ridge," Frank grunted.

Four additional goats worked up the ridge, toward the mountain summit where the small goat pointed.

"There are more coming," Jane said. Indeed, we counted five more, making thirteen overall.

"I've never seen so many goats on Chicago Peak," Frank said.

Jane decided to climb a low ridge beyond the lake in order to view the basin beyond. Frank went with her. I lagged behind to watch the little tyke who appeared stranded.

A nanny peeled away from one of the group of goats to pick her way across a ledge. The little one saw her coming and began bouncing up and down in apparent glee. Then they were together; he began nursing.

Because she was impatient, Jane missed the final act of the drama; missed watching the lost baby find his real mother; missed learning that we really know little about wild creatures. ∎

Anomalous Adventures

The first rule of outdoors adventure is that a guy named Murphy sometimes plays a key role. For instance, it's not uncommon to experience a modest degree of panic when a big patch blows off your inflatable raft while fishing in Iceberg Lake, three hundred feet offshore. I've also learned it's impossible to digest a leisurely breakfast when you're camped thirty miles from road's end and no horse bells have tinkled in the distance since you rolled from your sleeping bag.

Or contemplate this as proof of Murphy's Law: blow-outs on both of your loaded stock truck's left-side duals. Naturally you're halfway between home and your target trailhead. Naturally you have but one spare.

I've pulled into camp just at dusk and found the tents (erected a week earlier) flattened by unseasonal snowfall.

And I can't count the number of times one of my hunters ran smack dab into the bull elk of his dreams, snapped off the lens covers on his rifle's scope, only to discover the lenses fogged.

Mosquitoes cranky after a long winter? Guess when you're most likely to forget the repellent.

Rained for a week? During your week's canoe vacation, I'll bet.

Yet perversely, those trips are precisely the ones we most remember, most talk about, most laugh about. They're adventures! On the other hand, trips where everything goes as planned—you know the ones we most enjoy—are the exact same ones that merge into fond memories with no clear face.

My wife and I sold our outfitting business in 1990. We kept four horses—and you can be sure that out of the thirty head of ponies in our string, the four we kept were not the four worst. Each of those four present saddle and pack horses is experienced and reliable. Each has traveled thousands of miles over all sorts of trails in all kinds of weather.

Nowadays Jane and I can plan a personal wilderness pack-trip where we'll unload the stock at the trailhead and they'll stand like bored New York doormen while I sling saddles and packs. We're on the trail in minutes, traveling at a pace so steady NASA could set their clocks by it.

Nowadays we're always early into our planned campsite. Once there, Jane and I work like a well-oiled machine. She unmanties packs, and loads the patient ponies' nosebags with grain, while I jerk saddles and brush down the stock. She sets up our tent, I put up the dining fly. She lays out our bedroll. I string a highline and hobble and turn our horses out to graze.

Within an hour of our arrival, Jane has her kitchen in place and I have enough wood gathered for the first night. Within two hours, we're climbing a mountain or swimming in a river—depends on weather, mood, and circumstances.

And the particulars of the trip is forgotten a week after returning home.

The trips remembered in microscopic detail are which? The ones where the packstring blundered into a yellowjacket nest and rolled down a mountainside; where we helped bring a helicopter in on a mercy flight for an injured man from another party; where lightning crackled around us, knocking the top from a mammoth larch tree only a hundred yards from our tents.

Yeah, the guy Murphy can be annoying, but he plays an indispensable role in making lasting memories. ∎

Facing Down Dilemmas

The necessities of life are usually so convenient to present-day Americans that it's difficult to remember it wasn't always so for our fathers or mothers. Need shelter for the night? Check into a motel. Need to travel? We can drive to Salt Lake, Denver, or Seattle in a day; fly to Los Angeles in a morning or New York before midafternoon. Hungry? A restaurant is around the corner or a supermarket down the street.

Our old homesteader friends are long gone now, but during Jane's and my early married years they were our heroes. It was shortly after the turn of the century when the couple staked their homestead. They chose forest land far from civilization, and more than thirty years passed before a forest road nosed to their land.

We sat at Perry and Jessie Wright's knees, listening to stories of the old days. Once, while we were visiting, Jessie served delicious huckleberry pancakes. We raved over them. Jessie beamed. "Huckleberries are easier to get these days," she said. "Back in the old days, we'd take packhorses and spend a week or two picking huckleberries."

"You did?" Jane said. "What did you do with them? Sell them?"

"Sell them!" the lady exclaimed. "Sell them! Heavens no! We packed my canner and lots and lots of fruit jars. And we canned them right there at Bulldog Prairie or Bradley Lake."

"Canned them?" I cut in. "That must have been quite an undertaking to pack empty jars, then can berries over campfires. Why did you want to do that?"

Perry slapped the kitchen table with the flat of a hand. "Didn't *want* to do it, Roland. *Had* to do it."

"Had to do it? I don't understand."

"Scurvy," the old man replied. "We live up here where growing fruits and vegetables was chancy. We couldn't always run to town for a can of applesauce. Scurvy was always in the minds of people like us."

"And there was no way," Jessie added, "to get berries home from far-off places like Grassy Ranch or Bulldog Prairie before they spoiled. So canning right there in the mountains was the only way to do it."

I shook my head, thinking of packing fruit jars—empty or loaded—via horseback along some of the hairy trails I hiked while elk hunting. And later, after spending decades leading others to adventure and packing tons of camp supplies into the greatest wilderness in all the northern Rocky mountains, I'm still dismayed at the accomplishments of yesterday's homesteaders.

Most of today's hardships are confronted because someone chooses to test themselves against hardship via adventure. In Perry and Jessie's day, pioneers faced down dilemmas because there was no other way. They exhibited considerable ingenuity and industry while problem-solving, and it's appropriate that we venerate their deeds. It's not surprising, but also appropriate, that they seem supermen and superwomen to us.

What's remarkable is that the trial and conquest of early-day homesteaders took place so recently. Their descendants are scattered throughout the West—and East. They sleep in motels, eat in restaurants, shop in supermarkets, and take commuter flights to Paris. Though they're but one generation removed from those iron men and women of yesterday, it's rare that this generation remembers them. ∎

I used to climb mountains a little; been on top of the Grand Teton a few times, and Mt. Moran, and you get the same feelings when you get up on top of the world. We live in a beautiful country with a lot of pretty places to see and I'm sure that the folks that have gone on your trail rides and hunting trips will never forget their experiences.
                              Don R. Garner • Kalispell, MT

Madam Vanderbilt, Bill Gates, and Ogg the Mammoth Hunter

Ever wonder what's the secret ingredient that makes for a successful hunter? Why does one individual seem luckier than another? Is one more sensitive to nature's nuances? Has the successful hunter completed the equivalency of a doctorate in interpreting the chatter of pine squirrels or the raucous cries of whiskey jacks? Does he read shifting wind currents more accurately? Has he mastered big picture weather patterns known only to wild creatures?

Or does the successful hunter carry a bigger magnum to reach from one mountain range to the next? Or possess more pockets full of gadgets with manufacturers' success guaranteed (note, I said *manufacturers'* success): spotting scopes, GPS devices, buck scents, cow calls, camouflage designs?

Identifying and discovering reasons for the success of others is a common parlor game played by metropolitan society matrons, captains of industry, and connoisseurs of fields and forests. Uncovering the singlemost secret of competitors' success is the universal dream of Madam Vanderbilt, Bill Gates, and Ogg the mammoth hunter.

But the truth is there is no single reason why one captain becomes wealthy while thousands do not; why one matron is constantly copied while others are not; why one hunter seems phenomenally successful while you and your partners are not.

In the case of hunting and hunters, however, one can come nearer to reducing success to one single element than with Vanderbilt or Gates. That element is time.

Time afield is the common thread tying all really successful hunters together, whether they pursue chukars amid Snake River canyons, pheasants in South Dakota cornfields, honkers in Alberta stubble, or elk around the Yellowstone Plateau.

Who has the best-trained dogs? Certainly the person who spends time afield with theirs.

Who better understands the nuances of forest lore? Who else but those who give nature adequate opportunity to speak to them.

The guy who, year after year, stocks his freezer with elk ribs or venison chops is not your garden variety Sunday afternoon hunter. He's not the one who waits to read about the latest hunting "hot spot" in newspaper or magazine before making plans to venture afield.

Nope, he was tramping the hills while remnant snowbanks still clung in March, counted wedges winging north in May. He was out every chance he had in June, July, and August. And when September, October, and November rolls around, you'll never find him trading a moment of field time in order to watch the Broncos groan against the Seahawks from his living room sofa.

So forget about rifle calibers, optic qualities, and direction devices.

Dump the idea that the guy you envy somehow took a language course in wildlife-speak, or has a better "feel" for landforms because he has insiders' knowledge of USGS staff procedures. It isn't who you know, or even what you know, but how you learned it—by being out there and doing it.

Give Ogg credit where credit is due—that he took his hunting share as seriously as Bill Gates takes his market share. ■

A Place to Which We'd Like to Return

This story occurred on a Kansas golf course. The reason I tell you this up front is so anyone who doesn't care to read a heartwarming tale set in Kansas can set the book aside, pick up the newspaper and turn to the obituary page for their morning jollies.

The story begins with friends of mine I'll call Dale and Phyllis (which are their real names) driving across country, returning to Montana from a trip abroad. Dale and Phyllis are golfers—very good golfers. Of course their clubs were stashed in the trunk of their car.

An early morning sun was just beginning to warm the land as the couple drove along U.S. Highway 50, in extreme western Kansas. As they motored past the public golf course for the small community of Syracuse, Dale asked, "How about a round?"

Phyllis, who is a better golfer than Dale, readily agreed. They wheeled up to the clubhouse.

"Hello!" my friend called, pushing open the door. There was no greeting. There was a lady in the dining room, however, and Dale asked, "Can we play a round of golf?"

"Yes," the lady replied, making no move toward the clubroom.

Puzzled, Dale asked, "Well, what is the fee?"

The lady shook her head. "I don't know." Then she added, "I don't work here but I believe there's a fee schedule on the wall by the cash register."

Dale walked into the clubroom and sure enough, there was a fee schedule on the wall by the cash register. Then he went back to the dining room lady to ask, "Who will take our money?"

"Oh don't worry about that. It's an honor system around here. You can pay when you come back in."

So Dale and Phyllis put their clubs onto an electric cart and buzzed through nine holes of golf. Dale said they waved at a groundskeeper working on the number-seven fairway and a couple of other golfers in the number-four distance. He thought the course a good one: "Sort of like any well-kept course in any small town in America."

After they'd completed their nine, the couple strolled into the clubhouse to pay. There was still no one behind the counter. Nor, in fact, was anyone in the building.

"It seemed strange," my friend said. "Other money lay by the cash register, so Phyllis and I calculated the cost of our round—including our cart, then wrote a check for $30.51. We wound up placing the check atop the pile."

I shook my head in wonder.

"That's not all. There was a pop cooler against one wall. It had a lift-top and no coin slots. A customer was supposed to help himself and leave the appropriate change on the counter. There was a coffee machine full of coffee, too. Help yourself and leave the money."

"Syracuse, Kansas sounds to me like the kind of place to which a fellow would like to return," I murmured.

Dale grinned. "How true. I'd say that's one town where folks don't worry too much about locking their doors at night."

<hr/>

Now tell me, did the folks who chose the obituary page or the advertisements get half so much? ∎

The Last of the Old West

Ahh, Montana!" the pleasant-faced elderly man said wistfully as he eyed our sport-show display. "The last of the Old West." A silver-haired lady crowded close beside him, looking for all the world like she modeled for a "Grandma's Cookies" ad.

"Huh?" I said. His was a reaction to be expected, perhaps, from an Easterner. Or perhaps from a Midwesterner. Or even someone from California. But this particular show was in Edmonton, Alberta.

The man picked up one of our brochures, and the couple retreated down the aisle. Over his shoulder, the man said, "You're bloody lucky, you know."

I shook my head, puzzling over his remarks. About that time another man, this one in his mid-forties, slapped the counter, startling me. "My favorite place—Montana!" Before I could get my wits about me, he'd continued on his way.

Many others paused at our display during that five-day show. Most expressed the same sentiments: "Montana!" they would all say, usually rolling the word off their tongue so it came out sounding nostalgic. Often it was repeated in different ways: "The last frontier" or "the real West" or "the last of the pioneer West."

Finally I could stand it no longer, and thinking of the Hudson Bay Company and the Northwest Fur Company, trapping brigades and gold rush days and mounties and … and I said to yet another who'd just repeated that Montana is the Old West, "I thought Alberta fell in there somewhere."

He shook his head sadly. "No, no. We've done with it here in Alberta. It's all gone, the open land and cowboys and cattle ranges. No, you Montanans have the last of it, lad. And I suppose you'll be squandering it too, eh?"

That Edmonton show was more than two decades ago, but I've not forgotten what was learned there; about the frenetic rush for resource development going on to the north of us. Then, it was oil in Alberta. And grain farming. Now it's paper mills in their northern dog-hair forests. Tomorrow?

Montana! The last of the Old West. That's how we're thought of by folks from more developed regions. It's a perception that bewilders us Treasure Staters who sometimes seem aghast at *our own* unseemly haste to rip and tear and squeeze and gouge for the sake of "progress." We can look back over the last decade and see changes wrought on our Montana landscape and in our flavorful Montana culture.

But take heart. There's scant chance we'll catch the rest of the world, no matter how hard we try. Though some change is inevitable here in the Big Sky Country, more drastic changes are occurring outside Montana.

We'll always be the last of the Old West to those people who journey here because we'll always represent those values their state or province or nation held dear a few decades before.

At least I hope that's the way it will be in *my* Montana. It will if we pay close attention to the values others have already foregone in their rush to "improve" their way of life.

Paradoxical, isn't it? ■

Technology Wins One

There is no advancement in outdoors equipment equal to
developments in backpacks. Comparing today's lightweight aluminum, plastic, and nylon packs with yesterday's
Trapper Nelson or military rucksack is like comparing a sleek
modern submarine with a Mississippi paddlewheeler.

There are two distinct types of backpacks: external-frame
and internal-frame. Each has its advantages.

The external-frame pack is considered the modern "old
school" backpack favored by purists. It usually has an exposed
H-shaped aluminum frame suspended by padded shoulder
straps, a stretched backband, and a load-bearing adjustable
hipbelt. Straps or wired clevis pins attach the pack bag to the
frame.

An internal-frame pack uses flexible stays or an aluminum
or graphite sheet to transmit weight onto a padded, stiffened
hipbelt. A flexible plastic frame-sheet adds support and pro-
tects the spine against pressure from interior cargo.

The internal-frame pack rides tighter to the body than does
the external-frame. Because the internal-frame pack is carried
lower and snugs more closely to your back, it's considerably
more stable when balance is important—such as in crosscountry skiing or climbing or rock hopping. The internal-

frame's streamlined shape also allows better arm movement and will pass through tighter places where you'd be dragging an external-frame pack.

Although internal-frame packs appear to be mushrooming in popularity, they have drawbacks. One is that: because of the lower center of gravity of it's load, you must lean forward more when carrying an internal-frame than with the other type. Another drawback is price. As a general rule, internal-frame backpacks can cost twice the price of a good external-frame.

Aside from cost, the advantages of external-frames are better ventilation against your back, easier access to side pockets and compartments, and a more erect stance because the load is carried higher. The high center of gravity can be a negative, however, when bushwhacking or engaging in activities where balance becomes critical.

I started backpacking with an old steel-frame and canvas military rucksack. Looking back from the advantage of today's advanced backpacking technology, one can almost wonder how we won a war? Bob Frauson, who served with the 10th Mountain Division in World War II, told me the military rucksack was patterned after the Norwegian Bergen Pack. The pack was carried low on the hips because balance was so critical in most of their operations. Bob said, however, that many of his old companions in the 10th suffer from what is referred to as "rucksack back" in their lower lumbar regions.

He also began a ditty sung by the 10th while on the march. The tune is similar to that of "Bell Bottom Trousers":

"Ninety pounds of rucksack, a pound of grub or two; he'll schuss the mountain like his daddy used to do."

Bob Frauson shared this information while Jane and I visited him and his wife in their nearby home. The ex-mountain trooper said he'd sing the rest of the ditty for me when we're not in mixed company. ■

Who's Barney?

Barney was the best fisherman I ever knew. Put a willow pole, some string, and a bent pin in the kid's hands and there'd be fish in the pan come supper. When we were older and could afford commercial stuff, Barney had a passable outfit—but only one. Nickels were hard for the guy to come by because he spent less time working than fishing.

He was so-o-o sensitive. We'd have lines in the same hole—maybe only a few feet apart. I had no action, Barney's was constant. "There …" he'd whisper. "Go ahead and take … oh! I got another nibble. There's another, see?"

I could hold onto Barney's line and feel nothing. I might study where it disappeared into the water and see nothing happening. Then the guy would jerk his rig and laugh as it bent double. Soon he'd lay a 20-inch trout alongside the other two he'd already taken. Meanwhile I'd turn up my jacket collar, thrust hands deep into trousers' pockets and contemplate a distant mountain's navel.

Contrast Barney with the Midwest writer working on a magazine story who, during research, reached me by telephone: "Are you into ice fishing, Roland?"

"Nope. Not me. I tried it. Twice. Froze out, stove up, and didn't catch a fish."

There was silence on his end, so I added, "I've never tried an ice house, though. Maybe I could find winter fishing more tolerable from a cozy-warm shelter."

He chuckled. "That was what I was just going to say; I was just like you—ice fishing and me didn't get along until I tried it from an icehouse. The ones we use are of lightweight nylon, with an aluminum frame. They can be set up with a flip of the wrist."

"They'd never stand up to the wind at Duck Lake."

"Yeah they would. I've fished from 'em when the wind was blowing a gale."

I laughed. "The prairie winds take boxcars off the railroad tracks at Browning."

More silence. At last, he said, "Anyway, you ought to see how well set up we are. We have these little one-person ice houses that collapse onto a sled. Say a half a dozen of us go fishing out on a lake. We'll scatter, with each pulling his sled to a different spot. We drill holes, then pop up the ice house and drop our depth finder in …"

"What? Depth finder?"

"Yeah, it's got a fish locator on it, too. Mine's pretty sophisticated. You can see the fish coming."

"You've got to be kidding!"

"Each of us carries two-way radios, too," he said. "We keep moving and drilling holes until somebody finds the fish. Then he gets on the radio and pretty soon there's half a dozen ice houses clustered in a group."

"With depth finders and fish locators dangling beneath the ice?"

"Yep. We can heat coffee and talk on our radios and watch for fish coming our way. I'll bet you'd like that."

"Barney," I said. "What about the way Barney did it?"

"Who's Barney?" ∎

I love your program on the radio and listen as often as possible. We love your "laid back" voice and topics we can relate to. Thanks for taking us outdoors on our way to work.
Beth Brunson • Ellensburg, WA

Remember the Marker Layer

The angry whirr of a dozen castanets fetched an involuntary cry as Jane jumped back. The dog, ranging to the side, heard her and bounded toward her mistress. "No, Tess!" Jane screamed. It was too late; the Brittany leaped the tiny wash where the snake coiled. It struck. Fortunately, the sudden rush and leap of the dog from another direction surprised the reptile and it missed.

So goes fossil hunting in Garfield County.

The land is powder-dry and sun-baked. Our friend's ranch is covered with a bunch of sagebrush and a little bunchgrass and takes forty acres to the cow. But the cows there are hog-fat—provided they don't wear off the fat running back and forth to water.

It's hard to imagine how this parched, butte-dotted tableland could have grown redwood trees that were hundreds of feet tall and dozens of feet around. But the fossilized Sequoia cones Jane and her friend found in one tiny side canyon are proof positive. The triceratops horn and the serrated teeth of tyrannosaurus rex, the terrible lizard from the Jurassic, also mean something.

Visualizing this barren land as a lush near-tropical seacoast—much the same as Florida or Louisiana or the Yucatan —is tough. But it's the only way one can understand the evidence. To complicate things further, throw in occasional sharks' teeth and mix with fossils from other ocean-going creatures and you'll be exposed to just a couple of the many transitions this sparsely populated desert region has experienced.

There are coal seams here—part of the rich Fort Union deposit extending clear into Wyoming and points east. The seams lie exposed in the sidewalls of buttes and arroyos, sometimes downwarped from east to west—evidence the land was lifted from some obscure Dakota high point, draining seacoast and swampland.

The coal seams are, of course, the residue of decaying vegetative matter that accumulated and was pressed downward by subsequent accumulations, then covered and compacted by deposits from an encroaching sea. Deeper and deeper the vegetative debris was pushed and compacted. Then the sea retreated and another lush tropical forest grew and decayed and was pushed down by following decaying matter. The sea came again to deposit layers of sandstone and limestone and clay. Down, down, until the hundreds of feet of decayed vegetation at last became compressed into three-, four-, five-foot layers of poor but sulphur-free coal.

Then the land warped up. To the west, mountain ranges pushed to the sky—the Rockies, the Cascade Range, the Coast Range intercepting moisture-laden clouds and turning this land as dry as the inside of a flour bin.

The coal seams are considered marker layers. Above the coal, one might find, as I have, bones from recent prehistory. Below the coal layers are deposits from a much earlier epoch; one with giant thunder lizards that shook the ground as they walked.

There's a bunch of evidence missing. Why not dinosaur fossils *in* the coal layers, as often occurs in central Utah? Because when Fort Union coal was laid down by the lush vegetation of Eastern Montana and the Dakotas, the thunder lizards were gone.

Well, why not fossils from later species?

That's one thing about fossil hunting—it raises many more questions than answers.

Just remember the coal layer.

And remember to look for them on *private* land. ∎

I heard your whitewater fishing story yesterday—about the wife losing her fishing pole and saying it was her husband's fault. Really enjoy listening to these outdoor experiences.   Betty Siverhus • Maynard, MN

I want to tell you how much I enjoy your radio program every morning. You tell the story so beautifully. I really enjoyed last week's on the antlers of the elk and deer.
Mrs. B.W. Leaf • Elliston, MT

Generational Differences

Every so often, Jane and I do something unconventional—like leaving home at 8:30 in the evening for a week of hiking Utah's Canyonlands. Why not? Our vehicle was packed for an early morning exit. It was Jane's idea to leave early. It was my idea to drive to Salmon, Idaho, and then, the following morning, hike a mile-and-a-half to a neat little hot springs on U.S. Forest Service land.

The springs are popular with the college set, but since we would be visiting there on a weekday morning, we fully expected to have the place to ourselves. However, when we pulled up to the trailhead, a car with Montana license plates was already parked there.

And when we arrived huffing and puffing at our destination, there was a green pop-up tent pitched above the springs' deepest pool. The pool itself was also occupied.

The occupiers eschewed normal bathing attire.

I thought the young lady was agitating clothes, but she wasn't. Instead, the couple were engaged in an activity not normal to a public place.

Fortunately the hot springs had been used by countless previous visitors and stream channels had been diverted and dammed by enterprising bathers to create myriad other pools—albeit shallower and smaller than the one we coveted. We donned our bathing suits and settled in for a half-hour's relaxation. Occasionally, though, we cast envious glances at the deeper, larger pool. "I can't believe they're still doing it!" Jane said twenty minutes later.

I laughed. It was the water temperature—I could've pointed the problem out to the couple had they been more readily accessible to outside analysis. I could also tell the guy if he thinks he has trouble now, just wait until he reaches my three score and four.

Their ordeal—or idyll—ended ten minutes before Jane and I slung our daypacks and headed for Utah. It was on our way down the mountain when the thought struck that I'd lost an opportunity to engage in what could've been important generational research. I began chuckling.

For instance, there's little doubt folks from my generation feel somewhat inhibited about ameliorating lust in what could logically be construed as a public gathering place. But when that nude couple vacated the best pool on the premises, they didn't seem at all nonplussed to find they shared a proclivity for hot springs bathing with other visitors. It's routine, so I'm told, for birthday-suited strangers to share pools in this and similar hot springs. But we'd not properly analyzed our age and proclivity differences.

"What are you giggling about?" Jane said, blocking the trail and facing me.

I threw out my arms to encompass the world. "Has it occurred to you that the education of mankind might've been significantly advanced had we simply donned our suits, walked to the edge of their pool and cried in a loud voice, 'HOW'S THE WATER?'—purely as a matter of academic research, of course."

She laughed. "He might have jumped out of that pool and pounded the devil out of you."

"You might be right. But wouldn't that act alone provide important research relative to attitude differences between generations?" ∎

I am a lot more familiar with you than you are with me. I am Kevin Menz's oldest brother, Jeff. [Kevin was a former guide who was killed in a tragic Iowa highway accident.] I wanted to personally thank you for honoring Kevin's wishes and spreading his ashes over the Great Wall [cliff formation in the Bob Marshall Wilderness]. Kevin's being put to rest has eased my parent's suffering somewhat. My brother was blessed to have such a fine friend as you and he spoke of you often and with great affection. If ever I can do anything for you please drop me a note.

Jeff Menz • St. Peters, MO

Shared Experiences

This column may have been the most important one I'd ever attempted and I wondered if I had sufficient talent. The subject was our relations with the less fortunate. It wasn't about money or care-giving or social assistance. Instead, it was about sharing experiences.

"How is Lyle?" my friend Matt asked.

I shook my head. "Not good. He can't see well enough to drive or read, and he can't get much more than just the drift of a football game on television."

Matt shrugged. "A man can only play the cards he's dealt."

Yeah, right. Matt himself, my oldest friend, doesn't have too many more good cards left to play. The hand he's been dealt includes emphysema, arthritis, heart bypass, multiple angioplasties, cancer, diabetes, amputated leg. He'd once been a superb athlete, a member of the elite 101st Airborne and one of World War II's "Battered Bastards of Bastogne."

Together, Matt and I had taken dozens of horseback pack-trips into some of the most splendid mountain country in the world. We'd coached youth baseball together and built Little League and Legion diamonds that are in use today. We worked together and played together and drank beer together.

Now there's not much we can do together but visit about the "good old days." Yet here was a guy suffering from multiple afflictions who cared enough to ask about a mutual friend who is losing his eyesight.

"How long has Lyle's eye problem been going on?" Matt asked.

"It came with a rush. Apparently, blood vessels ruptured, maybe six months ago. It's been getting progressively worse since then."

"No chance for an operation?"

"His doctors don't hold out much hope. They say there's a chance an operation could make it worse."

Again Matt shrugged.

I continued: "We rode up Camas Creek in Glacier Park. It was mid-September—a beautiful day, with snow-dusted mountain peaks shining all around." I paused in recollection, then went on: "There were some late-blooming harebells growing along the trail and I thoughtlessly said, 'Look at the flowers. Aren't they splashes of blue?' Lyle cleared his throat and said in a subdued voice, 'You'll have to tell me about them, Roland. I can't see them.'"

My friend nodded.

"God, Matt, I felt so rotten. Later I had to slap a hand over my mouth to keep from exclaiming at the sight of particularly magnificent mountains."

Matt frowned. "You think about ..."

But I was on a roll: "Jeez, Matt, I have a hard time keeping from telling you about some of the adventures I'm still going on, now that you can no longer do them."

The frail man pounded his chair arm. "No! Dammit, man, you're not thinking right. Maybe I'll never again be able to do what we once did, but I can still relive those adventures, visualizing them through your eyes—if only you'll share with me! Don't you see that Lyle still wants to do all the things he once did or he'd not been riding with you? Don't you understand that by not sharing what you saw with him, you diminished his experience?"

I shed a tear after gripping my friend's shoulder and taking my leave. And I decided this bit of wisdom is something that also needs to be shared.

My friend Matt is finally gone, his great heart stilled. The man's indomitable will is but a memory where his unselfish self once towered. Even good things and great must end. And so my friend Matt, cherished by most, remembered by all, crossed over the Great Divide. He's a classic example of the power of the hereafter: of how one is thought of *here, after* he's gone.

This book has to end, also, but the telling of stories will go on and on. There are over a hundred different tales or incidents related within these pages, and there are many, many more where those came from. I've written *thousands* of newspaper columns and radio scripts. And the Good Lord willing and the creeks don't rise, there'll be many, many more in years to come.

For instance, there's the guy who wheelchaired through a wilderness; and the time Jane and I were bluff-charged by the Forest Service; and Roland's scientific theory of why ticks howl and coyotes crawl. There's the story of cognitive dysfunction—the male syndrome; the saga of mosquito collision; the art of being addled; the man who bathes snakes.

Matt's advice about sharing experiences strikes me as a good guideline for any storyteller, and I intend to keep it in mind. Far be it from me to diminish your experiences by not sharing mine.

So gather 'round.... ■

Use the order form on the reverse side of this page to order more of Roland Cheeks books.

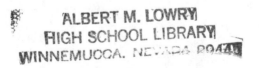

My Best Work is Done at the Office 320 pgs. 5-1/2 x 8-1/2 $19.95 (postpaid)
The perfect bathroom book of humorous light reading and inspiration to demonstrate that we should never take ourselves or our lives too seriously. by Roland Cheek

Dance on the Wild Side 352 pgs. 5-1/2 x 8-1/2 $19.95 (postpaid)
A memoir of two people in love. A "connecting" tale for anyone over forty who's loved and lived and struggled in pursuit of a dream.   by Roland and Jane Cheek

Phantom Ghost of Harriet Lou 352 pgs. 5-1/2 x 8-1/2 $19.95 (postpaid)
A key to finding elk with or without a guide; discovery techniques with insight into the habits and habitats of North America's second-most charismatic creatures; a guide to understanding that God made elk to lead we humans into some of His finest places.
by Roland Cheek

Learning To Talk Bear 320 pgs. 5-1/2 x 8-1/2 $19.95 (postpaid)
An important book for anyone wishing to understand what makes bears tick. Humorous high adventure and spine-tingling suspense, seasoned with understanding through a lifetime of walking where the bears walk, surviving while smelling the bears' breath.
by Roland Cheek

Montana's Bob Marshall Wilderness 80 pgs. 9 x 12 (coffee table size) $15.95
hardcover, $10.95 softcover (postpaid)
97 full-color photos, over 10,000 words of where-to, how-to text about America's favorite wilderness. by Roland Cheek

Telephone orders: Call Toll Free 1-800-821-6784.
Have your Visa, MasterCard or Discover ready.

Postal orders: Skyline Publishing
P.O. Box 1118
Columbia Falls, MT 59912
Telephone: (406) 892-5560   Fax (406) 892-1922

Please send the following books:
(I understand I may return any Skyline Publishing book for a full refund—no questions asked.)

Title	Qty	Cost Ea.	Total
_____	_____	$ _____	$_____
_____	_____	$ _____	$_____
_____	_____	$ _____	$_____
		Total Order:	$_____

Ship to: Name_____

Address_____

City_____ State_____ Zip_____

Daytime phone number (_____)_____-_____

Payment: ☐ Check or Money Order

Credit card: ☐ Visa ☐ MasterCard ☐ Discover

Card number_____

Name on card_____Exp. date___/___

Signature:_____